Against the State

Anarchists and Comrades at War in Spain, Myanmar, and Rojava

James Stout

AK PRESS

Against the State: Anarchists and Comrades at War in Spain, Myanmar, and Rojava
James Stout © 2026
This edition © 2026 AK Press

ISBN 9781849355452
E-ISBN 9781849355469
Library of Congress Number: 2025937163

AK Press
370 Ryan Avenue #100
Chico, CA 95973
www.akpress.org
akpress@akpress.org
510.208.1700

AK Press
33 Tower St.
Edinburgh EH6 7BN
Scotland
www.akuk.com
akuk@akpress.org

Cover photo by Linn Let Arkar
Cover design by Crisis
Printed in the USA on acid-free paper

For my grandparents, who taught me every stranger is a friend I have yet to make, and for all the people I have known and the many I have not who gave their lives for a chance to live free. And for my friend Pierre, who did just that before he had a chance to give me his characteristically direct feedback on this book, which he urged me to write.

Contents

Preface vii

Acknowledgments xi

Introduction 1

1. Mountains 13

2. Spain 25

3. Myanmar 75

4. Rojava 113

5. Discipline among the Anarchists 151

6. Arming the Anarchists 171

7. Solidarity 199

8. Logistics 219

9. Gender 233

10. Death and Other Endings 251

    Glossary 263

    Suggested Further Reading 265

    Notes 269

    Index 275

Preface

War, as it is conceived of today, is a conflict between states. It is a contest to see who can use violence to force another actor to concede the monopoly on legitimate political violence in an area. Wars are not fought by states, of course, but by people on behalf of states, mostly young people. Some are compelled to fight by sentiment, ideology, or even a sense of adventure. Many are compelled by force, or by economic circumstance, which amounts to the same thing. States can die in wars, but the blood spilled in conflict is overwhelmingly that of young and often working-class people.

Yet people alone are not sufficient for warfare in the modern era. Wars today involve massive amounts of materiel. The state and the corporations have spent centuries honing new and more efficient ways to kill people, from the intercontinental ballistic missile to the thermal optic, from the fighter-bomber to the guided artillery shell. These innovations, developed with money extracted from working people in the form of taxes, have made war more efficient and concentrated the ability to kill in the hands of the wealthiest states on earth.

The machines with which war is conducted are supplied to the state by capitalists. The names of the companies that make them are written in blood across the history of the twenty-first century: Raytheon, Lockheed Martin, General Dynamics, Northrop Grumman. War is an industry, and like any other industry under capitalism it must continue to grow to deliver dividends to its shareholders. For most of my life, the states in which I have lived have waged wars far from the metropole against the Middle East. All my life, they've been at war with someone. Peace has been a privilege of the colonial metropole, war a reality of the postcolonial periphery. This has allowed unprecedented growth and influence for companies whose primary business is killing, and, of course, such profiteering has been met with opposition from across the political spectrum, especially from the left.

One of my earliest news memories is of watching, on a tiny TV in rural England, British Challenger 1 Main Battle Tanks fighting in Iraq. Like most children lucky enough to grow up in peace, I didn't know the reality of war. I liked machines, I liked shooting cans with my air rifle, and I liked being outside, and war looked like an adventure. But war, in its realities, soon loses the sheen of adventure. War is by turns terrifying and boring, and sometimes— rarely—the most incredible adrenalin rush available to humans. War is far too often associated with glory, yet for most it brings nothing but misery.

Everyone whom war touches loses something. Some lose a part of their body, others their peace of mind; some lose their childhood, others a loved one or their own life. For those sitting far away in boardrooms and banks, war is not a tragedy but a steady generator of income. It keeps stock prices high, retirement funds growing, and investments returning. In humbler settings, parents worry their children won't be returning. For these reasons anarchists have denounced war as a racket. They have often faced state violence for this position, and at times war has been used to heavily censor and surveil the libertarian left.

When anarchists have fought, it has not been as armies but as guerrilla bands. This form of struggle, without the profit incentive and state support offered to large armies, is often celebrated on the left. From the Pyrenees to Kurdistan, small bands of dedicated guerrillas have wreaked havoc on the state and opened up significant spaces for liberation. This model is easy to make compatible with horizontal and consensus organizing, being not that distinct from the anarchist affinity group. However, it is in moving from the mountains to the plains, and from the band to the battalion, that anarchists have struggled. Yet if the goal of a guerrilla campaign is to liberate significant territory, then to succeed it must organize its fighters at scale.

Modern state war relies on the integration of aircraft, armored vehicles, infantry, unmanned aerial vehicles, and indirect fire. Assembling such an apparatus is a considerable logistical challenge and comes at significant cost. For non-state actors, including the ones studied here, organizing at such a scale is vital if they wish to replace state actors, but the transition to this style of warfare has eluded many movements that were successful in guerrilla warfare. Guerrillas rely on speed and stealth, they can carry out missions and then disappear, but no amount of speed and stealth can replicate the brute force of state armies when it comes to holding territory. To liberate an area, by definition one must be able to organize openly and freely there. This is antithetical to guerrilla warfare. This is not an easy transition, and it is one that has eluded many anarchist groups.

In this book, I look at three groups that have found themselves, through circumstances not of their choosing, at war with the state. Over time, they managed to organize their people into standing armies that liberated towns and cities and held terrain. Their experiences, ideologies, and wars have been different, but they all offer us a chance to learn. The questions they have faced, about discipline, logistics, equality, and war materiel, have been answered differently in different times, places, and ideologies, but they all have in common a desire to liberate space and a struggle against the state.

Acknowledgments

Without the support and diligence of my editors at AK Press, this book would have been impossible. Their financial support and considerable labor have made it possible for me to share the stories of these revolutions and the people who fought in them. Andy, his brothers and partner, Khabat, and Diwar all played a huge role in helping me understand these revolutions from the perspective of their participants, without them this book would be very different. Without the music of the Manic Street Preachers and the Clash, I'd never have been drawn to the Spanish Revolution or anarchism in the first place. I also received financial support for my archival research in Catalonia, conducted long before this book was even a concept, from the University of California, the British Spanish Society, and the International Olympic Committee.

Against the State

Introduction

The flower of the word will not die. The masked face which today has a name may die, but the word which came from the depth of history and the earth can no longer be cut by the arrogance of the powerful. We were born of the night. We live in the night. We will die in her. But the light will be tomorrow for others, for all those who today weep at the night, for those who have been denied the day, for those for whom death is a gift, for those who are denied life. The light will be for all of them. For everyone everything. For us pain and anguish, for us the joy of rebellion, for us a future denied, for us the dignity of insurrection. For us nothing.

—Subcomandante Insurgente Marcos,
Fourth Declaration of the Lacandon Jungle

A few days short of the seventy-ninth anniversary of the death of Buenaventura Durruti, arguably the most beloved anarchist of the twentieth century, I went jogging in a park in Madrid. Donald Trump had been elected president of the US (for the first time) a few days before, and I was finding it hard to shake the ghosts of Spain's Civil War from my thoughts. I figured some time alone would help. I was hoping to jog my way through the battlefield where, two generations before, on a similarly icy morning, anarchists in arms had fought one of the decisive battles of the twentieth century. It's not that hard to run from Casa de Campo, where Durruti died, to the Puerta del Sol, where one could argue the seed of the Occupy movement was planted. Still, between the cold air and my anxiety-induced effort, I could taste blood in my mouth. My anxiety wasn't helped by a slight delay caused by an animated disagreement with some Real Madrid fans—whose club has often been associated with a racist and fascist vision of Spanish identity and who had been upset by an FC Barcelona hat I was wearing and a particularly repugnant sticker that I was removing. Soon, instead of paying homage to Durruti, I was fighting a battle of my own to make it back to my flat in time for work.

Having barely squeezed in a shower before I caught the metro to an academic conference on the Spanish Civil War, I found myself listening to presentations on the Occupy movement and the civil war and wondering why so many anarchists have eschewed the topic of war when discussing the theory and practice of the libertarian left. As a historian of the Spanish Civil War and as a reporter covering conflict, I've always been fascinated by the anarchists who fought in Spain. In general history books, they're often dismissed as naive idealists, tilting at windmills amid a conflict too serious for such high-minded ideals (although inaccurate, we must concede that the Cervantes comparison is not entirely unwarranted given that one affinity group of anarchist youth in the Spanish Civil War did call themselves los Quijotes del Ideal—the Quixotes of the Ideal). However, when anarchist militias or units do appear in books more focused on military history than political ideology, it's not as logistical failures or as naive cannon fodder. Anarchists, from the first days of the war in Barcelona to the last battles in the Serra de Pàndols, appear in books when they defy expectations, when they don't suffer from the collapses in morale that plagued the more conventionally organized units or the tactical naivete that plagues so many militias.[1] Even in the accounts of foreign communists, many of them violently opposed to the libertarian leftism that thrived in Spain, the anarchists who came from all over the world to fight in Spain earn a grudging respect for their bravery and tenacity.

Conversely, when Spain's anarchist militias appear in movement texts, it is often in the form of icons rather than people. Too often, the temptation to resort to hagiography to create heroes has compelled us to overlook the divisions and shortcomings of the Confederación Nacional del Trabajo (National Confederation of Labor, or CNT) and the Federación Anarquista Ibérica (Iberian Anarchist Federation, or FAI), to blunt our criticisms, to oversimplify, and as a result to learn less than we could from their lives and deaths, which in a sense renders their sacrifice less valuable. This is not to say that excellent histories of the various anarchist columns that fought in Spain do not exist; one could probably form an effective barricade out of excellent history books, as the International Brigades who fought in Madrid's university did with philosophy books in 1936. I certainly do not claim to have turned over any new historical ground in this work.

Rather, I hope to join some dots in praxis between then and now, between research in dusty and disorganized archives as an academic and conversations in less tranquil spaces with fighters whose dreams, lives, and deaths are often overlooked by the legacy media. In Spain, I learned about the past, but in my time with the teenage rebels of Myanmar with their 3D-printed guns and homemade drones, I sometimes feel as if I am opening a window to the future.

My journey to these pages certainly didn't begin on a jog in Madrid. Although I can't claim to have anything like the tenacity of those fighters, I found academe to be an unwelcoming place for someone interested in the creation of democracy without the state. I ought to clarify here that by "democracy" I do not mean a set of institutions or practices but instead a substantive commitment to individual and community autonomy and the placing of power in the hands of the people. The sine qua non of anarchism, to me, is the creation of systems that allow people to care for one another without reinforcing systems that allow people to control one another. It's a commitment to mutual aid, consensus organizing, and horizontal structure. There is a discussion to be had, and it will be had in these pages, about the extent to which these principles can be set aside to achieve victory or as part of an alliance, but they ought to be core to any group that claims to use the left libertarian model in its organizing as well as in its envisioned utopia. The means used to achieve human liberation cannot be so far apart from those ends that we excuse oppression now in order to be free some time in the future; as the twentieth century has shown, state communism has used this logic to justify some of the worst crimes in the history of humanity. If anarchists and left libertarians are true to their beliefs, they must adhere to them even in times of great difficulty. In doing so, they show they value of their convictions, and they allow everyone who joins them to live a beautiful life. In this way, even if they are not successful or—as is inevitably the case—if not everyone who fights for freedom lives to see victory, they will have known what it is to live free and died for something worth fighting for.

I have been skeptical about the state from a young age. At sixteen, I volunteered in an orphanage for neurodivergent young people in Romania, fixing bikes and teaching kids to ride them, sharing the joy of flying along on two wheels with other young people who had been treated as human byproducts by the natalist state and brushed away to a remote orphanage in the mountains.

Should the state have such control, I wondered? As an undergraduate, I began by asking questions that I later recognized an anarchist would ask. My chief question was why, in response to assumptions made by many friends and colleagues about the necessity of the state. Perhaps my skepticism about the state as a vehicle for human improvement came from my experience in Romania or the Emma Goldman book my history teacher in high school gave me to read after I came back. Over time, and after reading hundreds of books, I began to say things an anarchist might say, chiefly that I did not believe the state in its current inception was as necessary as many believe it to be. I spent time in Caracas and became thoroughly disillusioned with the idea of the party and the state as vehicles for human liberation. I began to talk with friends about a model that didn't allow the abuses of power I'd seen in Venezuela and elsewhere. These discussions, alongside participation in mutual aid, developed my own set of beliefs about the possibility and necessity of a society devoted to people helping one another without controlling one another. The state, at its core, aims to monopolize legitimate violence and to use this to the ends of the parts of society that control the state. Through reading and reporting, I have seen the state use violence to further the interest of capital and the people who own it, at the cost of a great deal of human suffering. This is antithetical to the definitions of anarchism I have advanced and the world I want to live in.

But I never quite worked out where conflict fit in. Certainly, anarchists should not exercise violence on behalf of the state. Even after years of writing this book, interviewing dozens of anarchists and other libertarian leftists fighting all over the world, and making several reporting trips to conflict zones, I am not sure if I have anything approaching a coherent response to the question "How do anarchists go to war?" I certainly can't hope to answer why they should. But through experience and research, I have something of a grasp of how they have gone to war, and I think that is enough to begin a conversation.

I don't intend this to be a guide or even a complete history. In Ukraine, Mexico, Korea, East Africa, and China—regions I do not write about in this book—people have also fought wars without the state. However, the areas and times I cover in this book do represent good case studies of movements that are both new and old, intertwined and independent. Some of these movements have developed ideologies, others are finding their ideology as they fight. All of them have learned, changed, and grown through exposure to conflict and taking control of liberated spaces. From Spain, we can learn from the past and the mass organizations of anarcho-syndicalism; in Kurdistan we can see people struggle with questions of community, gender, and ideology forged in the most brutal conflict of the century. In Myanmar, we can see young people compelled by a sometimes inarticulate but always fierce rejection of the state and its violence find a future for themselves and perhaps for all of us in the mountains and jungles of a war that rages on outside of the headlines. These are the places my life has taken me, the revolutions I have known and shared, and the stories I feel best equipped to tell. They may not always offer coherent solutions, but they offer us the chance to learn from the experiences and mistakes of others so we don't repeat them.

An anarchist community can and should defend itself. This is undisputed in most serious discussions on the issue. But there is little discussion of how anarchists are to respond to conflict between states, or within states, which seems to be a constant companion to the statist hegemony that has been the primary global paradigm for centuries. It is easy for us to assume that anarchists would remain aloof from such conflict, but often that is not an option. Conflict is terrible, and nothing I write here should take away from that. I do not mean for a second to glorify it. But war often provides us with an opening, a crack of daylight in the darkness, which one can widen to gain a little more autonomy until, sometimes, the darkness disappears altogether.

Violence should not be used as a means of obtaining liberation except as a last resort. It is inherently antithetical to the idea of consensus organizing to use force to obtain compliance or control. However, any political movement would be naïve to reject violence entirely, as it is the bedrock of the state and especially common in totalitarian states. In particular, in totalitarian cases, people are compelled to respond to the state in the language it speaks. Where the state has ignored the people's words, it cannot overlook their weapons. In the rage, chaos, and violence of conflict we must never forget that the means and the ends are to be kept in focus; we should not glorify or embrace violence or carry it out for its own sake. Even Ramon Rufat, an anarchist guerrilla operating behind enemy lines in the Spanish Civil War to rescue fellow anarchists and others in danger, staunchly refused to kill, though his refusal came at great risk to his own life. We cannot justify anything but the minimum use of force, the minimum acceptance of hierarchy, and the most temporary embrace of both.

This book is composed of stories, many of them stories about war. When we tell stories about war, we try to tell the truth. But sometimes the things that happened don't contain the whole truth; they're just the canvas on which our truth was painted. Stories sometimes take the things that happened and add the things that might have happened, the things that should have happened, or the things we were convinced were happening. That's not because the stories are intended to embellish or mislead; it's because the storyteller wants their readers to feel what they felt, to see war through their eyes. Many of the stories I've been told weren't stories I was there to see, but even if I had been there, what I saw and what I remembered might have been different. Finding an objective truth is nearly impossible when all we have are firsthand accounts, and this is not a book that seeks objective truth. Rather it's a series of feelings, fears, and hopes that I have tried to weave together and give a little meaning to.

My first example, perhaps the most obvious one, came to me mostly through stories told and told again, and through those few that were written down. When we think of fighting anarchists, we nearly always rush to revolutionary Spain for our examples. Often we go specifically to the unit Durruti led, the Durruti Column, which marched from Barcelona to Aragon and then to Madrid to defend a revolution that had occurred at the same time as a civil war began.[2] Perhaps we consider the Makhnovists of Ukraine, riding their horses and tachankas across the battlefields to face down both monarchism and state communism in places that today are once again seeing death and destruction.[1]

I first conceived of the need to stitch together this book's disparate stories and abandon a project that focused exclusively on Spain while I was talking with a young fighter named Zaw, whom I'd met because he live-streamed his combat in the jungles of Myanmar on Facebook. I didn't know much about his political outlook, and I don't think he would have had a name for his worldview if I'd asked. We were chatting over a terrible connection on an encrypted line. He was showing me a puppy that his unit had adopted, and a teddy bear they'd found that seemed larger than any of them. They were training, he said, and trying to stay out of the rain. Like soldiers everywhere, they were bored, hungry, and shockingly young.

---

1.   In early 2025, as I edited this book, an anarchist friend fighting in Ukraine sent me a photo of a large black flag with Nestor Makhno emblazoned on it flying on the front lines. Weeks later, I received the sad news of his death, another life lost in pursuit of liberty.

When I asked Zaw who commanded his unit, he said nobody did. Intrigued, I asked how they made decisions, and he told me they talked together. Later, with a translator, he told me they sat down to discuss attack plans and generally those with more experience offered their views before the group came to a plan by consensus. It reminded me of the books I'd read about anarchists in Spain, but Zaw and his Gen Z army certainly hadn't read those books. Rather, these were young people who respected each other and had come into the jungle to fight against the harsh authoritarian military of their country that had enacted a coup months before. In their struggle to keep the boot off their necks, these young people, both men and women, had removed authority from their military organizing as well. And, just like the Durruti Column, they had proven very effective.

Like most of the people you'll hear about in this book, Zaw and his friends had not sought out conflict. The state had increased its level of violence toward them, and they responded to the state in the language the state spoke to them, which used bullets and bombs instead of words. War is an obvious consequence of state competition under capitalism, and anarchist communities have a long tradition of defending themselves or other people who are not causing harm to anyone against state and non-state actors who would seek to harm them. Often these ruptures have created an opening for anarchists, or simply for people opposed to tyranny, to organize and conduct mutual aid on a large scale, increasing the reach and impact of their ideology. In Syria, for example, as the state crumbled in all its aspects, community councils sprang up to replace it, and people began to conceive of a future without the state.[3] These councils came from a basic desire for autonomy, liberty, and equality rather than the pages of a particular work of theory. The task of this book is not to advance any new theory but merely to document a phenomenon that has long existed.

In moments of war, all radicals face a choice between pursuing their revolution alongside the war or putting their principles aside in order to fit into a more conventional military model and win the war using conventional means before returning to their radical goals. Often they are forced into alliances with groups that have incompatible ends, and they may have to adopt the means of their allies to survive. I will attempt to show here that this choice, often presented as a dichotomy, need not be dichotomous. In Spain, anarchists were presented with two distinct paths, each violently opposed to the other. Some anarchists and anarcho-syndicalists joined the government

and urged their comrades to accept the increasingly authoritarian regulariza-
tion of the military, and in doing so they abandoned what was core to their
ideology. Those who refused often found themselves facing the troops they
had fought alongside, either as firing squads or in the internecine struggles
of May 1937 in Barcelona. By the end of the war, the remaining anarchists
were left with a choice between two sides who both wanted them dead, and
they had little other than the fear of a death sentence from their one-time
comrades to keep them fighting.

Women in Western Kurdistan didn't wait for their revolution. In the tur-
moil of one of the longest and cruelest civil wars of the twenty-first century,
they chose to stand up not only against the state but also against patriarchy.
In doing so, they created a system that was worth fighting or even dying to
protect. Women and men from around the world have traveled to join them,
risking their lives to preserve an experiment in what anarchist anthropologist
David Graeber called "democracy without the state." Despite everything that
the Turkish state, which controls second-largest army in NATO, and the
Islamic State, the most powerful terrorist group of the century, have thrown
at them, they continue to exist. Even as bombs fell every night during my
time in Rojava in October 2023, the organizers of the women's movement
continued their work against domestic violence and patriarchal attitudes. At
the start of 2025, they face unprecedented threats from the Turkish state, but
they continue to live and fight according to their principles and have not laid
them aside to support their war effort.

In Myanmar, young people across the left face a series of daily nego-
tiations between ideology and practicality. They must negotiate their way
through extraordinarily broad popular fronts, both on the ground and internationally. Some find themselves in units with strict authoritarian structures,
others can organize on a small scale within their units, and still others fight in
horizontally organized and gender-inclusive units that fight not only to defeat
authoritarian governments but also to prove the value of building a future
without authority and oppression.

Anarchists have always called into question the state's monopoly on legitimate violence. In many cases revolutions have begun with people in the streets
advocating for what might be seen as anarchism with a small "a." From Syria
to Spain, people have sought to bring governance closer to the community.

In countless examples around the world, a movement that began in the
streets without leaders ended up in the corridors of power, with the state even

stronger than before. As I write, the Syrian revolution that once established community councils and interfaith solidarity has installed a man into power without even the performance of elections and is considering a constitution that ensures the president will always be of the Muslim faith. Months after Assad fled, the multiethnic country remains the Syrian Arab Republic. As in many revolutions, those who continued to advocate for a stateless society, or substantive democracy of any kind, face a precarious future

It might behoove anarchists to consider how to defend freedom and to look at cases where state repression has been held off and the people have retained self-governance. Yet anarchist theory has done little to incorporate what those fighters have learned, instead choosing to avoid complexity and reassert ideological absolutes or to cede the terrain entirely to vertical organizing. This leaves gaps in organizing and condemns anarchists to repeat the mistakes of the past rather than benefiting from the lessons bought with the blood of those who have gone before them. Understandably, theories of liberation have focused on methods that do not frontally challenge the state's monopoly on violence, as more often than not these lead to little more than death and the destruction of a movement. But it does not follow that because war is undesirable it should be set aside entirely as a terrain for learning and thought, especially given how many libertarian projects have been forced to fight for their existence. David Graeber, normally one of anarchism's strongest and most beloved defenders, in his essay "The New Anarchists," posits that anarchism is ill-equipped for war. "The 'short twentieth century' was, by contrast, probably the most violent in human history, almost entirely preoccupied with either waging world wars or preparing for them. Hardly surprising, then, that anarchism quickly came to seem unrealistic, if the ultimate measure of political effectiveness became the ability to maintain huge, mechanized killing machines," he writes—before going on to add that "this [managing the logistics of warfare] is one thing that anarchists, by definition, can never be very good at." And then he cedes this ground to "Marxist parties —who have been only too good at it."[4]

I would argue that Graeber cedes this terrain to the authoritarian left (who are admittedly rather well known for their affinity with tanks) a little too readily. While the conventional narrative of the twentieth century holds that the industrial might of the Soviet Union saved the world from fascism, this fight was not one that anarchists were absent from. War industry and war supply chains are fundamentally not distinct from any other industrial operation, and if we believe that workers are capable of cooperative self-management in peacetime, why should we abandon that belief in conflict? Certainly, as we shall see, the Spanish anarchists were not burdened by the same lack of confidence as Graeber when they turned a car factory into an armored car factory in a matter of days after the revolution.

We should not forget that during the Second World War, it was Spanish Republicans fighting as the 9th Company of the Régiment de Marche du Tchad who first liberated Paris. (And they had wanted to name their armored vehicle *Buenaventura Durruti*, but their French officers forbade it.) It was anarchists in Barcelona who beat back the Spanish army in 1936, and a broad popular front of Italian anarchists and communists who beat their own country's fascists at Guadalajara a few months later and remained in the mountains of Italy until they eventually defeated fascism there. Spanish Republicans, including anarchists, were a thorn in the side of the Nazis because of their crucial role in the anti-fascist Maquis, who fought the Nazi and Vichy state from behind enemy lines throughout the Second World War.

As Graeber argues in his essay of the same name, much of the "new anarchism" that emerged in the early years of this century learned its methods and strategies from countries outside the imperial core. The new anarchists, of which I suppose I am one, drew heavily on the inspiration of the "small a" anarchist Zapatista Army of National Liberation (Ejército Zapatista de Liberación Nacional, or EZLN) in Chiapas. Why, then, should the new anarchists cede the capability for defense on a scale larger than that of a small community to state actors and authoritarian systems?

Around the world today, wars offer openings for liberatory projects. War is a time when states must prove their value to citizens, and this inherently leaves space for anarchists to question their value altogether. Anarchism, by its nature, does not ask the state to change but rather challenges its right to govern. I am concerned in this book with challenges that occur on a small scale as well as a large one. Although fighters' visions for the future interest me, their methods for organizing now interest me more. A structure that allows a diverse group of people to fight alongside one another and operate horizontally on a consensus basis is one that we can all learn from and implement in scenarios far beyond armed conflict.

Throughout this text, I have used the colloquial term "anarchists" for a variety of left libertarian antistate actors, whom I do not wish to misrepresent.

This means that their ideology will likely differ from what readers see as doctrinaire anarchism. It is not my intention to gatekeep or even strictly define anarchism but rather to show examples of ways the legitimacy of authority has been undermined in times of conflict. At times I use anarchist anthropologist James C. Scott's "anarchist squint" to explain movements and moments that seem inexplicable when one applies state logics.[5] In their essay "Anarchism, or the Revolutionary Movement of the Twenty-first Century," Graeber and anarchist world systems theorist and historian Andrej Grubačić write that revolution in the twenty-first century is "less about seizing state power than about exposing, delegitimizing and dismantling mechanisms of rule while winning ever-larger spaces of autonomy and participatory management within it."[6] Years later, inviting me to cover their cooperative coffee and tea operation, young Burmese rebels told me, "You will love the feeling of being in the liberated zone."

It is these liberated spaces, where the world becomes more equal and the exercise of power less arbitrary, that I have sought for over nearly a decade as a journalist and longer as a historian. It's in conflict and crisis that I most often see the best of humanity: mutual aid, communities supporting themselves without arbitrary hierarchy or capricious authority. It's these openings that have inspired me as I have continued to cover a great deal of human tragedy, and it's from these spaces that I believe we can build the new anarchism of the twenty-first century that Graeber and others have pointed towards. In the liberated mountains of Burma, which inspired James C. Scott—Mutual Aid Myanmar counted Scott as a board member—but which he did not live to visit in their current iteration, young people are building our futures today. Their guns—at least at first—came not from the arms industry, but from the internet, and their politics from experience more than from books.

I am aware—perhaps too aware—of many anarchists who would condemn the revolutions I have documented here as not anarchist enough. They use the opposite of Scott's anarchist squint and look down their noses at the people fighting the state. I don't concern myself unduly with these people's opinions. When people are in the street fighting the state, and other people are on the internet criticizing them for not doing it the right way, I don't have to ask myself which of them is doing anarchism. As Graeber has noted, these people have no faith that an actual revolution can occur, and so they would rather criticize the revolutions they see than stand in solidarity with them. Nobody, as far as I am aware, has liberated themselves by tweeting, and at best these criticisms are a distraction from our natural impulse toward solidarity and support.

While the twentieth century left, with notable exceptions, was largely dominated by the idea of the revolution as a distinctive break and in practice as the violent seizure of state power according to the Marxist-Leninist model, the twenty-first century has embraced the need for revolution to occur every day and at all levels of society. As a young leftist at the beginning of this century, I was profoundly inspired by events in Chiapas and by the history of anarchism in Spain. In particular, I was taken by the antiauthoritarian vision of building a new world day by day, in their actions and practices, building their own power rather than, or as well as, seizing power through conquest or overthrow of existing structures. It's this vision of an anarchism that moves towards freedom as it grows, rather than in the storming of a palace or the seizure of a city, that I have seen in my work and that I want to relate here.

I am concerned here with "small-a anarchism," which spends less time on theory and more time on action, and which learns as it moves forward. Crucially, this small-a anarchism rejects capitalism and the state while it embraces a way of organizing that mirrors the world it wishes to create. It's this definition, broad as it is, that allows us to learn from the consensus-based decision making of Gen Z fighters in Myanmar, the men and women who fought ISIS and the patriarchy at the same time, and the anarchists of Barcelona who long ago took on their nation's army in the city streets and showed the state that its supremacy in matters of force was far from certain.

War is terrible, and it forces us to do terrible things. I don't hope to tell anyone what to do with this text, or how to do it, but I hope that I have given an honest account of what others have done and that this is in some way useful. I have tried to structure each chapter so that those with an academic or personal interest in a particular struggle can read them separately, but I hope you'll read the whole book as I have gone to great lengths to collect these stories around the world, and they give me a great deal of hope for a better world.

1

Mountains

Ethnicity and tribe began, by definition, where sovereignty and taxes ended. The ethnic zone was feared and stigmatized by state rhetoric precisely because it was beyond its grasp and therefore an example of defiance and an ever-present temptation to those who might wish to evade the state.

—James C. Scott, *The Art of Not Being Governed*

There isn't much to Feysh Kabour: a few single-story flat buildings, a dusty courtyard, a small taxi rank, and a giant flag for anyone who has failed to notice that although the Tigris River runs through Kurdistan, the Iraqi autonomous region of Kurdistan and the Autonomous Area of North and East Syria (AANES, better known as Rojava) are not in agreement about very much. On the eastern side of the border, two intelligence officials from the Kurdistan Regional Government, a more neoliberally aligned government that controls an area of Iraq as practically a separate country and has deep ideological differences with Rojava, quizzed me for more than an hour about my intentions in Rojava. "All the areas you are going to are under heavy bombardment," one of them told me. "I advise you not to go." It was surreal to hear about the bombing from a very smartly dressed man relaxing on a leather sofa while I sat across the room trying to squeeze my 6'3" frame into a comically small chair. In the time since I'd boarded the first of a series of flights, buses, and cars that had carried me from California to the bank of the Tigris River, Turkish drones had struck dozens of targets inside AANES territory. Those targets were not military facilities but civilian infrastructure in the middle of cities. Power stations, oil wells, and a cooking gas bottling facility had all been bombed in the quiet of the night when death fell from the dark sky with no warning. Electricity was intermittent, and water wasn't running in some cities. This happens every autumn: Turkey steps up its assaults on the independent Kurdish region that is sees as a threat to its ability to control Kurds within Turkish borders. It's a concerted effort on the part of the Turkish state to make sure the democratic confederalist experiment in Rojava ends in failure. Despite this and other difficulties, Rojava still exists as a society trying to build democracy without the state. That's why I was there.

I suspected the intelligence agents knew that I already knew what was going on in Rojava, and that it was part of why I was going there, but I knew it was their job to tell me not to go. They weren't wrong; it was dangerous. As far as I could tell, I was entering at the same time as the handful of other journalists working in the region were leaving. Kurdish people are remarkably hospitable, so in addition to asking me probing questions about my past, the agents also invited me for lunch and offered me the wi-fi code while they debated whether they would allow me across the floating bridge over the Tigris. I politely declined the offer of lunch; I had no desire to delay my trip and drive in Syria after nightfall, especially as we were going through regions and along roads where people had been killed in drone strikes the night before. But I gladly accepted the wi-fi code, booted up my Tor browser, and tried to work out if my hotel was close to any power stations.

Looking out the window and across the river, I thought about how much I wanted to visit Rojava and breathe the air in a society that was trying to do away with the state. In the eleven years since the Kurdish-majority cities in North and East Syria managed to expel most regime forces in a bloodless show of force, the conflict in the region morphed from one about the character of the state in Syria to the existence of the state in Syria. In this conflict, the embattled Ba'athist regime, the increasingly authoritarian Turkish regime, the remains of the so-called Islamic State (IS), and Iranian proxy militias in Syria have all found themselves at war with one another but united in opposition to the projects in Rojava and elsewhere in Syria that seek to redistribute power away from the state and toward the people. It was these people, who had managed to emerge from the fire of a burning country and the darkness of the so-called Islamic State to secure their liberty, autonomy, and equality, that I wanted to visit. But first I had to persuade the two intelligence officers who were scrolling my Facebook page that I wasn't off to join the Islamic State.

While I pondered if I had wasted my entire book advance, the intelligence agents called for a round of chai—a cinnamon-infused black tea served in a tulip-shaped glass with a generous helping of sugar, a drink that seems as crucial to human existence as oxygen in this part of the world. Iraqi Kurdistan's teahouses served as public spaces where, even under the repressive Ba'ath regime of Saddam Hussein, Kurds could gather and share their stories. Later they became places where Peshmerga—a term that is translated as "Those Who Face Death," the much-revered fighters of Iraqi Kurdistan—could gather, plan, and even recruit. The intelligence office at the border was no teahouse; it didn't even have the requisite domino table, but the intelligence officers still shared their stories as we sipped our tea. Soon enough, I was looking at Polaroid photos that had been immortalized through the miracle of social media. One agent's uncle was a Peshmerga leader, famous for his abilities with a rocket-propelled grenade. I briefly considered offering the Kurmanji word for the weapon as he searched for the English one. I make a habit of learning as much of the language as I can before I travel, and I had been particularly charmed by the word *Bixfing*, which Syrian Kurds use for the rocket-propelled grenade. But my grandmother had been arrested entering Syria half a century before, and I decided that showing too much knowledge of weapons systems would be risking the same result. The other agent's grandfather had fought for years as a guerrilla against the Ba'athists, bravely holding out when the world had left the Kurds to die in their thousands. "At that time," the agent said to me as he leaned across the sofa to emphasize the point, "our only friends were the mountains."

These days, the more statist conception of Kurdish identity that is predominant in the Kurdish autonomous region of Iraq has descended from the mountains and resides in the giant villas and skyscrapers of Hawler, the region's capital (which is called Erbil in Arabic). The government and its friends have built skyscrapers in the city with corporate logos that light up the sky at night just like the drone bombs lit up the night sky in Rojava. However, the mountains of southern Turkey and northern Iraq have remained home to the Kurdistan Workers Party, better known by its initials in Kurdish, the PKK (Partiya Karkerên Kurdistanê) for decades. In 1984, the group began an insurgency against the Turkish state in an attempt to establish their own. However, over time, the group and its leader Abdullah Öcalan, have moved beyond a state-based conception of their struggle and instead have embraced an ideology of radical feminism, environmentalism, and what they call democratic confederalism. It was this ideology that had brought about the revolution and eventually the self-administration of a huge chunk of Syria. This way of thinking had come down from the mountains, swept across the plains, and defeated the Islamic State. Now, having gained so much, it was being bombed so heavily that its future was in doubt, and I wanted to see the only multi-ethnic democratic project in the Middle East before its adherents had to retreat to the jagged peaks that I could see through the dusty afternoon in Feysh Kabour.

Eventually, after a prolonged conversation about the care and breeding of sheep, including questions from the agent's family members who were now attending my interrogation remotely via WhatsApp, I was allowed to cross into Rojava. Growing up with livestock didn't seem abnormal or all that useful to me as a child, but I've been pleasantly surprised with its ability to open doors in the most unlikely places.

With my interview completed, I began a circuit of small offices where people would stare at me for a few seconds, look at my passport, write something down, and send me forth to another official who would do exactly the same thing. It felt like an unconscious parody of the state's capacity to turn every action into an office visit and a form to be filled out. Eventually, I was sent to a small waiting room, and then to a long-suffering bus that had just dropped a full load of people from Rojava on the eastern bank of the Tigris. On its return journey, I was the only passenger. The driver pointed across the river, and I nodded. He took a huge draw on a terrible cigarette and set off across the shaky bridge that floats on oil drums and spans the Tigris.

In Rojava, my fixer Khabat and her brother Diwar greeted me with smiles and, as is often the case, a remark about my height. We showed my passport to an official, who smiled and addressed me in English to welcome me to Rojava and send me to the immigration office, where I would be given a sort of permission slip that allowed me to travel freely throughout the region. The role of the officials at the border in Rojava is not so much to check for visas and the payment of import taxes as to ensure those entering are not a threat to the community, in a manner not so different to Catalan anarchist militiamen who seized border checkpoints between Spain and France in 1936. The Rojava officials' permission slip also asks other groups in the area to accept their assessment that I was safe and should be treated as a guest. Because I was entering a country that is not recognized by other countries, nobody stamped my passport.

After offering me a cigarette, the man across the desk from me politely answered my questions about the half-dozen yellow- and green-framed portraits, and little laminated cards hanging from a tree, in his office. "All friends," he told me, "all *şehîd*." *Sehîd*, I soon learned, means "martyr"; you can't come to Rojava and not learn that word. Fifteen thousand people, some of whom had come down from the mountains in 2011 to join the Syrian revolution, or in 2014 to take on the task of ridding the world of the Islamic State, had lost their lives in the process. In Qamişlo, the capital of the AANES, şehîd are everywhere. Their portraits, yellow-backed for men and green-backed for women, smile at you from billboards on every roundabout, reminding you that many of the people who died to rid the world of IS would be too young to get a drink in a bar in the US. Lined up in neat little rows in the martyr's graveyard in Qamişlo, they remind you that there is no such thing as a "surgical strike" and that grandmothers and children of the region paid with their lives for the crime of living near a power plant or being on the street at the same time as a recognizable military leader.

I spent the next few days in Rojava, hearing martyrs' stories from their friends. I met leaders in places where they thought we might be safe from bombing, nervously waited to hear if they had made it home safely, and sat in my hotel at night wondering if the bangs and flashes were bombs in the distance or streetlights blowing their bulbs. I got up every morning with the fajr to prayer reminding us all that we'd made it through another night and now had to start another day that would inevitably begin with news of the people who were not waking up this morning. Every morning before Khabat arrived, I would walk through the market, ducking under canopies that were too low for my head, as if I needed a reminder I wasn't from here. But despite standing out like a man with two heads, I felt welcomed by everyone. Every morning I shared cups of tea and war stories with strangers and faced a pop quiz from merchants who seemed to have taken on the inestimable burden of improving my Kurmanji Kurdish via the pedagogical medium of pointing at vegetables and shouting their names. Later in the day, Khabat and Diwar sat with me for hours as we sipped tea and shared our stories, hopes, and fears.

With Khabat and Diwar I conducted interviews across Rojava. In Qamişlo, we heard a mother cry as she told me how her fifteen-year-old son had been a promising goalkeeper on his local football team until a missile from a drone landed next to the garage where he was repairing his motorcycle. Now he was another martyr, another grave in the cemetery, and another yellow-backed photograph on a grieving mother's wall.

In the mountains, there are caves and tunnels. Places where you can look out at the world without anyone looking down on you. In the city, there are houses, plazas, markets, and shops. Places where people sit at night with no idea if they'll wake up tomorrow. After ten years of war it's normal now, but sitting in my hotel listening to new friends play old songs on the tambour—a traditional stringed instrument—I was struck by the sadness of it all. The only thing most people here I met wanted was a better world for their children and a chance to influence their own futures. Having been attacked by the Iraqi, Iranian, Syrian, and Turkish states, they no longer wanted a state at all. Because they had reached this very reasonable conclusion, the states of the world wouldn't trust them with anti-aircraft missiles, the only tools with which they could prevent the slow destruction of their infrastructure. Instead, they were to be left alone to freeze or die as drones they were powerless to stop bombed their power stations and picked off their children one by one.

After several days in Rojava, at the urging of colleagues and family, I departed. It was sad to be leaving this hopeful, friendly, and hard-won place. A friend who fought against IS in Rojava told me Rojava is special because it is real. He was right, of course. The fact that Rojava is not just a utopian dream in the mountains or an idea in a book but daily reality for millions of people is remarkable. That Rojava has held onto its gains rather than retreat into the mountains is admirable. As a young leftist, anarchism existed for me only in history books, in mutual aid groups, in the woods, and in the moments when we stood in the street and saw the police back away. Now, young leftists around the world can pack their bags and come see for themselves the gains, and incredible struggles of organizing without the state.

Long before the Kurdish freedom movement took up arms in 1984, the mountains were an ally of anyone looking to escape the state. In his 2009 book *The Art of Not Being Governed,* James C. Scott, one of anarchism's few defenders in academe, developed the idea of uplands as areas that are inherently harder for the state to exercise control over and where people can go to choose a life without the state.

States, Scott argues, spread out from urban centers into areas that didn't impede their roads and railways and they left the upland areas relatively untouched until much later in their consolidation. These areas were harder to generate revenue from and harder to make legible for the state in terms it understood, like grain sent to granaries, taxes extracted from people, or soldiers drafted into armies. The state, as he argues in *Seeing Like a State,* might seek to make these areas more legible, but it meets resistance from free people who reject the need for fixed family names, units of measurement, and documented land ownership in favor of their free association according to mutually agreed upon norms. This slower and incomplete state expansion into the mountains, at times met with the active resistance of free people, allowed for what Scott calls "shatter zones" to emerge where people could seek refuge from the control and coercion of states. In *Two Cheers for Anarchism*, Scott argues that these people need not and often did not identify as anarchists, but that through the use of an "anarchist squint" we can understand their actions and worldview in a way that explains them much better than the state perspective, which simply sees these people as "backwards," "unruly," or, as one Burmese guerrilla commander put it to me, "wild."

In states, and in histories that consider the state the inevitable and final form of human society, the free people who resist the state's attempt to make the uplands into legible areas are cast as the domain of "barbarians" or "unruly hill tribes." These descriptors are applied as readily to the Picts and Scots of the United Kingdom as to the Karens of Burma or the fictional peoples of George R. R. Martin's *Game of Thrones*.

If we start from the assumption that the state is the final form of human organization, it follows that people outside the state are "behind" the people inside it. Scott argues that if we view the state as a choice, we can see the people outside it as having chosen to avoid the state and instead to make their lives in the freedom offered by terrain that is less capable of what the state sees as quantifiable production, terrain where they can often exist outside the state's monopoly on the legitimate use of violence. It was in just such a mountain range, one that remains beyond the control of the state to this day, that the ideas I had traveled so far to learn about were born.

Sitting at a wobbly outdoor table in a town in Kurdistan, in the shadow of the mountains where the KCK (the Koma Civakên Kurdistanê or Kurdistan Communities Union), still maintains its strongholds, Zagros Hiwa, the group's spokesman, told me that he'd taken a long and risky journey from the group's bases to meet me.[1] The region had been hammered by Turkish drone strikes against KCK-affiliated leaders all month. The KCK is an umbrella organization

---

1. The Kurdistan Communities Union is an organization that brings together the different elements of the Kurdish freedom movement that differ by the state they work in and the way they interpret the movement's ideology.

that brings together the various Kurdish armed and political groups dedicated to implementing their leader Abdullah Öcalan's ideology of democratic confederalism, making the KCK's representatives high-value targets for the movement's enemies. "I smuggled myself into town," Hiwa told me, "because coming to my place would be too risky."

Hiwa and the friend who accompanied him sat across the little wrought iron table from me, all of us seated on those small metal chairs that seemed custom-made to make me look as awkward as a giraffe limbo dancing. Both Hiwa and his friend seemed aware the situation was high-risk for them, and our conversation was marked with pauses as cars or pedestrians passed by. Every time a shopper neared us we fell silent, and our conversation picked up again only once they had gone on their way. Cars parking or any movement above were met with furtive glances. Such was the degree of concern that we were even eschewing the chai this time. When it's safer, Hiwa promised, I will be able to come and meet him in the mountains.

We talked for an hour about gender, the state, the French and Spanish revolutions, and the situation that was unfolding in Gaza at the time. Many of the insights you'll find in other chapters of this book came from that hour, in which Hiwa seemed to weigh every word against the risk he'd taken to join me and his years of experience in the Kurdish freedom struggle. He was glad I had come to Rojava because it was important for me to see proof that people could exist without the control of the state even in places that had once been subject to it. Before we parted ways, he passed on a recommendation for a museum that I should visit on my travels, one with exhibits on the genocidal campaigns pursued by the Ba'athist Iraqi state against the Kurdish people following the Iran-Iraq War.

A few days later, I found myself at loose ends and decided to travel to Slemani, one of the largest Kurdish cities and certainly one of the more charming, to visit the museum he'd recommended. On entry, after walking through a hall filled with thousands of pieces of broken mirrors, each one representing a life cut short by state violence, I walked into the Peshmerga museum. The first room simply houses a black-and-white photo of the snow-capped peaks that my driver insisted on taking me to see on the drive to Slemani. On the wall next to the photo, a museum label repeats, in English and Sorani Kurdish, what the intelligence officer had remarked on: "those days when we had no friends but the mountains."

Over years of reporting on revolution and war, I've made a lot of friends in the mountains and often reflected on Scott's theories. I was particularly excited to visit Myanmar, where Scott had worked extensively as an anthropologist and to see the revolution he supported until his passing. When Scott published *The Art of Not Being Governed* in 2009, many of the freedom fighters in Myanmar whom I spoke with on a trip there in 2022 would have still been in middle school. Even if they had been older then, or especially precocious, it would have been very hard for them to read Scott's work because access to the internet and literature was heavily controlled by the military government. Twelve years later, in 2021, they would find themselves in one of the very shatter zones that Scott was talking about.

The hills of the Thai-Burmese border, where I met these freedom fighters, arch up from the Moei River that divides the two countries. The steep and densely wooded slopes are hard to farm, harder to pave, and harder yet to control. They stand in sharp contrast to seven-lane motorways and giant pagodas of Nay Pyi Taw, the capital city that the military began building in 2002 to create an impenetrable fortress in the country's arid central plains. After the coup, young people seeking to escape the reach of the state fled Myanmar's cities for these mountains and jungles, places where the Burmese state never really enjoyed the monopoly on the legitimate use of violence that characterizes the Weberian state.

Following the coup and the bloody repression of the youth's demands for democracy, it was from Yangon, Mandalay, and Nay Pyi Taw that young Bamar people—the majority ethnicity that has long dominated the military and governance of the country—fled, and it was in the mountains that they found safety and refuge from the state. On a Zoom call with Sayar Mohn Tine, a leader in the Mandalay People's Defense Force (PDF), an armed revolutionary popular front formed after the coup to fight for a genuine, bottom-up, substantive democracy for all of Myanmar's ethnic groups, he wanted to make very clear to me that they were not "wild people." This, he said, had been a constant refrain from the military junta they took up arms against in 2021.

The young, city-dwelling Bamar people had come to the mountains, where the state had told them wild people lived, because they wanted human rights and democracy. Ironically, these things that are supposed to be guaranteed by the state were only available to them because of the assistance of the people the state deemed ungovernable. When the Bamar city-dwellers arrived in the mountains they had been warmly received by the Ta'ang National Liberation Army (TNLA), whom they had long been told hated

Bamar people. When Mohn Tine left Mandalay, he was nervous. "He expected some problems because of the [different] races," his translator Nine Nine told me. They'd been told most of the ethnic minority groups in Myanmar hate the Bamar people. "But when he actually reached the Ta'ang region, he found out that there is no hatred for the Burmese people," Nine Nine said. Instead, he found the TNLA was a "well-formed military" and that they were also following a code of conduct. Mohn Tine found that the TNLA was happy to stand shoulder to shoulder with him in his battle for a form of democracy based on bottom-up community empowerment, not strict majoritarianism and the appearance of elections, and, to his great surprise, "most of the leaders from the TNLA have liberal ideas and they also want to welcome the young leaders from the revolution." He did run into one problem though: "[The Ta'ang region is] very cold for the people from the Mandalay region! So we are still having problems with the weather, but now we're getting used to it."

Mohn Tine's assumption that the Bamar people would be discriminated against was typical. Andy, my fixer and friend who seemingly never tired of my asking him to explain the complexities of race, language, and identity in Burma, told me he'd had similar ideas growing up. He says the hate he was taught eventually had a way of making itself manifest even if it has no basis in reality. "It was a really harsh reality for them [the minority ethnicities]," Andy told me. "It's not just the Burma military, it's also Burma's people that didn't care or didn't do anything while they're [minority ethnic groups] being killed. So then they have this hate against Burman people, which is very understandable."

At first, Andy didn't question where the hate had come from, and he assumed hostilities between ethnic groups were natural. He says he began to question this in 2017. "The Rohingya thing happened in 2017. I was seventeen. I started getting phone calls from my friends in the Western countries, Westerners. They would be like, 'Hey, what's happening in your country? Why are you killing all the Muslims?' I'm in Mae Sot, Thailand. And I'm like, 'I don't know what you're talking about. I've never heard anything like that, right?' And then I tried to learn a little bit more, but everyone had such intense opinions about it. That at some point I'm like 'Ah fuck, I don't know anymore.' Because the military was still in control at that time still. So, they controlled the news, they controlled the media." It wasn't until Andy experienced repression himself that he realized that, just like he was, many of the minority ethnic groups were victims of state violence misrepresented in state propaganda. "You're a kid, you're trying to get by day to day, so you didn't really think about it. And for me, that went on for a long time until the military coup happened in Myanmar," Andy said.

In reconsidering his politics, Andy also reconsidered his own identity. He spent much of his childhood in a refugee camp just across the Myanmar–Thailand border where most of the refugees were Karen. "I'm half Bamar, half Karen," he said. "I don't identify myself as Karen anymore because when we're in the [refugee] camp, we got so much shit for being half Bamar. So that was the time when I was, like, 'fuck Karen people.'" In changing his view of ethnicity, he has also changed his view of politics and of the once revered Bamar Aung San Suu Kyi. "She's not really a part of this revolution anymore, I think, especially for us. People will say different things. If you ask someone else about their opinions about her or the NLD, the NUG, they would say something different.[2] But for me, I focus more on the ethnic groups and try to learn more about how they feel, and what they feel. And I speak for them when I speak."

In Mae Sot, I met Andy and his brothers. Every night, after long hot days of heart-wrenching interviews, somewhat clandestine meetups, and the occasional car bomb, we'd meet to eat street food in tiny plastic chairs and drink cheap beer that was pretty good and cheap whiskey that was pretty awful. On our last night, after being systematically humiliated at both pool and our impromptu karaoke singing, we talked about politics. I told Andy I don't vote often, that I'd rather spend my time doing something with my hands and I see voting as more a harm reduction tool than a meaningful chance at political expression. My explanation of anarchism wasn't my best work, but perhaps a young man who has experienced so much state violence is well placed to understand it through his own life experience. A few months later, he asked me for some books to read. A few months after that, I saw him on social media engaging with friends in Rojava.

It wasn't until I was waking up to the call to prayer in Qamişlo, more than a year after I'd met Andy, that I realized how much his thinking on the state had

---

2.   The National League for Democracy, a party built around Aung San Suu Kyi and the neoliberal and somewhat protracted transition to procedural democracy. The National Unity Government, a still mainly Bamar organization of elected lawmakers ousted by the coup and sometimes erroneously referred to as a government in exile; it claims the legitimacy of the 2021 electoral mandate and in theory commands the PDFs.

evolved. With eyes blurry from lack of sleep, and a faint buzz puncturing the half-light that might have been a drone or just the half-dead air conditioning making a valiant effort to defeat the desert heat, I saw an unusual number of encrypted messages on my phone. Andy had sent a video, and I rushed over to the chair in the corner of the room that I had to stand on to get good wi-fi signal. As the video loaded, I saw the young men and women of the Karenni Nationalities Defense Forces, a unit formed after the coup to fight against the junta and for the people. One of them stepped forward and began reading a speech which, to my great surprise, expressed their solidarity with the people of Rojava. From a world apart and without the help or recognition of the "community" of states, these two groups had found one another. Soon, I was suggesting readings on Myanmar to interested friends in Rojava, and readings on democratic confederalism to teenage guerrillas in the Burmese jungle. After so many years, and so many lies from the US and other allies who abandoned them after they stopped being useful, the people of Rojava had finally found a friend other than the mountains.

2

Spain

It was a fight for the most profound and original social transformation
of our century. A new society had just started to be constructed, the
unjust society was disappearing, and some historians ... not only have
demonstrated a lack of objectivity in their descriptions of these important events but did everything possible to ignobly and maliciously
discredit the positive achievements of the revolutionaries. In 1936 I was
fifteen years old ... 50 years have passed, but I still feel the atmosphere
of that epoch ... 17th and 23rd of July, 1936.

—Eduardo Vivancos

In Barcelona on the evening of July 18, 1936, Pau Casals—the father of the
modern cello—was leading the final rehearsals for the opening ceremony
of the Popular Olympics. The choir and orchestra had already practiced the
hymn of the Popular Olympics, a song co-written by a Catalan composer and
an exiled German-Jewish lyricist. The latter had fled fascism in Germany, the
former was standing against it at home. With the hymn finished, Casals moved
to a familiar favorite, the final movement of Beethoven's 9th Symphony, better
known as the "Ode to Joy." The music began with quiet strings that resembled
an orchestra tuning up, and the singers from a neighborhood choral society
took their places, drew in a deep breath, and prepared to sing. Before they
could, the performance was interrupted.

"I had just called the chorus onto the stage to sing the chorale," Casals
wrote in his memoirs, "when a man rushed into the hall. He handed me an
envelope, saying breathlessly, "This is from Minister Gassol, an uprising is
expected at any moment in the city." Casals continued:

I read Gassol's message. It said our rehearsal should be discontinued immediately . . . all the musicians should go straight home . . . the concert scheduled for the following day was to be canceled. The messenger told me that since the message had been written, an insurrection had started in Madrid and fascist troops were now marching on Barcelona. I read the message aloud to the orchestra and the chorus. Then I said, "Dear friends, I do not know when we shall meet again. As a farewell to one another, shall we play the Finale?" They shouted, "Yes, let us finish it!" The orchestra played and the chorus sang as never before. . . . "All mankind are sworn brothers where thy gentle wings abide!" I could not see the notes because of my tears.[1]

Before dawn the next day, the city woke to the sound of gunfire. To most of the working class, this wasn't a surprise; most of them probably hadn't gone to bed at all. The members of the anarchist affinity group Nosotros ("Us")—Buenaventura Durruti (who had checked himself out from the hospital five days before and was still recovering from a hernia operation), Francisco Ascaso, Juan García Oliver, Aurelio Fernández, Ricardo Sanz, Gregorio Jover, Antonio Ortiz, and Antonio Martínez—stood ready. They had robbed banks and killed archbishops and prime ministers; they didn't fear the state, in fact through years of gunslinging for the greater good, they had taught the state to fear them. Their war with the state had begun more than a decade ago, but now they stood ready to lead the five thousand members of the anarcho-syndicalist Confederación Nacional del Trabajo (National Confederation of Labor, or CNT) in a decisive battle.

The Spanish military, unwilling to accept the result of the 1936 election, had risen against the state. Among them were monarchists, radical Catholic Nationalists, and fascists. Fascism was still young in Spain, but no sooner had Spain formed a fascist party in 1934 (a merger of the Falangists and the right-wing unions) than the socialists and anarchists, informed by the many German and Italian exiles among them, decided the correct response was to begin killing the fascist party's members. The Spanish Second Republic, which was now collapsing, was known in the streets as the "Republic of Order."[2] In its short existence, it had swung from the liberal left to the hard right and back to the left, but it never looked favorably upon the anarchists. The Second Republic's history is generally broken down into three biennials. In the first, reformist millennium, a progressive-socialist coalition established an ambitious social reforming agenda. By 1933, the reforms had gone too far for some and not far enough for many. This resulted, predictably, in a loss of support in parliament for the government and a snap election that returned a broad right-wing alliance. The Spanish Confederation of the Autonomous Right (Confederación Española de Derechas Autónomas, or CEDA) emerged as the largest party, but Spain's president declined to invite their leader to form a government, as his monarchist sympathies were clear. This government's harsh policing led to rebellion in Asturias and Catalonia and a massive state crackdown. This, in turn, led to the victory of a broad Popular Front in the 1936 elections, which in turn led to a coup.[1]

In Catalonia, the Esquerra Republicana de Catalunya (Republican Left of Catalonia, or ERC), the left Republican coalition that had controlled the legislature there since 1931, took to the streets in 1934, but the anarchists remained at home. Without the anarchist pistoleros, the Catalan uprising of October 1934 lasted only a few hours. That same month, Asturian miners occupied cities and set up revolutionary committees and abolished money, standing against the state for two weeks before the government's Regular troops (the name distinguishes them from auxiliaries) from Spanish Morocco were deployed against them. In a sign of things to come, the military chose not to use conscripts from the peninsula because it feared they would refuse to fight their own people.

The anarchist movement, and particularly anarcho-syndicalist movement, in Spain had become the dominant political ideology of the Spanish workers by the time the civil war began. The Spanish section of the First International was founded in 1869 and quickly anarcho-syndicalist organizing gained such a strong foothold that it left little space for the Marxism-Leninism that was taking root in unions and parties elsewhere. In the early twentieth century, the anarcho-syndicalist CNT was born, and, through its unions, anarchists dominated labor organizing in the Basqueland and Catalonia, Spain's industrial provinces. By the time of the revolution in Russia, anarchism had eclipsed other left ideologies in Spain and Marxism-Leninism struggled to establish a foothold among the workers, especially in Catalonia. The two pillars of anarchism in Spain were a strong stance against the total domination of the Catholic Church on all sectors of society and its active role in subjugating

---

1. It is with great regret that I must summarize the history of the Second Republic so briefly, but this is not a book about the state. Readers interested in knowing more about the topic will find a wealth of resources in the bibliography.

the peasants and workers, and opposition to the brutal excesses of Spain's industrial and agricultural bosses. These were enemies it shared with some left Republicans, but that was where their similarities ended. While the Republic tolerated the existence of anarchists, they were far from friendly to the libertarian left and created new police forces to suppress anarchist uprisings in the first years of the new republic.

Anarchism, as happens everywhere, was met with repression and violence. In the years before the Civil War Spanish anarchists had responded in kind. Since the end of the nineteenth century, Spanish anarchists had embraced the bomb and the pistol alongside the union and mutual aid. In the early twentieth century, the CNT formed various direct action components to fight back against state violence. The core of its direct action capacity was the affinity group, a small clandestine group that planned, executed, and took credit for daring direct action missions that included robberies and violence against bosses who abused workers. In addition to these affinity groups, action groups were directly funded by the CNT to retaliate against boss-funded assaults and the intimidation of workers by paid thugs, resulting in an era known as "pistolerisme" in Barcelona that peaked in the 1920s. Finally, defense committees were the cells which the CNT established to defend the revolution and dedicated themselves to preparing for a broader conflict. These groups showed their value in July 1936. In addition to these group activities, so-called "lone tigers" undertook individual acts in an attempt to unlock the mechanism of history and spark revolutionary uprisings.

By 1936, in what would be the final election of the Republic, both sides were very clearly committed to the outcome of the game more than the rules by which it was supposed to be played. On July 18, as the fascist rebels sought to take Barcelona, General Fernández Burriel's IV division marched to Plaça de Catalunya, where the people lay in wait. Anarchist fighters remained in constant communication with the CNT and the anarchist FAI. The uprising had begun in Morocco on July 17, and tension had been building in the crowded slums where Barcelona's workers lived cheek by jowl. Union Radio had called a general strike the day before, and despite the refusal of the Republican government to acknowledge how deep the trouble they were in was, the unions were under no illusion as to the stakes. They demanded they be armed against the nationalist, fascist, and monarchist forces of the uprising. The state refused.

Despite being outgunned, the anarchists had a plan. They would let the troops march as far from their barracks as they could before their barricades blocked the troops' way, then they would block the troops' retreat and leave them with a choice of surrender or death. Each neighborhood's defense committee would defend its area, turning the tiny winding streets of working-class Barcelona into a shooting gallery. The Catalan government refused to arm the people, and so they armed themselves. On the July 17, the CNT ignored censorship and published a call to arms. Workers had begun raiding boats in the docks and gunsmiths in the city. When a company of armed police came to recover some of the stolen rifles, Durruti told them, "There are times in life when it's impossible to carry out an order, even when the person giving the order is very high up. By disobeying, man becomes civilized. Civilize yourself by making common cause with the people. Your uniform doesn't mean anything anymore. There is no authority other than the revolutionary order and it demands that the rifles are in the workers' hands."[3]

The armed police, particularly the Assault Guard, were the shock troops of the Republic. In the four years since they had been founded, they had gained a fierce reputation for putting down riots and strikes. They were much better trained than the country's conscript army, and more accustomed to fighting in cities than the rural Civil Guard, whose loyalty to the Republic was questionable. Now, with the Republic that formed their units under threat, the Assault Guard's cops found themselves on the same side of the barricades as their old foes, the anarchists.

The members of Nosotros had abandoned attempts to negotiate with the government and instead retreated to an apartment where Jover lived, deciding their usual meeting place in Cafe Tranquilidad might be too much of a risk. At Jover's flat, they ate spicy sausage sandwiches, sipped red wine, and chain-smoked cigarettes. Ascaso, too nervous to eat, drank coffee and hurried his way through several cigarettes instead. They readied a machine gun that anarchist troops had stolen from the barracks piece by piece, and they checked their Tigre carbines. The Tigres were Spanish replicas of lever-action Winchester rifles that had gained fame in the hands of Pancho Villa's Mexican revolutionaries; this legacy, along with the rifles' relatively high capacity and reloading speed, made them a popular choice among the CNT's gunslingers.[2]

---

2. A quirk of Spanish copyright law made foreign patents unenforceable on products not made in Spain, and thus direct copies of US made weapons were common in Spain.

Outside the Catalan Ministry of the Interior, workers were gathered demanding weapons. While the government had been saying for days that they wouldn't provide the people with rifles, it miraculously found some pistols just as word reached them that rebel troops were en route to the city. The Assault Guard officer posted in front of the ministry, finding himself suddenly aligned with the very anarchists his organization existed to repress, looked at the rifle on his shoulder and the pistol on his belt before passing the latter to the crowd. "Take it," he said. "We'll fight together!"[4]

Radios blared out updates across the city, and the people prepared themselves. Old rifles and pistols, and the bombs that the anarchists particularly loved, were dragged out of the bottom of drawers and from behind false floorboards. Red and black sashes—based on the diagonally split red and black flag that Ascaso had designed—were hastily tied over the workers' blue overalls to avoid being mistaken for a foe. Defense committees established by the CNT been preparing for this moment for years; now they put their plans into action across the city. Over the next few months, they would form the core of not only the combat arms element of the CNT but its logistics and support as well.

In October 1934, in Asturias, a combined force of socialists and anarchists under the banner of the UHP, a somewhat flexible acronym that denoted a popular front between anarchists, socialists, and communists, had taken up arms against the state and held significant territory for two weeks, necessitating the deployment of the Army of Africa (including the first known combat deployment of a helicopter, under General Francisco Franco, to suppress the revolution). The success of the Asturias miners underscored the possibility of armed revolt and, at the same time, likely signaled the beginning of the end of the Second Republic. For the next two years, it was not a question of whether the regime would be toppled by force but instead when and by whom.

Focusing on the losses of the previous four years and the lessons learned in Asturias, the CNT had a plan for its defense groups. Each included up to six militants, with a secretary who took notes and networked, a comrade who worked on identifying enemies in the area, a comrade who looked at the buildings used by those hostile to the revolution and their potential weaknesses, another who researched the strategic points of the city such as bridges and underpasses, one who focused on public transit networks, and the final member, who occupied themself with the work of obtaining arms and supplies. These six-person groups allowed trusted comrades to plan for revolution without concerns of being infiltrated to do the work that would allow them to become the shock troops of the people, opening the way for other workers to enter into combat against the state.[5]

Each neighborhood defense committee would network with others and form a national network. In Barcelona, anarchists from the CNT and other groups formed a local committee for the preparation of the revolution to study tactics, methods, and tools used by other revolutionaries. For the FAI—the anarchist purists who rejected any compromise with the state or with authority—these two groups were the ideal foundation and endpoint of a revolutionary military.

In the months leading up to the revolution, the anarchists knew a coup was coming. In a meeting of the Catalan Textile Union, all the members of the Nosotros group were present and the issue of creating an army came up. García Oliver proposed the creation of an anarchist army, but Durruti felt that the risk of it becoming disciplinarian was too great. In the end, *Solidarid Obrera* published a piece by Sebastian Faure outlining the ideas behind a revolutionary army, including the "centuria" of one hundred fighters, the unit of which the anarchist militias would be composed, but Faure did not suggest that the CNT should begin creating these units. Choosing to remain pure to their ideals and organize only at the six-person defense group level, the anarchists began their preparations for the war they could see coming.[6]

The idea of an anarchist army was not a new concept but merely a formalization of a long-standing tradition of being able to confront the state. Horacio Prieto, who would go on to be secretary of the CNT, began writing about the need for discipline and even for obedience during war, and how this would include workers as well as soldiers. Discussion about defending the revolution popped up in anarchist publications across France and Spain, reflecting on the events in Russia and Ukraine that had seen anarchists destroyed by the ready and well-organized capacity for violence of the Soviet state. The debate on the experiences of their foreign comrades resulted in some agreed-upon characteristics for a revolutionary army within the CNT before it needed to form one in earnest. It had to be voluntary, they decided, as well as class-based, self-disciplined or disciplined in a revolutionary fashion according to a code of conduct established by the volunteers.

In the Spanish anarchist press, which often carried long missives and pseudonymous op-eds, a writer by the name of GEOFILO A. N. T. opined, "[We must avoid] the great mistake of creating a standing army, it must be the workers themselves who change their tools for weapons when the situation demands it."[7] Another, writing in *Tierra y Libertad*, called the idea of a revolutionary army "pure fascism" and asked, "Where will we stop? . . . Poor libertarians, who have to have liberty imposed upon them by a 'well-disciplined army.'"[8] This debate about how far the revolution's defense justified actions that contradicted the revolution's goals was by no means settled by 1936, but the fact that it had existed at all shows that the anarchists in Spain were not merely reacting to circumstances that July morning. They had spent years preparing to defend their revolution, and their success in Barcelona can be attributed to this organization as much as it can to their bravery or tactical acumen.

In Madrid, a city with a larger socialist population and proportionally fewer anarchists, things were even more desperate. The government had failed to arm the workers, but some young army officers led by Lieutenant Colonel Rodrigo Gil Ruiz had taken matters into their own hands and distributed 5,000 weapons to the UGT (Unión General de Trabajadores or General Workers Union) and the CNT. The next day, as it became clear that the Republic needed every fighter it could, new Prime Minister José Giral ordered the government's reserve of 65,000 rifles be given out. The rifles were quickly located, but their bolts were nowhere to be found. It turned out they were stored separately, in the Montaña Barracks, where Colonel Moisés Serra refused to hand them over and effectively signaled that the uprising in Spain's capital had begun. Cipriano Mera, the beloved anarchist leader, had just been released from prison and went straight to the construction union to begin organizing the defense.

On the night of July 18, socialist dockworkers of the UGT identified a boat in Barcelona's port that had dynamite on board. They stormed it, seized its payload, and began distributing explosives all over the city for the manufacture of homemade grenades. Some members of the Assault Guard, perhaps hearing Durruti's reasoning, went against orders and sneaked rifles out to members of the CNT and FAI. Lluís Companys, the president of Catalonia, who earlier that evening had refused to open the armories, realized he had become irrelevant and powerless. He decided to go for a walk and, pulling a felt hat across his face, he set off down the Ramblas. The iconic Barcelona promenade, where today one cannot move for tourists and street performers, was filled with a different crowd that summer morning. Anarchists, Marxists, and socialists were busily putting up sandbag barricades and preparing their balconies as firing positions.

At four in the morning on July 19, members of the Requeté—a highly conservative Catholic and Carlist group—reported to the San Andreu Barracks. Meanwhile, at the Pedralbes Barracks, officers roused their troops with a ration of rum and told them they were being mobilized to quash an anarchist uprising in the city. They marched, in formation, down Avignuda Diagonal, and towards Plaça de Catalunya at the heart of the city. Cavalry and dragoons left their barracks on Calle Tarragona a little later, planning to join up with the conscript infantry. As they went, they shouted "Viva la Republica!" in an attempt to confuse their enemies. They failed at both these aims.

Instead, as the sirens on factories around the city sounded the alarm, the Spanish army's conscript soldiers who thought they would seize the city without much of a fight met up with sniper fire, homemade bombs, and barricades. The construction workers, woodworkers, and dockworkers all knew how to hastily construct these fortifications using tools that had served the interests of their bosses the day before but now became weapons in the fight against fascism. At these barricades, the troops met men and women armed with everything from modern machine pistols to blunderbusses and slingshots. Many troops were forced back into their barracks; others made it as far as the telephone exchange, and the hotels Ritz and Colón in the center of the city.

With the threatened fascism finally manifesting itself, the CNT defense committees sprung into action. Barcelona's Raval, the densely populated district just off the more tourist-friendly Rambla, had become known as the Barri Xinès (Chinatown). This was not because a notably large Asian population lived there but because locals had seen gangster movies about Chicago's Chinatown and thought their own streets were every bit as mean.[9] As the sun rose above the Mediterranean on July 19, 1936, with the military marching towards the city and many a balcony in the Raval quickly becoming a sniper's nest, every rifle was needed at the barricades. The Spanish and Catalan police took a break from killing anarchists, and instead significant elements of the Mossos d'Esquadra (the Catalan autonomous police), Guardia Civil (the Spanish national police), and the Assault Guards grabbed their handy carbines—rifles with names like "Destroyer"—and took to the barricades to fight alongside the very anarchists they had been murdering months before.

For years, the police in Barcelona had done violence on behalf of the people who own things against the people who make things; they fought the unions with vicious campaigns of violence and staged the escape of prisoners to justify shooting them in the back. Now the police had to stand side by side with the workers to have any hope of defeating the army.

The heroes of the day were not police, though; they very rarely are. Instead, the heroes were the ordinary people of Catalonia who rushed to the barricades to fight off the soldiers marching on their city. The role of the armed anarchists, both in terms of the cohesion and organization of their unions and the bravery of the men and women of the CNT and the FAI, was pivotal. This was their home turf, and, in many cases, they had more experience manipulating their weapons than the conscript infantry soldiers they faced

Across Spain, the police hung back from street fighting in the early days of the war. Where the working class took decisive actions, the paramilitary police joined them. Where the military seized control quickly, soldiers often found the police standing alongside them and supporting the coup. The Assault Guard, a newer police force under the Republic, tended to be more loyal to the Republic, but it also only existed in cities where the working class tended to be more organized. The Civil Guard tended to be less loyal but also found itself in rural areas where resistance was less organized. In Barcelona, it was not until the army had been turned back and only a few units held out in hotels and headquarters that the Civil Guard, in a grand gesture, came out to defend the Republic.

The working class in Barcelona had no need for police by mid-morning on July 19. In Avinguda d'Icària, barricades made from huge rolls of newsprint stopped the mountain cavalry—a unit that included troopers on horseback and light artillery pieces—in their tracks. The newsprint rolls had been placed there by dock workers using their electric forklifts. As the workers resisting the coup advanced toward the soldiers, they rolled the paper forward, firing from behind it as they went. They were joined by fellow workers on the balconies, all trying to shoot Captain López Varela and Commander Fernando Urzué, the officers in command of the Nationalist troops, who were beginning to see that the odds were not in their favor. As the soldiers retreated, trying to fight their way back to their barracks, a small group of workers and an individual Assault Guard closed the distance between themselves and two 75 mm field guns held by the military. Holding their rifles above their heads, the workers and the Assault Guard officer signaled their desire to talk, not fight. One of them offered a passionate speech informing the soldiers they had been lied to and that they should not fire on their brothers. Whatever they said worked, and very slowly the seed of class consciousness was planted, sprouted, and bloomed in the time it takes to turn a 75 mm gun 180 degrees and fire it at one's own barracks, where officers were sheltering after sending their men out to die.[10]

Far from Avinguda d'Icària, bullets whipped and cracked across the wide boulevards that cut through the regimented grid of the Eixample neighborhood. Finally offered an opportunity to strike back, a group of German anti-fascist exiles raided the homes of Nazi diplomats in Barcelona and found stashed weapons. Elsewhere, foreign anti-fascists found each other in the streets or joined up with preexisting affinity groups to form centuria. These centuria were broadly based on language and took the names of famous leftists like Tom Mann, Karl Marx, and Gastone Sozzi. Later, some of the centuria would be regularized and placed under the command of officers as they formed the nucleus of the International Brigades, the army of the Communist International. Others would join the anarchists and even give their lives in the revolution for the chance to build a world with neither gods nor masters nor officers or commissars.

As it became clear that the initial attack had failed, the members of Nosotros gathered in Arco del Teatro to discuss their next moves. They were joined by Sergeants Manzana and Gordo, who had fled their barracks and brought ammunition to the anarchists. Together with these soldiers, and members of the Transport and Woodworkers Unions, they broke from their meeting to assault the Hotel Falcón from where they were taking sniper fire. Having cleared out the marksmen, they reloaded their weapons and returned to their meeting and discussed what to do about the reports of workers pinned down by machine gun fire further along the Avinguda del Paral·lel.

It was decided that Ascaso should lead one group, and García Oliver another. They'd approach from different streets while Durruti, still recovering from his operation, would remain in the Plaza del Teatro to coordinate the fight and to provide backup as needed. Ascaso's group took heavy fire from three machine guns and would have been doomed had García Oliver not snuck around the machine guns and their crews, whose arc of fire was constrained to the street they were pointing down and assaulted them from behind. Ascaso shot the machine gun team's captain, one of the army corporals shot his own lieutenant, and the machine guns fell silent. The members of Nosotros, who had begged the state for arms not a day before, now held cannons, machine guns, and thousands of rifles.

At 11:00 a.m. General Goded landed from Mallorca. He had hoped to command the city, which the nationalists had seen as a soft target. Instead, he rushed to the military headquarters where he found other generals unwilling to support his coup. Troops had been told they were fighting against an anarchist uprising, and the lie was becoming apparent. In his rage, Goded muttered, "Abandoned, abandoned!"[11] General Llano de Encomienda reminded him that he had not been abandoned but defeated. Without consulting Goded, other Nationalist officers raised the white flag of surrender. But when Assault Guards approached to take them prisoner, a machine gun on the balcony opened fire on the crowd that surrounded the headquarters.[3] At the direction of Companys, Goded was then detained and transported to the Catalan Parliament, where he was told to make a radio announcement telling his troops to stand down. But it was too late, the civil war had begun and a few weeks later Goded was executed by firing squad. In the garrison in the Montjuic castle, the troops began shooting their officers, and they opened their armory to the CNT.

The Catholic Church in Spain had a long history of violence toward the left, and the left had an equally long history of violence towards the Church, the institution that had been key to repression under the monarchy and, after the civil war, would be key to decades of oppression under Franco. As troops withdrew from Barcelona in July 1936, anarchists took revenge against the Church. Nuns' corpses were disinterred, priests accused of collaboration were executed by firing squad, and the afternoon sky filled with smoke as churches burned. Often those priests and the churches themselves were subject to popular trials or *checas*, but sometimes the executions were more rushed. In rural areas, where priests themselves knew poverty and shared material conditions with the workers, this violence occurred less often. Where churches were flagrant in their cruelty, the reprisals were no less cruel.

By lunchtime on July 19, Spain had gone through three prime ministers, and the coup had taken control of much of the country. But in Barcelona soldiers lay dead in the streets, and their commanders had fled or been arrested. The city had no need for politicians or police, having dispensed with the state in a few hours and seized power for the people. On the barricades and cars they captured, they wrote the names of their parties, or the initials "UHP" which variously stood for Uníos Hijos del Proletariado, Unión

---

3. The crowd wanted to storm the building, and it was only through the intervention of Caridad Mercader—a communist whose son later killed Trotsky—that Goded's life was spared.

de Hermanos Proletarios, or Uníos Hermanos Proletarios (Unite Sons of the Proletariat, United Proletarian Brothers, or Unite Proletarian Brothers), depending on whom one asked. Regardless, they really meant one thing: a shared working-class unity against fascism and against the attempt to weaponize the state against working people.

"Siblings" might be a better term than "brothers." Women had been making steady and significant gains in the Republic. Anarchist women, like the group Mujeres Libres, were at the forefront of the gender revolution and had long demanded that the libertarian left apply its concepts of equality to gender as well as class. Despite their efforts, misogyny remained ingrained in the social structure of the nation, including in many left spaces. Undeterred, women established their own groups, outside the state and within it. Throughout the Republic, the Catalan popular sport movement had long strived to bring the people together in anti-fascist sporting unity and explicitly advocated for women's inclusion in sporting events. In a letter inviting anti-fascist athletes to Barcelona's alternative to the Nazi Olympics in Berlin,[4] the organizer wrote, "That sport, and above all sport of a general, popular character, is one of the best and most important means of achieving women's freedom, cannot be open to doubt . . . The participation of many women in the Peoples' Olympiad is therefore one of the most important objects which this great institution has to fulfill."[12] Now, those young women who had learned equality on the playing fields of Catalonia would made their case for equality behind the barricades.

Many women who had seen that invitation set about defending the freedom they'd found amid the chaos and joy of the revolution that morning. July 19 was slated to be a day when the city witnessed "the uniting of all anti-fascist sportsmen from whatever camp they may come" at the Popular Olympics.[13] These anti-fascist alternative games aimed to show the strength of the Popular Front with a series of events, from those you might expect to special events designed to reward nations with a healthy working class, not just a few freak athletes. The organizers hoped to show that the anti-fascist movement was composed of healthy, strong, and committed young people from around the world who were capable of standing up to fascism in the conflict that

---

4. Many of the communications of the organizing committee are digitized through Warwick University's excellent collection, which can be found at https://cdm21047.contentdm.oclc.org.

increasingly seemed inevitable. They didn't realize that some of them would spend the very next day doing so.

At the games, nations would compete instead of states. This meant that the exiled German Jews and anti-fascists who were living in Barcelona would not compete under the flag of the countries that expelled them but instead under the banners of the Jewish Workers' Sports Club and the Germans Against Fascism. From the US, a team of trade unionists came, mostly East Coast communists. They included Charley Burley, a soon to be legendary biracial boxer who refused to compete in Berlin, and Dot Tucker, a Black woman from the Bronx who ran her union local and the 100-meter dash. The organizers, keen to include Black Americans in their anti-fascist struggle, had paid the travel costs for the American team.

Continuing the Revolution

But the games that were expected to bring 20,000 anti-fascists to Barcelona never happened. George Orwell, who would find himself in Barcelona a few months later, called sport "war minus the shooting," but all pretense was dismissed with on the morning of July 19, and for the thousands of anti-fascists who had come to Barcelona to show the strength and diversity of the movement, the time to switch from running shoes to rifles had arrived.[14]

The Americans, many of whom were there to compete as boxers and wrestlers at the games, awoke to gunfire not far from the Boqueria Market. If you have been to Barcelona, you've probably walked the streets that turned into battlegrounds. Today one can see bullet holes in some of the cafés there; some are from July 1936, and others are from a different and altogether sadder battle a year later. Popping out of their hotel rooms onto their balconies, the American team drew fire from both sides until they shouted in English that they were Americans. Once the fighting lulled, they ventured out into the streets. They saw the horses that had been expected to parade down the Rambla lying dead in the street and used as makeshift cover. Their riders had long since died or fled.

Charles Burley, the son of a Black American woman and a white Irish miner, knew what it was to have to fight for equality. He didn't speak Spanish, but he showed his support by joining the crowds pulling up paving stones and stacking them across the street, forming barricades so strong that they could withstand light artillery. The Catalan workers had perfected them in the numerous uprisings since the Tragic Week of 1909 and numerous confrontations with the state since then.

Eduardo Vivancos, a gymnast, Esperantist, and anti-fascist, had been practicing gymnastics in the Olympic stadium that morning. He, like many Catalan anarchists, had learned Esperanto to do away with the barriers that divided the people of the world, and on that morning in July he was excited to use his skills to help fellow anti-fascists communicate. Half a century later, he shared his memories of revolutionary Catalonia in the quotation that opened this chapter. Vivancos died in Canada in 2022. To my knowledge, he was the last surviving Popular Olympian, and with him died a vision of bringing the people of the world together to play so that they wouldn't have to fight.

On July 20, Vivancos and thousands of others saw the sun rise over a Barcelona that was entirely in the hands of its own people. Runners carried messages between the barricades in the predawn half light, unions met and planned to collectivize their workplaces, and the remaining rebels holed up in their barracks and fortresses to decide between death and surrender. The members of Nosotros had assembled again at the Atarazanas Barracks. Other barracks had been taken, and workers from the cities around Barcelona had arrived to play their part in the revolution using the rifles they had liberated. Ascaso, Durruti, García Oliver, and other anarchist militants agreed that the people needed to move quickly to take the remaining barracks and their arsenals of weapons. Following German anarchists who had captured a machine gun from their fascist countrymen and staged the weapon on a flatbed surrounded by mattresses, Ascaso, Durruti, García Oliver, Pablo Ruiz, Sanz, and Fernández accompanied the vehicle down the Rambla. Approaching the barracks from the northwest, on streets today filled with tourist cafes and ice cream stands, the anarchists were very exposed.

Ascaso led the attack, using the wooden carts of booksellers as concealment. He quickly advanced ahead of his comrades and signaled to them his intent to kill the sentry stationed outside the barracks. He then made a dash for a truck parked on Montserrat Street, which would provide him cover for his shot. The sentry spotted him and fired several times as Ascaso made his dash, but the sentry missed. Ascaso paused for a second to return fire with his Mauser rifle before continuing his run for cover. Just as he reached the truck, the sentry's bullet struck him in the forehead and his revolutionary life of thirty-five years came to an end. Soon after, the Atarazanas Barracks were stormed and their rifles seized.[15]

So intertwined were Durruti and Ascaso's lives that they had both met their respective partners in the same bookshop in Paris on the same day. But the members of Nosotros had little time to mourn, as word was reaching them that the coup had succeeded in other cities. The last vestiges of the state's power were lying on the floor of the barracks, and the city was in the hands of the people. Now they needed to decide if they were going to stay in Barcelona to consolidate their gains or march south to liberate their comrades in Zaragoza. Even with the barracks seized, they lacked rifles. As night fell, CNT patrols set off around the city; each group of five shared a single pistol and a single grenade.

That evening, the General Commissioner of Public Order, Federico Escofet met with Companys. The coup, Escofet said, had failed. But that did not mean that Companys still held power. "President, I promised to stop the military rebellion, and I've done so," he told Companys. "I carried out my pledge. But an authority needs the power of coercion to make itself obeyed, and we don't have that power. There is no authority."[16]

A few streets away, still wearing their blue overalls and drenched in the blood and sweat of the battle, Durruti, García Oliver, Diego Abad de Santillán, and several others were gathered in a tiny office at the Construction Workers Union building. A depressed Companys called them and requested a meeting with anarchist delegates. To discuss this, the most well-loved anarchist leaders and those in positions in the regional committee met at the Casa Cambó, which at the time was held by the committee and became known as the CNT-FAI house.

Still in their battle-worn clothing, the men of action decided to take the meeting and set out to negotiate, although they had little need for the state. They took one of the CNT's newly requisitioned automobiles a few hundred meters to Generalitat. Inside, they met Companys, who seemed pointedly aware that he was no longer in charge of Catalonia. He'd prepared a speech for their arrival:

> Firstly, I must say that the CNT and the FAI have never been treated as their true importance merited. You have always been harshly persecuted and I, with much regret, was forced by political necessity to oppose you, even though I was once with you. Today you are the masters of the city and of Catalonia because you alone have conquered the fascist military… and I hope that you will not forget that you did not lack the help of loyal members of my party. But the truth is that harshly oppressed

until two days ago, you have defeated the fascist soldiers. Knowing what and who you are, I can only employ the most sincere language. You have won. Everything is in your power. If you do not need or want me as president of Catalonia, tell me now and I will become just another soldier in the fight against fascism. However, if you think that in this post—which I would have only left if killed by the fascists—that I, my party, my name, and my prestige can be useful in this struggle—which has ended in Barcelona, but still rages in the rest of Spain—then you can count on me and on my loyalty as a man and politician. I'm convinced that a shameful past has died today and I sincerely want Catalonia to march at the head of the most socially advanced countries.[17]

Not everyone in Spain woke up in the absence of the state. Much of southern Spain fell into the nationalist rebels' hands, and the reprisal killings of anyone loyal to the Republic were as brutal as they were swift. In Córdoba, Granada, Valladolid, Zaragoza, and Seville, thousands of workers were marched to the cemetery, executed, and thrown in mass graves after the cities fell to the rebels.[5] In his daily radio broadcasts, rebel general Queipo de Llano made threats of sexual assault, and celebrated the mass rape of working-class women that had already occurred. "Our brave Legionaries and Regulares have shown the red cowards what it means to be a man," he said. "And incidentally the wives of the reds too. These Communist and Anarchist women, after all, have made themselves fair game by their doctrine of free love. And now they have at least made the acquaintance of real men, and not fa**ots of militiamen.[6] Kicking their legs about and squealing won't save them."[18]

While it did succeed in many cities in southern Spain, and in the anarchist stronghold of Zaragoza, the coup was not successful within the Republican

5. Violence against noncombatants occurred on both sides of the war in Spain, but the overwhelming bulk of the violence was perpetrated by the rebels. Crucially, the mass murder of leftists, liberals, and those deemed to be part of a "Jewish Masonic conspiracy" was sanctioned and encouraged by military leadership. By contrast, violence in the Republic was sporadic, spontaneous, and often unsanctioned when it occurred.

6. The slur in this quotation is often translated as "milksops" but this is not an accurate translation of Queipo de Llano's homophobic and sexist tirade. While there were indeed gay men fighting for the Republic, it is much more likely that this is a reference to the idea that any men who would fight alongside women must be less "macho" than the deeply sexist general and his forces.

navy. The day before José Giral, the minister of the navy, had received an intercepted transmission from Francisco Franco, asking naval officers to join the uprising. Giral responded by telling all naval radio operators to "watch their officers, a gang of fascists." On the battleship *Jaime I*, officers supporting the coup were overwhelmed, imprisoned, and in many cases shot. The command of the ship was ceded to a committee. This led to a memorable radio transmission from the crew of the ship to the Ministry of Marine. "Crew to ministry," the radio transmission began. "We have had serious resistance from the commanders and officers on board and have subdued them by force. . . . Urgently request instructions as to bodies."[19]

It was a few days before battle lines became clear and it became obvious that, although the coup failed in Barcelona and Madrid, the Civil War had just begun. Without boats, the Nationalist rebels seemed to be in big trouble, but Germany and Italy came to their aid, undertaking the first airlift operation in military history using German planes to move the Army of Africa from Spanish Morocco to Andalusia. The Republic, with more troops and more access to supplies, seemed better positioned for a war of attrition, but quickly it would be cut off by the governments of France, the UK, and the US, who all agreed to a pact of "non-intervention" in line with their policy of appeasing fascism at the time. Abandoned by the states of the world, Spain's future was left in the hands of individual volunteers and heavily armed fascists.

Building a People's Army

On July 21, Companys signed the decree that authorized the formation of militias in Catalonia, an occurrence that he could do little to prevent given that it had already begun on a massive scale. The Central Committee of Antifascist Militias of Catalonia (Comité Central de Milícies Antifeixistes de Catalunya, or CCMAC) doesn't seem to have been an official part of the Companys decree but rather a result of the meeting that occurred on July 21. In the meeting, anarchists and other leftist groups expressed a desire not to go for broke with a revolution but to maintain the anti-fascist front that had defeated the coup in Barcelona and do the same across Spain.

On the first day of the committee's existence, Jaume Miravitlles, who came as a representative of the ERC, was shocked to find his new comrades had not decided to conform to the usual sensibilities of bourgeois governance.

"We came dressed as typical bourgeois intellectuals—tie, jacket, and fountain pen," he wrote in his memoirs decades later, "and suddenly found ourselves facing a group of anarchists who entered the room. They were unshaven, wearing combat uniforms, and carrying revolvers, submachine guns, and ammunition belts from which they hung their dynamite bombs."[20]

The CNT's "men of action," organized in affinity groups and with whom Miratvilles was now faced, were more than familiar with bombs and bullets. They had a role in the CNT, alongside comrades more devoted to organizing or theorizing. In previous years, when the state chose to confront the people with violence, the men of action had been at the forefront of the people's response. But the challenge facing them now was to move from the affinity group to the column, the brigade, and the army.

Each political faction had been allotted a barracks by the CCMAC and weapons with which to train and equip its members. The anarchists took the Pedralbes Barracks, the Sant Andreu Barracks, and those on the docks and Lepant Street. On the Avinguda Diagonal, they renamed the Cuartel del Bruc the Bakunin Barracks, after the Russian insurrectionary anarchist. Columns formed not at the CCMAC headquarters or the Generalitat but at the offices and gathering places of their respective syndicates and political parties, and then they trained at their own barracks. This created a difficult situation in which the theoretically united front was impossible to actually unite in one place or around one mission. While the military was united in its uprising, the opposition remained fractured in its response. Only in Asturias, where the lessons of 1934 had shown the value of unity, did columns form of anarchists, socialists, left Republicans, and the numerically insignificant communists.

In the factories around Barcelona, workers' committees took control as bosses fled to France or went into hiding. Across the country, collective factories added a third shift, and boilermakers churned out steel for armor plating vehicles at the Hispano Suiza automotive factory. The network of committees sprang up like wildflowers in spring across the areas where the coup had failed. This was not a spontaneous organization but rather the result of decades of anarcho-syndicalist organizing. Much as the wildflowers wait for the rains of spring to bloom, so the workers movement waited for a break in state and capitalist control so anarchism could flourish.

It was at the CCMAC's first meeting that the group proposed sending columns of volunteers to liberate Zaragoza, and Durruti volunteered to organize the first. Durruti asked that he be accompanied by Enric Pérez i Farràs, a former artillery officer who had been detained for his support of the Catalan separatist uprising of October 1934. A week previously, Pérez i Farràs had been in command of the Mossos d'Esquadra, the Catalan police force. Now he was attached to a volunteer column of anarchists, riding in commandeered trucks and "tanks" up-armored by the workers in a boiler factory.

García Oliver, in a speech broadcast on the radio, whipped up morale for the battle. "Our comrades must be the vanguard fighters," he shouted out of radios in homes and factories across Catalonia. "If we have to die, then we have to die. . . . Activists of the CNT and FAI have to carry out the duty demanded by the present hour. Use every resource. Don't wait for me to stop talking. Leave your home. Burn, destroy, defeat fascism!"[21]

The response was not so much a small vanguard as a mass mobilization, as the battle cry of "A Zaragoza!" echoed throughout the sticky heat of densely populated working-class Barcelona that week. The city saw unprecedented popular voluntarism as men and women rushed to their unions to sign up to play their part in what they saw as the beginning of the end for fascism, and perhaps the state as a whole in Spain. Football pitches around the city became training grounds as workers learned to operate the bolts on the various antique and imported weapons from the stashes amassed by the committees. Soon it became clear that if every volunteer took off for the front, there would be little labor capacity in the rear and fighters would not be supplied.

At the CNT-FAI house, a command post set up in the offices of the Construction Union at the Casa Cambó in Barcelona, a sign hung above the door. "Comrade," it read, "be brief, we make revolution by acting not by talking!"[22] With popular enthusiasm far outstripping the capacity of the CNT or the CCMAC to organize, defense committees took on the role of organizing their neighborhoods. Understandably, volunteers grouped together with others they knew they could trust; people from the same factory, union, or youth group, or just their neighbors in the working-class slums that had popped up as Barcelona's precocious bourgeoisie-built industry that far outstripped the rest of Spain and hoovered up unemployed and desperate workers from across the country. Pérez i Farràs occupied himself with finding loyal members of the military and police who could serve as advisers, while the foot soldiers of the revolution roamed the streets searching for more rifles, bombs, and comrades in arms.

While the militias assembled, the athletes of the Popular Olympics also gathered in their hotels and billets across the city. Some, having seen the coup summarily defeated, assumed the games would be held in a few days in a newly liberated city. Some attempted to hold their events ad hoc in the Montjuic Stadium, others planned their return in October when the coup would surely be forgotten about and the workers in control.

Not all the athletes could go home. The Spanish contestants were often unable to return to their homes, which were now under the control of the rebels, and many Spanish contestants rushed to join the Catalan militias to liberate their hometowns. Alongside them, German and Italian athletes, who knew only too well that fascism couldn't be countered with strong words and debate, rushed to arm themselves and meet fascism in Spain with bullets and bombs.

Of those who could go home, some chose not to. Bill Scott, an Irishman who had come for the games, was convinced that "a victory for fascism in Spain [was] a victory for fascism in Ireland."[23] He decided to stay in Spain, and he fought in the bloody Battle of Madrid, where he survived being shot in the neck. Otto Bosch, lover of novelist and poet Muriel Rukeyser and a Bavarian cabinet maker, sprinter, Red Front fighter, anti-fascist, and now militiaman, also stayed. He fought and died for the Republic. Other athletes went home but regretted leaving behind the city where the workers were in charge and where the army ran in fear from the people in arms. Some came back to fight as it became clear that the war in Spain would not be short or simple and that German and Italian fascism would throw everything they had at the people of Spain while the capitalist countries did nothing to help the Republicans. Others raised funds and awareness at home.

Among the Germans was Clara Thaelmann, a Swiss German swimmer who had come to Spain to represent a workers' sport club in the Popular Olympics but who rejected the Stalinism and anti-anarchism of many of her fellow German athletes. While the majority of German volunteers would go on to serve in the Thälmann Centuria and later in the Comintern's International Brigades, Clara chose to join the non-Stalinist POUM (Partido Obrero de Unificación Marxista or Party of Marxist Workers Unity) militia.[7] The POUM was composed of independent communists who opposed Moscow's strict

---

7. The Thälmann Centuria was not named for Clara but for Ernst Thälmann, the KPD (Communist Party of Germany) leader who was imprisoned and later killed by the Nazi regime for his anti-fascist organizing.

control of its people and the movement.[8] The party had formed in 1935 as a fusion of the Spanish Communist Left and the Workers and Peasant's Block and quickly became an influential actor in Catalonia. Later, along with her partner Pavel, Clara Thaelmann joined the international group of the Durruti Column, which also included Simone Weil and numerous other anarchists of lesser fame but no less value.

On July 24, Durruti took to the airwaves to ask the people who wished to join him to assemble on the Passeig de Gracia, and to tell the workers of the CNT to remain in control of the buildings, institutions, and rifles they had captured a few days earlier. Even five days into the war, he knew that their fight would be against the state trying to claw back control in the rear-guard as well as the army trying to claim terrain on front lines and that they must defend the revolution's gains as well as roll back those of the coup plotters to the south.

Before setting off, Durruti made an appeal to the people of Barcelona to bring food items for distribution. "Enthusiasm," he said, "is the revolution's most powerful weapon. The revolution triumphs when everyone is committed to victory when each person makes it their personal cause."[24] The old distinctions, between soldier and civilian, no longer applied.[9] Certainly, the military was not shy of targeting civilians in areas it had captured, and in Barcelona, civilians and fighters stood together as the backbone of the new people's army.

Durruti left Barcelona with a red and black flag at the head of the procession and the centuria of metalworkers leading the way, then miners who would soon become sappers, then maritime workers soon to distinguish themselves

---

8. The POUM is not and never was a Trotskyist party, despite Stalinist claims to the contrary. Sadly, these claims are repeated in many histories of the civil war despite their open disagreement with Trotsky.

9. There is a famous quotation to this effect in an interview supposedly given to Pierre van Paassen who at the time was working as a journalist. Van Paassen's work has come into some scrutiny in recent years, and some of the more famous quotations in his writing I have omitted as there seems to be good evidence they are fabricated and it seems van Paassen may not even have been to Spain. For a narration that is written from a genuine front-line perspective, and a place of solidarity, not spectacle, we are lucky to have the works of Emma Goldman and so many other anarchist writers. For more on van Paassen, see Danny Evans, *Anarchist Studies* (blog), October 12, 2022, "A Pile of Ruins? Pierre van Paassen and the Mythical Durruti," https://anarchiststudies .noblogs.org/article-a-pile-of-ruins-pierre-van-paassen-and-the-mythical-durruti.

in guerrilla warfare, and textile workers, and finally an old militant known as "el Padre" who had fought alongside Pancho Villa in Mexico and assembled a centuria to go to battle again. All of them had seen street fighting and years of violent state repression, some had seen war, and few were ready for what was coming. Durruti sought to remind them that they had to adapt to this new form of conflict, and to do this he attempted to lead from the front lines by example as his friend Nestor Mahkno had told him an anarchist leader ought to.

The column consisted of thirty cars, sixty lorries packed to the gills with volunteers, four tankers from the metropolitan petroleum company CAMPSA, one water tanker, and fifteen vehicles carrying the various pieces of artillery that had been liberated the day before. They were joined by ambulances, four vehicles that had been rapidly up-armored in the Hispano Suiza luxury car factory, and a vehicle with telegraph equipment. It's impossible to know exactly how many volunteers joined the motley parade as they left the city, but the best estimate is that around 2,000 men and women of the CNT left the city that afternoon.

Although it was officially known as the Durruti-Farràs Column, the vast bulk of its members were proud anarcho-syndicalists, and they gave their unit the name of their noted and respected revolutionary comrade, Buenaventura Durruti. Indeed, by mid-September the old soldier would abandon the column altogether and return to Barcelona. Durruti placed more faith in an anarchist artillery sergeant named Manzana, who had been with him since the beginning, to help rectify the great deficiencies in tactical know-how in his column. The CNT had created a generation of anarchist street fighters who were proficient in the urban guerrilla tactics that had helped them resist and defeat state violence for decades. But the men who could throw a bomb or spray a machine pistol from a moving car knew little about how to assault a fixed position, make efficient use of artillery, or dig a trench. For the conduct of military maneuvers, they relied on the soldiers who had remained with the Republic, and the anarchists who had been forcibly conscripted and managed to escape their units and join the ranks of the revolution.

Eight hundred more anarcho-syndicalists, led by Antonio Ortiz, left later that day on a train. In total perhaps 3,000 anarchists headed to the front, one of the greatest assemblies of libertarian power at arms in history. The columns grew as they traveled south. Generally, military doctrine suggests that a three to one advantage in personnel is the minimum optimal ratio for an assault, perhaps more if assaulting a fortified position like the city of

Zaragoza and fighting against an entrenched and well-trained enemy. This would have required 12,000 fighters, double the highest reasonable estimate for the total number of fighters Durruti amassed. However, the Generalitat retained much of its force in reserve. One could surmise this was an attempt to guard Catalan soil and not sacrifice Catalan blood for Spanish soil, or perhaps that they felt more than happy to see the best of the anarcho-syndicalists throw themselves against the fixed positions, artillery, and machine guns of the army in Zaragoza.

In the next few weeks, the Durruti Column were joined by other columns, composed mostly of male and female workers and some soldiers. Most shared a commitment to democratic organizing, revolutionary self-discipline, and little to no differentiation by rank. They neither saluted nor marched, but they all came to fight. The overwhelming feeling among the anarchists was that the war would be short, their victory complete, and their reliance on other groups or parties unnecessary. They had, after all, defeated whole columns of troops in Barcelona, and persuaded soldiers to turn on their own officers. With the momentum on their side, they reasoned, why would they not be able to do the same across the country?

On July 25, the column arrived at Caspe. The town had fallen to the coup thanks to the Guardia Civil there siding with the plotters. Local militias had been in intense fighting for a day when the anarchists arrived, and the massive weight of their numbers quickly forced the coup plotters to beat a hasty retreat. It was here, in the town hall, that the various columns met and decided their next steps. The Durruti Column, it was decided, would remain on the left bank of the Ebro and reinforce that area of the front.

Soon their triumphant advance encountered the realities of warfare when they were strafed for the first time. The attack, however, was tactically insignificant, causing only a dozen casualties. However, the column broke ranks, and many volunteers panicked and ran. Reflecting on this, and perhaps the loss of his comrades, Durruti withdrew his troops to Bujaraloz. There, he addressed them from the balcony of the town hall, saying: "Friends, no one forced you to join the Column. You chose your fate freely and the fate of the first CNT-FAI Column is quite thankless indeed. García Oliver said it over the radio in Barcelona: we're going to take Zaragoza or die in the attempt."[25]

It was in Bujaraloz that they began to establish the concrete structure of the column. The basic unit was one of ten fighters, a "decuria" or section (later these became platoon-sized elements of twenty-five fighters), which would elect a delegate who was subject to recall at any time. Ten groups made up a century or centuria of roughly 100 fighters. These formations often followed union or industry affiliations and elected a delegate on the same terms and also had a committee formed of the squad delegates and the century delegate. Five centuria formed a group that also elected a delegate. Each group had a committee of the elected centuria delegates and an elected group delegate. These group delegates also participated in a war committee that also included Durruti, who was the general delegate of the column and other notable anarchists (Rico Rionda, Miguel Yoldi, Francisco Carreño, and Lucio Ruan) as well as their advisers. In addition to this, there was an international group which, though smaller than the other groups, acted as an autonomous group federated with the other groups and represented at the war committee by its own delegate. There was also an intelligence group, composed of metalworkers and led by José Bueno Perez that conducted intelligence in the rear. Delegates had no privilege, status, or special uniform, and the only orders the column gave were tactical in nature; the rest was organized democratically, with Durruti chosen leader by his comrades.

Fighting in federation and solidarity with the column but often in different areas were distinct guerrilla bands such as the "los Dinamiteros" (miners from Figols and Salent), "Los Hijos de la Noche," and "La Banda Negra." These guerrillas smuggled vulnerable people out of Zaragoza and sabotaged enemy infrastructure far behind enemy lines. They fought in the more traditional anarchist way, in small and clandestine groups that aimed not to take and hold territory but rather to operate behind enemy lines and execute specific missions before melting back into the mountains.

Many of these groups, generically known as "Children of the Night," reached deep behind enemy lines to carry out daring raids. One such collective, led by anarchist bricklayer Ramon Rufat Llop, adopted the slogan "you can't lose any more, you can only lose your life" and conducted missions deep in occupied Zaragoza.[26] As the military took control of the city, a huge wave of violence against anyone so much as suspected of being a Republican took hold. Franco famously said he would happily kill half of Spain to rule the other half, and in Zaragoza that seemed to be what was happening. In early October, Rufat Llop smuggled himself from the ranks of the Durruti Column and into Zaragoza. Once there, he connected with other anarchists to form a network that smuggled people out of the city through the Devil's Canyon to Republican lines. At one point, the group disguised themselves in the uniforms of the fascist Falange and shut down a whole neighborhood by closing a bridge. They were able to retrieve 108 people and make it to the mountains before the actual fascists realized they had been deceived. Not all attempts were so well fated; the men and women of the group paid with their lives when captured, either by summary execution in the field or after imprisonment, torture, and a kangaroo court death sentence.

Much of the libertarian press argued against the formation of a front and formal units, instead suggesting the columns should fight as guerrillas. While the image of the guerrilla is no doubt heroic, guerrillas cannot hold significant territory or confront an army in battle. Guerrillas behind the coup's lines continued to sabotage its efforts throughout the war and the decades afterward, but the anarchists also needed an army. Along with the need for conventional formations came difficult questions about autonomy, ideology, and capability in the anarchist columns. By the end of the summer of 1936, the structure of the Durruti Column was adopted by others, including the Iron Column from Valencia, the Ortiz or Sur-Ebro Column, the Torres-Benedetto Column, the Ascaso Column, and the Red and Black Column. The Iron Column, however, did not have groups, only sections and centuries.

While the pause to restructure undoubtedly helped to avoid the shameful spectacle of fighters running in all directions under air assault, it also delayed the march to Zaragoza and gave the troops who had taken the city time to prepare. The choice to delay in Bujaraloz, along with the decision not to cross the Ebro at Caspe and push directly to Zaragoza was undoubtedly a tactical concession. In Zaragoza, the workers were in general strike and establishing an effective opposition to the coup. But they desperately lacked weapons and ammunition. While the columns reorganized in Bujaraloz, their comrades died in Zaragoza, and the weapons which had once been trained inside the city were pointed out and in the direction of the advancing anarchists.

On August 8, the column marched again with its new order and little opposition in front of it. Within a week, it had liberated a large swath of territory and seen no opposition. The column now stood just twenty kilometers from Zaragoza. The columns on the south of the Ebro encountered stiff resistance. Again, the Durruti Column waited. Still, they found themselves with only enough rifles to arm two out of every three of their fighters. In front of them, the nationalists purged the Republican supporters in Zaragoza, blew up the bridges over the Ebro River, and reinforced their forces with 3,000 Carlist Requetés from Pamplona.

The same day that the Durruti Column marched out of Bujaraloz, another anarchist column left Valencia and Alcoy bound for Teruel, this was the fabled Iron Column. The column grew as it marched, and enthusiasm was much higher than the ability to arm the volunteers, who were at first not organized into any units. At the town of Sarrión, they first saw battle. Elias Manzanera, one of the column's fighters, describes taking up positions in an old farmhouse. As he stood guard, another comrade played "Farewell to Life," from the opera *Tosca*, on a piano they had found. Their reverie was punctured by an artillery barrage and an onslaught of machine gun fire. "Our young people continually pushed forward," he wrote thirty-five years later, "with the four old rifles we had."[27] They fought hand to hand in several places before the more experienced fighters, who had formerly served in the army they were now fighting against, noticed a weakness in enemy positions. Under their advice, the Iron Column pushed an attack on the left side of their sector, capturing a machine gun and forcing the enemy into retreat.

After a disorganized first experience of combat, the Iron Column formed centuria based around trade unions. They also had committees dedicated to transport, supplies, food, and information. The column's war committee was headed by Lt. Col. Pérez Salas and made tactical decisions for the column, which grew to more than 18,000 adherents albeit with only 3,000 rifles. All fighters, regardless of their position in the column, received the same pay.

At the former monastery of San Miguel de los Reyes, they liberated a prison and released its inmates, many of whom joined the column having been incarcerated for their anarchist activities in the Republic. It is for this and other actions that the adherents of the Iron Column are described in the *Encyclopedia of Spanish Anarchism* as being well known for their "forcefulness in putting the social revolution and libertarian communism into practice."[28] They established their own newspaper and radio station in order to explain decisions and foster debate, later in the conflict they attempted to remedy their shortage of weapons by requisitioning them from police units in the rearguard, and they saw the collectivization of territory they liberated and the liberation of more territory as of equal importance.

A few days later, they fought again outside Teruel. Their ammunition ran low, and they ran out of water. Villagers helped them assuage their thirst, which Manzanera describes as "spitting feathers," but could do little to help with the ammunition shortage. Things were made worse when a group storming a trench saw the enemy surrender and advanced to accept their surrender only to be fired upon beneath a white flag, an act of extreme cowardice and duplicity that the Manzanera recounts as an "irreparable loss" of a much-loved comrade.

At about the same time, a group of anarchists from France, Cuba, Argentina, Germany, and Austria set off across the ocean for the Balearic Islands. The operation was not approved by Madrid but had the support of the Catalan government and the CCMAC.[10] The initial beachhead they gained after the amphibious landing was pushed back once Italian fascist planes destroyed Republican aviation and then set about strafing and bombing the Republican militias who were forced to yield the territory they had gained and retreat.

Having failed to liberate the Balearic Islands, many of the surviving anarchists joined what became the international group. Among the group they joined was Bruno Salvadori, an Italian anarchist who went by the name Antoine Gimenez. He used this name for the rest of his life, it's how his comrades and friends knew him, and how I'll refer to him here. He'd been working as a bricklayer in a village outside Lerida when the war broke out and had rapidly found a way to get involved. With other newfound friends, he'd helped storm the convent in the village and liberate the nuns who were told they were now free women and could go where they pleased. Having liberated their village, Gimenez and the anarchists he had joined made their way to Llerida, and from there they joined the Durruti Column as it passed through town.

While the anarchists were sweeping south through Catalonia, a new government was formed under the socialist Largo Caballero in Madrid. This government immediately began the work of reestablishing the control of the state in the rearguard while the anarchists fought at the front. Meanwhile, the CNT declined an offer to join the government and instead proposed a series of councils in parallel to ministries, and a national defense council composed of Republicans, anarchists, and socialists. But these plans were rejected with a nudge from the Soviet Union's ambassador. It was after this that the general secretary of the CNT, Indalecio Prieto, began bargaining

10.   They were joined in a parallel but apparently uncoordinated mission led by Alberto Bayo y Giroud, a man who deserves his own book, which would surely include his expulsion from the Spanish military for dueling, his publication of several novels and books of his poetry, and his participation in the Cuban revolution alongside Castro and Guevara.

with Largo Caballero to negotiate the previously unthinkable anarchist entry into government.

It was only in Aragon that the anarchists really took steps to form concrete institutions that formalized the gains they had made against the state in July. On October 6, unions and militias came together at the Durruti Column's headquarters to form the Regional Defense Council of Aragon. The council formalized the collectivization that Aragonese peasants had implemented before the arrival of the anarchist columns from Catalonia in some cases, and in other cases had implemented in part out of fear of reprisals.

On August 11, the war committee signed what became known as the Decreto de Bujaraloz, which transferred the land, machinery, and capital goods of large landowners to the people and created a model in which collectivization was the new normal. That previous normal had been a system largely indistinct from the Middle Ages in which the vast majority of land was owned by large landowners or caciques. Literacy was low among the peasantry, something the column sought to address by setting up night classes, but their political engagement was unhindered by this. Much of the land collectivized was, therefore, not taken from families and smallholders but instead from landowners who had fled, been killed, or joined the coup.

In an interview given to the CNT's publication *Solidaridad Obrera* in Madrid on October 4, Durruti summarized his position on the war and the revolution.

> We're making the war and the revolution at the same time. We're not only taking revolutionary steps in the rearguard, in Barcelona, but right up to the line of fire. Every town we conquer begins to transform itself in a revolutionary way. . . . The defeat of my column would be horrifying. It couldn't just retreat like a typical army. We would have to take with us everyone who lives in all the places that we've passed through. Absolutely everyone! From the frontlines to Barcelona, there are only fighters on the path we've followed. Everyone works for the war and the revolution. That's our strength.[29]

The Durruti Column and other anarchist units, thanks to a constant lack of weapons and ammunition, often rotated troops from the front line and sent them to help in the collectivized communities. This may have given the impression to some that they were there to enforce or inspect progress, but to others it was a chance to see the revolution being implemented and know more about what they were fighting for. In one case, Durruti himself stopped in a collectivized village on the way back to Barcelona. Wearing his unremarkable uniform, he approached the town committee to request fuel for his car. On his way to the town hall, he met two older women whom he asked for directions and whether Mass was being said at the church. Abel Paz gives an account of their conversation:

> "No, no," they responded. "There's no priest. The priest is working in the field with the other men. Kill him? Why kill him? He isn't danger-ous. He even talks about going to live with a town girl. Besides, he's very happy with everything that's happening.
>
> "But the church is right there," said Durruti, pointing.
>
> "Ah, yes, the church. Why destroy it? The statues were removed and burned in the square. God no longer exists. He's been expelled from here. And, since God doesn't exist, the assembly decided to replace the word "adios" [with God] with "Salud" [cheers]. The Cooperative now occupies the church and, because everything is collectivized, it supplies the town."[30]

The collectives though, could not provide the fighters with the rifles they needed, and Durruti told a *Pravda* correspondent that they had to rotate fight-ers out of the front due to the lack of rifles. The rifles they did have were all of different chamberings, making logistics a nightmare.[31] In these circumstances, the guerrilla units within the column became vital in the war effort. They could impact the enemy while consuming very little in the way of resources. Through the use of dynamite, they could destroy enemy fortifications and equipment that would have cost many lives and bullets, but very often these clandestine missions cost their lives.

Aside from those daring operations, a lack of war materiel limited the actions of the Durruti Column to skirmishing and clandestine missions to loot weapons from the enemy. Even if they'd been able to acquire more weapons, there was a critical shortage of ammunition. If they did get into a firefight, they collected empty brass casings in the hope that they could be reloaded. While the metallurgical and chemical industry of Catalonia began to refit and prepare itself for war production, the enemy began to court its fascist friends in Germany and Italy, which would deliver a huge and insurmountable advantage in terms of access to war materiel. Desperately, the CNT and other anti-fascist groups on the Aragon front tried to press their advantage before more weapons and planes arrived from abroad. They considered conscription and bringing older workers to the front to do manual labor. But it was not the capacity for work or a lack of bodies that held them back, it was the fact that, when the war began, all supply lines to the Republic were severed in months, whereas the fascist states churned out weapons and war materiel for the rebels at the highest possible tempo. Ultimately it would be German and Italian troops, tactics, and munitions that turned the tide in the war. The collective industry of the Republic could no nothing to compete with the state apparatus of three countries focused entirely on destroying the small island of liberty that was built in northeastern Iberia that summer.

With German and Italian aid flowing to Franco, and the French government having sold a few outdated planes to the Republic, France began to propose a nonintervention pact. On August 7, the so-called anti-fascist Popular Front government declared unilaterally that it would not intervene in Spain. It was joined by the UK, Czechoslovakia, the Netherlands, and Belgium. The US also committed to nonintervention, albeit briefly delayed by a single senator who filibustered until a shipment of aircraft had left. Soon Italy, Germany, and the Soviet Union had signed the pact in extremely bad faith. Rarely has an international agreement done what it claims to, but this one seems to have been uniquely duplicitous.

This was not helped by the refusal of Madrid's government to relocate munitions factories from Toledo, which soon fell to the rebels. Meanwhile, the government of the Soviet Union had organized a workers' collection, which was sent to the prime minister of Spain in Madrid. On learning of this from a *Pravda* journalist, Durruti chastised him. "The meaning of our war is clear," he said. "It's not about supporting bourgeois institutions, but destroying them."[32]

At the same time as the anarchists were searching for weapons, the bourgeois-liberal Republicans were taking action to prevent them from getting them.

Both Madrid and Paris chose to reinforce the status quo, rather than reinforcing the troops on the front line fighting fascism. One incident that makes this commitment clear is the attempt by the CCMAC to supply the militias of the Basque town of Irun, on the border with France, with munitions that Madrid had failed to deliver. The Catalans, undergunned themselves, sent a convoy to Irun on a route that ran through France. The vehicles were searched in France, and the machine guns and rifles were confiscated. The militias of Irun were bombed by Italian and German planes as they tried to conserve ammunition, battleships bombarded them from the ocean, and artillery fired from the land. The planes came back with leaflets, threatening to repeat the massacres of Badajoz, where civilians and fighters alike had been rounded up and executed in the bullring, with as many as 1,000 people killed on the first night the city fell into the hands of the rebels. Frustrated, the Catalans demanded an aircraft from Madrid. Again one was promised, but it never came. After nine days of hot and relentless fighting, the militias in Irun fired their last cartridges and retreated across the border to Hendaye. A week later the rebels took San Sebastian/Donostia, and they soon took all of Gipuzkoa, capturing much of the Spanish arms industry of the region as well as a vital border crossing with France.

While the borders of France were closed even to Spain's own weapons, the country's wealth flowed out freely. When the military first rose up, the country had about $700,000,000 worth of gold (in 1936 prices). Within a week of the coup, transfers of the gold to Paris in exchange for war material had begun. These transfers were not stopped by the nonintervention pact that France and other liberal democracies signed in August 1936, with the gold now being exchanged for hard currency in Paris and then used to purchase weapons elsewhere.

The anarchist columns, under-equipped and facing a war of attrition, desperately needed rifles. With the help of French anarchists, they had found arms dealers willing to sell to them, but they lacked the hard currency required to buy weapons. So, they reasoned that when the state relied on their bodies to fight for it, they were entitled to the state's resources. Thus, these anarchists hatched a plan to take the state's gold reserves and use them to purchase weapons.

Fortunately, 3,000 armed and trustworthy anarchists of the Land and Freedom column had been sent to Madrid to aid in the defense of the capital, and to be the strike force of the anarchists should the government there begin to abuse the trust of the libertarian left.[11] With scant regard to operational security, they hatched a plan called "Operación Banco de España."

Durruti, who had no small amount of bank-robbing experience, hitched a

---

11.   At first called the Red and Black Column, the column was later renamed as another column had already used this name.

ride with French novelist and later minister of cultural affairs André Malraux who was flying to Madrid. However, word of the plan reached other comrades, and there was a great deal of concern about the possible consequences, including open warfare between Madrid and Catalonia. Days later, as the anarchists paused to consider, the remaining gold was shipped first to Cartagena and then to Moscow on the direct orders of Joseph Stalin. Once there, it funded the purchase of weapons, some modern and some hopelessly outdated—like the WW1 rifles captured by the Russian army and now held by the Soviets. Few of these would reach the anarchists on the front, and with the gold left the last chance of arming the militia without complying with Soviet demands.

As the gold was leaving the country, the Aragon front also began to change. A unified command of all the various political columns was created to bring together the various factions and militias. At the same time, the insurrectionist military began to attack. On October 8, a column well supplied with infantry, armor, and air support tried to split the road between Monegrillo and Osera de Ebro. There they met centurias from the Durruti Column armed with ancient rifles and using many different kinds of ammunition and a few captured pieces of artillery. This time, the anarchists showed considerable bravery and discipline as they held off their numerically superior attackers, dodged strafing runs, and conserved their ammunition until reinforcements arrived. When night fell and the enemy withdrew, most of the militia members found themselves with just a handful of cartridges and would have soon been forced to retreat. The next day, they faced a much larger attack, supported by armor and artillery. "The battle was intense," wrote José Mira, a delegate of the first *agrupación* (a group of five centuria within the column). "Although our relatively small number of men in the area fought well, they had to give ground due to the enemy's enormous superiority."[33]

The anarchists were in danger of being overrun, and quickly a relief column was organized, taking ammunition from less intense areas and arriving when the enemy cavalry was about to outflank their comrades. Mira's account of the battle illustrates how the anarchists were able to stop the attack using weapons they'd captured: "One of our light batteries placed its artillery on the road, in front of their trucks, and opened fire." This direct fire method was used extensively in the Second World War and required significant infantry support for the artillerymen while they set up their weapons. When executed well, as it was in this case, the direct fire method forced the enemy to make "a hasty, bloody retreat." Nazi use of 88 mm guns in this role was one of their most feared tactics throughout the Second World War, but here we see anarchists using the tactic just weeks after the first "88s" arrived in Spain and before they are reported being used in this role by the Condor Legion.[12] The Republic's meager air force was able to bomb the retreating columns, turning the retreat into a rout and allowing the anarchists to capture significant numbers of weapons and Falangist and Carlist prisoners.[13]

A few days later, the Lenin Column of the POUM was in a similar position and was forced to fall back from a firefight when they ran out of ammunition. The Durruti Column moved to cut off supply lines and facilitate the Lenin Column's counterattack, attacking Perdiguera on October 16. As was often the case with the various Republican columns, the attack was led by international volunteers serving as storm troops and facing the highest casualty rates. In Perdiguera, their already dangerous job was made much more so by the centuria to their left, which failed to advance, leaving the internationals quickly stranded.

Antoine Gimenez recounts in great detail how the battle played out. Gimenez's group first occupied a shepherd's hut outside the village. The previous day they had captured a machine gun from the enemy, and now they had turned it around to defend their position. They were attacked by cavalry, with each horse carrying two men. "Bullets were flying all around us from every side, mowing down men who had not taken cover in time," he recounts. The group's leader asked them to hold the position for fifteen minutes to allow for others to fall back and for reinforcements to arrive. After fifteen minutes, they were left with only four men and two women. The women were working as medics and refused to leave the wounded as the others fell back.

Gimenez made it back to a barn where about forty fighters had holed up, pushing stones out of the ancient walls to create loopholes from which to fire.

---

12. The Condor Legion were German Nazi troops directly engaged in combat in Spain. They provided tanks, field guns, aircraft, and naval capacity to the rebels as well as valuable experience to the 19,000 Nazis who saw the front lines in Spain and used their time there to hone their tactics for the blitzkrieg of Europe.

13. It is perhaps this battle that Emma Goldman discusses in her obituary for Durruti. In her pieces, she says: "At daybreak Durruti, like the rest of the militia with his rifle over his shoulder, led the way. Together with them he drove the enemy back four kilometers, and he also succeeded in capturing a considerable amount of arms the enemies had left behind in their flight."

They defended their position with dwindling ammunition against a much larger force. From their loopholes, they looked at their comrades left behind in the hut and watched as the men and women were all shot or captured, which quickly amounted to the same thing.

"After that, there was no more talk of surrender from anyone," Gimenez wrote.[34] The group was running low on ammunition, and Gimenez had already watched two comrades throw their last grenades and fire all but one round in their rifles before using the final round to end their lives on their own terms. The fascists in the fields around them were using hats on sticks to try to draw fire and encourage the internationals to waste their last ammunition.[14]

Eventually, they concluded that if they waited until nightfall the enemy would sneak close enough to set their building aflame. "When it comes to dying, I'd prefer to go down fighting," said La Calle, a Spanish anarchist raised by the streets that gave him his name. The wounded begged them not to leave them alive, and four more of them chose to kill themselves rather than be captured alive. The wounded who could do so provided covering fire and the rest of the group made a dash for the Republican lines.

"I ran, and as I ran I could see the comrades ahead falling down," Gimenez wrote. "As I kept moving I could feel the bullets whistling past me, close to my ears."[35] With his comrades falling around him, dying while firing their weapons, Gimenez continued running, eventually falling into a ravine where he was recovered the next day by a Republican patrol. He was one of three survivors, including an Algerian comrade, Ben Sala. The women in the group had all perished. Some were captured and executed; others died tending to the wounded or in the withering fire the cavalry directed at the first hut. Later, they would hear from deserters that the enemy's commanding officer had been killed in the exchange of fire, but it is likely brutality would have been used against them whether or not this was the case.

Mathieu Corman, a Belgian journalist who had joined the column, wrote, "We improved our lines by eight kilometers, but the territory gained did not compensate for the Column's losses."[36] Indeed, the heavy human cost provoked much anger among the internationals, who believed they had been betrayed. It remains unclear if an order to retreat had not reached the internationals

---

14. His book, *Sons of the Night*, is a wonderful account of his time in the international group that has been beautifully and thoroughly annotated by younger anarchists influenced by his example.

but had reached the other centuria or if the internationals' comrades simply didn't come to their aid out of confusion. However, a rumor took hold that Lucio Ruano, a delegate and member of the war committee, had deliberately left them to die. Ruano, an Argentine whose parents had sheltered Durruti from the law during his time in South America, had well-documented fallouts with international volunteers, including the American Carl Marzani, later in the war. Ruano would go on to lead the column but not without a series of similar incidents leading some to distrust him.

Militarization and Madrid

The breakdown in communication in Perdiguera was not uncommon in the war, nor is it unheard of today, but it came shortly before the government decreed, without consulting the militias at the front, that they must militarize by late November or be cut off from all central government provisioning including that of arms and ammunition. Militarization would mean accepting a vertical command structure, ranks, and the associated differences in pay and status. Anarchists were deeply divided about this order, some feeling that it meant abandoning the goals of the revolution, others that it was the only way to defeat fascism. The government took steps to issue pay to paymasters on a battalion level by late October. Because the ardently anarchist Iron Column lacked battalions, it seemed clear their soldiers would be paid only what their unions could muster.

Due to a lack of pay and weapons, the Iron Column began to rotate more forces out of the front line and pursue other goals, including burning property and police records in Valencia in a giant twenty-four-hour bonfire, and an attempt to disarm the Civil Guard and reassign those weapons to the front lines in late September.[15] Along with trying to remedy their lack of armament by liberating weapons from the police, they also seized gold from jewelers to buy weapons, as they needed hard currency to access the international market. This infighting perhaps further sealed the conflict between the state and the libertarians.

15. The latter action was, in part, inspired by a mixed column that had set forth earlier in the war, only for the anarchist members to be executed by the Civil Guard members who then defected to the nationalists.

As the deadline for militarization approached and reserves of ammunition dwindled, the anarchists showed little intention of complying. The Durruti Column sent a letter on the first of November explaining that it was operating well without militarization and that changing to the practices of the pre-revolution military would be a step backward. On November 4, Durruti gave a speech defending the revolution against compromise. He coupled this with a stark warning, saying, "You who talk about iron discipline ought to come to the front lines with me. There you'll find those of us who accept no discipline because we each know we have to fulfill our duty. You'll see our order and organization. Then we will come to Barcelona and ask to see your discipline, your order, and the control that you don't have."

Durruti had been clear on his stance for some time, having told Pérez-Farràs in Bujaraloz:

War has been imposed upon us and this battle will be different than those we've fought in Barcelona, but our goal is revolutionary victory. This means defeating the enemy, but also a radical change in men. For that change to occur, man must learn to live and conduct himself as a free man, an apprenticeship that develops his personality and sense of responsibility, his capacity to be master of his own acts. The worker on the job not only transforms the material on which he works, but also transforms himself through that work. The combatant is nothing more than a worker whose tool is a rifle—and he should strive toward the same objective as the worker. One can't behave like an obedient soldier, but as a conscious man who understands the importance of what he's doing. I know that it's not easy to achieve this, but I also know that what can't be accomplished with reason will not be obtained by force. If we have to sustain our military apparatus with fear, then we won't have changed anything except the color of the fear. It's only by freeing itself from fear that society can build itself in freedom.[37]

While the various anarchist columns wrestled with a theoretical choice between abandoning their principles or abandoning their fight against fascism, they made the practical decision to comply in appearance, if not in spirit, with the Soviet-backed policy. While they may have, in theory, added officers' ranks and billets, Durruti told an interviewer that "we don't need any of that. Here we are anarchists."[38]

A system for order was already in place. Obvious and heinous crimes, like theft from the unit or rape, were punished harshly, sometimes by death. However, Durruti used his status as the column's delegate and leader to keep repressive violence to a minimum. He repeatedly inveighed against spontaneous executions, which continued, albeit at a much lower rate than they were occurring in the zone occupied by the rebels.

However, the column's newspaper warned fighters not to fire without a clear target or advance without orders, suggesting that both had occurred at least once as overenthusiastic fighters launched spontaneous assaults. A constant issue seemed to be the fighters asking for leave, wanting to return home, or simply walking off. Many of them viewed the fight as a pastime or a way to generate income at ten pesetas per day—which made them comparatively rich at home. The newspaper sought to persuade them that they had to discipline themselves and accept the revolutionary weight of their roles.

As the militarization deadline came and went, Companys proposed to send Durruti and his column to Madrid. Durruti was strongly opposed, saying Madrid had only political and not strategic value. Meanwhile, as they urged the anarchists to fight for the city, in Madrid the government ministers were planning to flee the city. The CNT would not flee, and Horacio Prieto told the ministers as much, forcing Prime Minister Francisco Largo Caballero to negotiate with him from a position of weakness. It was in these discussions that Prieto secured the rather remarkable concession of four cabinet seats for anarchists and then took the distinctly undemocratic decision to fill them with his chosen people. He also promised to send Durruti to Madrid.

On the fourth of November 1936, the world learned that García Oliver, the designer of the red and black flag and a man who had once planned to kill Mussolini, was now minister of justice. He would be joined in the halls of power by another ardent FAI anarchist, Federica Montseny, and two moderate anarchists, Juan López and Juan Peiró. Prieto set off to Bujaraloz, where he tried to persuade Durruti. Durruti, having been advised of the new "anarchist ministries" by his friend and comrade García Oliver, dismissed Prieto and the wishes of the National Committee, saying he wished to stay on the Aragon front and to liberate Zaragoza.

The same day the anarchists entered a cabinet that was already making plans to flee Madrid, all the Catalan militia leaders met in Barcelona. They suggested that Durruti give a radio speech to raise morale. He did, but, instead of focusing on platitudes or slogans, he talked about the need to focus on the battle ahead and avoid infighting. He criticized the militarization decree and again invited the ministers to visit the front lines to witness the discipline of the anarchists.

The politicians would not have to travel far, indeed in Madrid the front lines were coming to them. The cabinet again proposed leaving for Valencia. García Oliver, who not so long ago had a rifle in his hands as he led his comrades against machine guns in Barcelona, proposed that they stay and join the people of Madrid on the barricades. Predictably, this was not taken well, and the cabinet began turning on Largo Caballero for including the anarchists. Eventually, the CNT ministers agreed to leave, on the advice of the national committee. Outside the government offices, CNT and UGT workers had no intention of ceding an inch and busied themselves turning paving stones into barricades and balconies into firing positions. The streets were strung with banners proclaiming that Madrid would be the tomb of fascism.

The ministerial convoy fled the city on November 6, passing through Tarancón on their way to Valencia and relative safety. The town was in the hands of the CNT, whose militants were in the business of stopping cars and ensuring that weapons and fighters were not being taken away from the front. The fighters were told to make way for a ministerial convoy on the night of November 6 and refused to do so. Instead, they disarmed and detained several of the ministers, threatening to send them into battle the very next day with the militias. After several hours, Prieto himself intervened to allow the ministers to leave for Valencia and Madrid to face the fascists without the burden of government.

"Viva Madrid sin gobierno!" proclaimed the radios in Madrid, while in Valencia the people prepared to receive the elderly, young, and injured in their homes as they fled the city. At a plenum of local CNT committees in the central region, the assembled delegates chose to ask Durruti to come to Madrid to boost the morale of the city's defenders. The national committee, seeing the impact that the arrival of the International Brigades to the battle was having and fearing that the Comintern's army might help the communists gain further power in Spain, also urged Durruti to join in the city's defense.

The fighting in Madrid was fierce. The well-uniformed and Soviet-led International Brigadiers fought from house to house, and office to office in the university. Famously they used books as barricades, and grenades and bayonets as much as their long, unwieldy rifles. Many of them died in Madrid, but their legacy lived on in the murals and memories of the city, and their passports lived on in the hands of Soviet spies.[16]

Persuaded that he was needed in Madrid, Durruti made the decision to leave the front lines in Aragon and return to Barcelona with some of his fighters to form a column of various political stripes and lead it to Madrid. Durruti had heard of some new weapons in Barcelona: Winchesters, some Swiss Vetterli rifles, and Lebel rifles chambered in the antiquated 11 mm cartridge.[17] The Winchesters were model 1895 lever-action rifles chambered in the Russian 7.62x54r cartridge, a much larger-caliber version of the Tigres that Durruti and his fellow gunslingers had preferred for urban combat. Their stocks were made of fragile wood, but their five-round magazine and relatively rapid rate of fire made for swift follow up shots. Durruti elected to have his troops leave their antiquated collection of weapons at the front line, barely functioning as they were, and collect new ones in Barcelona. To the great disappointment of the Soviet Consul, the anarchists were thus equipped with the weapons. Durruti's stratagem stopped the weapons from remaining in the rearguard in Catalonia while also ensuring that the anarchist forces in Aragon kept their rifles.

Durruti could see that the longer the war continued, the more chance the old ways would have of creeping back. It had already become clear that the government would choose to reinforce the institutions of the state rather than his fighters at the front. He felt that by pushing for victory he could also maintain the revolution's momentum. And so he set off, a Spanish anarchist leading a Catalan column armed with American rifles sold to tsarist Russia and then resold by the Soviet Union to Republican Spain.

Sadly, the rifles were not the only things that the USSR sent to Spain. By the winter of 1936, their military "advisors" were taking the reins of a new Republican Army. When CNT's ministers had entered office, the ministers had felt that they could ensure the relative autonomy of militias under the war committee. However, the increasing pressure for "militarization" coming from Soviet advisors and their Spanish allies had swept any possibility of a

---

16.   The volunteers of the brigades were often obliged to turn in their passports on arrival. If they did not survive their time in Spain, these passports, sent out of Spain in Diplomatic envelopes, were used to provide cover to Soviet spies.

17.   In this instance, "chambered in" refers to the specific type of ammunition a rifle uses.

more revolutionary structure aside. Instead, the CNT's government officials scrambled to limit the damage. Seeing the struggle for control of the army and knowing that the stakes were of the highest possible order, they rushed to find a settlement that was not entirely premised on the destruction of the libertarian columns and their members. In their haste, they circumvented the plenums, committees, and processes that they felt would take an unacceptably long time to make a decision on, compromising things that were so close to the sine qua non of anarchism.

By this point, it seems clear that the CNT had gone too far down the slippery slope of collaboration in its attempts to remain relevant in the Republic. Not only had they entered into positions of authority, they had also ceased to be delegates and had become, at best, representatives. They made decisions on behalf of the CNT without consulting the people of the CNT, and they acted like the bourgeois politicians they associated with and not as anarchists. Of course, they could not always obtain consensus for government decisions, but gradually the provision for individual decision making on behalf of the collective when time was of the essence grew into an assumption of power, and their adherence to core principles of the CNT eroded over time as they became more ministers than anarchists. The reality was that the anarchists had, by late 1936, lost much of the impetus and power they had held. With few weapons and little ammunition, and having not seized the gold that would have allowed them to be better armed and equipped, they were no longer able to stand up to the state and its forces. While the anarchist columns had been throwing their resources and bodies into the battle to liberate their comrades in Zaragoza, the Republican state had been devoting its resources to building up its means of violence and coercion. When faced with a choice between reinforcing the anarchists in Aragon and the repressive mechanisms of the state in the rearguard, the Republic had chosen the latter. Now Durruti and his comrades were forced to make concessions that would have seemed impossible on the morning they walked into Companys's office in July of the same year.

A few months later, militia members on leave met in Barcelona at the CNT-FAI house to discuss militarization. Their meeting is well documented and gives us some insight into the debate among anarchists. There was, among many, a sentiment that discipline and better training were needed to meet their foes' increasing use of German and Italian weapons, practices, and tactics. Domingo Ascaso—Francisco's brother—told the group, "Spanish anarchists need to accept the necessity of discipline and responsibility." Another said that the process of militarization had largely been nominal: "We acknowledge that we in the Durruti Column have officers who conduct themselves like true comrades." "The Spanish Anarchist organizations have preferred to come to an accommodation with the moderates instead of fighting them, because this was the only feasible solution," argued another volunteer. "The spirit of the militia is unchanged," this volunteer said, and he argued that militarization was only a "formal concession." Others argued for what they called "technical delegates" who could give advice but not orders.[39]

It was amid this lively debate that Durruti and his column made their way to Madrid. Many of them felt they were no longer defending their community but instead the Republic that had fought them for the previous half decade. Others felt that fascism had to be stopped in its tracks and that Madrid was the place to do it. Some saw the war as an impediment to the revolution and felt that the only way to stop the creeping concessions given to the state was to defeat the coup and then continue with the revolution, using the arms that were already in anarchist hands. With all these views and more, the Durruti Column entered the most hellish urban warfare that any of them had ever experienced. Some of them had fought in the trenches of the First World War, others in the Russian or the Mexican Revolution, but little could have prepared them for the biting cold of a Madrid winter and the ferocity of the house-to-house, room-to-room, and hand-to-hand combat that lay ahead of them.

The speculation about what happened to Durruti in Madrid could fill a whole chapter or perhaps a whole book on its own. What we know for sure is that the fighters in Madrid were in a living hell that autumn, and that Durruti spent his days dashing between the front lines and command posts. On the last day of his life, he discussed the idea of military discipline with Cipriano Mera, seeming to approve of some of Mera's suggestions of a more conventional discipline. Just as he was planning to leave in his Packard for a meeting of the defense committee, he heard the news of a setback and a captain ordering a retreat in the battle at the Hospital Clinico. He rushed toward the front, hoping his presence could unite and encourage the troops. On the way he stopped to talk to some militiamen. What the militiamen were doing is contested, with some sources saying they were fleeing, some saying it was just one militiaman on his way back for stretchers to carry the wounded, and others that they were resting behind cover.

Whatever the reason, Durruti's conversation with the fighters would be among his last, and within seconds the Packard was rushing to the Ritz Hotel, now serving as a hospital, with Durruti bleeding from his chest. At the hospital, doctors assessed that the wound, one colloquially referred to as a "through and through" injury as it enters on one side of the chest and goes through both lungs, was likely fatal. They were scared to operate, knowing that he would likely die on the table and that they would be blamed. The wound, even today, is among the worst a fighter can suffer.

Durruti passed away at 4:00 a.m. on November 20, four months to the day after his dear friend Ascaso, and thirty-nine years to the day before Franco. His autopsy found a large-caliber bullet in his chest, one that the physician determined to be 9 mm Largo, a caliber common to several Spanish submachine guns and pistols. This alone is enough to dismiss the theory he was shot by a sniper. Such a shot would have to have been taken at close to a kilometer, far beyond the accurate range of any weapon chambered in a pistol caliber and likely beyond its ability to do so much damage to a man whose friends called him "Gori," short for gorilla, due to his well-developed musculature. It seems then that either someone on the Republican side, a spy or double agent among the Republicans, or someone entirely accidentally fired the bullet that killed him. Some have suggested it was an anarchist, upset by his implementation of discipline, others that it was the communists, and others that it was the cocking handle on a Naranjero machine pistol catching on a car door. Who fired the shot doesn't really matter, because that is the nature of war, it cuts down the best and the worst with little rhyme or reason, and in being there we all know that death is a risk we must face in each moment.

The way Durruti died is less important than the way he lived. This was evidenced by his funeral, which was executed with little respect to schedule and a great degree of passion. So large were the crowds that the militiamen carrying his coffin could barely leave the building they were in. Two bands were in attendance, each unaware of the other, and quickly they became dispersed in the crowd. It took hours to walk the few blocks to Plaça de Catalunya, and in the process, his guard of honor became mingled with the hundreds of thousands of people who had come to pay their respects to their hero. The crowd was estimated at half a million, more than half the population of Barcelona according to the 1930 census. They stood for speeches and followed his coffin to the cemetery. It took so long to get there that he was interred the next day, alongside his brother in arms, Ascaso. He remains there to this day, watching over the people of Barcelona. I visit Durruti and Ascaco often, and it's a rare day when I don't find their memorials covered in flowers, flags, and other gifts from around the world. It's ironic to see so many little trinkets on the memorial to a man who so abhorred leaderism that he asked people not to clap at his speeches and who, at the time of his death, had nothing more than a change of clothes and a razor in his suitcase.

Durruti's last words were, reportedly, "I renounce everything but victory," a statement that has been seized upon by collaborationists and communists to use as a cudgel against anarchists. But, whatever his words, his message was clear. So clear that on taking Barcelona, Franco's forces destroyed his burial niche and threw his remains, with those of Ascaso and many others whose names are not as well known, in the mass grave at Fossar de la Pedrera. It seems appropriate that even in death, Durruti was united with the people. Today his grave has been reconstructed, alongside Ascaso's and that of anarchist educator Francesc Ferrer, and it bears the message "They symbolize and remind us of the many people who gave their lives for the ideals of freedom and social justice."

The anarchists faced a range of challenges after Durruti's death, not least the shameful choice of one column to execute, by way of revenge, fifty-two prisoners they had been holding at a convent, even though Durruti had argued against such measures. The growing demand for militarization eventually divided the anarchists, with a group in Pina de Ebro who accepted the principle of militarization, albeit with elected officers and significant rights allocated to troops, and a group in Gelsa who refused to accept orders. The latter group would go on to become the core of the Friends of Durruti, an affinity group that attempted to steer the revolution back to its libertarian path and away from collaboration with the state.

Throughout the spring of 1937, after driving the rebels back from the gates of Madrid, the anarchists continued to try to liberate Zaragoza. They hatched a plan to insert 1,000 troops in the city to begin an uprising at the same time as they attacked from the north, but they lacked the munitions to carry out this daring assault. Had they tried this earlier, with reasonable supplies, it might have succeeded. Instead, they defended their lines and launched smaller assaults, such as the international company's assault on the Hermitage of Santa Quiteria. The attack looked to have been successful until rebel planes beat it back and the promised Republican aircraft never arrived. Disheartened, the anarchists saw this as another sign of state sabotage.

In March 1937, the Generalitat published a wide range of decrees that reclaimed power for the state. Crucially, they dissolved the Patrullas de Control, a mostly CNT safety patrol that was established by the CCMAC. They aimed to recentralize violence under government control with an Internal Security Corps, the members of which could not be affiliated with unions or parties. Ultimately this attempt failed and resulted in the withdrawal of the CNT from the government in Catalonia.

Tensions in Barcelona crept up. A communist militant was captured trying to steal armored cars from a CNT barracks, supposedly on orders from his superiors. A socialist militant was shot dead at a roadblock, and the CNT was blamed. At Puigcerdà, on the border with France, the anarchist leader of the town's committee was shot by the Assault Guard, as were three other *cenetistas,* as members of the CNT were called. Previously, they'd held up socialists coming to volunteer, but that practice had long since stopped. Soon after, trucks full of police arrived in the town to occupy the border posts and to reclaim them for the state.

It was in this climate that anarchist newspaper *Solidaridad Obrera* published an article that did not mince words. "Disarming the people is stepping onto the enemy's side of the barricades," it thundered. It continued, "Workers, don't let anyone disarm you, for any reason! This will be our slogan, that nobody should disarm!"[40] Despite this, the CNT called off May Day parades because it was certain that not doing so would cause a riot.

The next day, Catalonia's socialist minister of public order presented himself at the telephone exchange with a detachment of Assault Guards and orders from the Generalitat's minister of internal affairs to seize the building. It has often been said that when Indalecio Prieto, a minister in the Madrid government, called and asked for the Generalitat that morning, an anarchist operator told him there was no government in Catalonia, only a defense committee. Whether or not this is true, the telephone exchange was an important node of worker power, having been collectivized the previous July. Not only was it a symbolic institution, it also allowed the CNT—which dominated the workers' committee in the building—to listen in on calls made by other groups. In one incident, a call between the president of Spain, Manuel Azaña, and Lluis Companys was cut off by an anarchist operator, leading the Generalitat to believe—probably correctly—that their calls were being spied upon. All of this came to a head as two hundred Assault Guards poured into the building. Taken by surprise, the workers on the lower floors were disarmed. But those higher up began to fire down at the Assault Guards.

Quickly, the Assault Guards called for help and were joined by two Patrullas de Control and other state forces. A truce was negotiated by the less radical cenetistas in the patrols, and communications vital to the war resumed. However, the standoff still remained, with the anarchists on the second floor and the police holding the first. The police sent sandwiches to the anarchists; the anarchists dropped grenades from the balcony onto police cars.

The tension, however, was too high, and the barricaded telephone workers were soon joined by other workers in the street, and weapons hidden for almost a year resurfaced. By nightfall on the third of May 1937, the civil war within a civil war had begun. Barricades sprang up across the city, and the POUM proposed an alliance to the CNT. Doubtless they sang the CNT anthem "To the Barricades" and its verse "Arise, working people, to the battle, we must topple the reaction! To the barricades! To the barricades for the triumph of the confederation!" These barricades were the stage for what has become known as the May Days, a five-day-long battle between the state and the workers chronicled in Orwell's *Homage to Catalonia*.

The Friends of Durruti rushed out leaflets urging the anarchists to stay in the streets and fight the forces of the Republic. They called for the shooting of those who tried to seize the telephone exchange, a rejection of state collaboration, and a return to revolutionary order, the destruction of the state in Catalonia. "We will never cede the streets," the leaflet read. "The revolution comes before everything else. Greetings to our comrades of the POUM, who have joined us in the streets. Long live the revolution! Down with the counterrevolution!"[41]

Orwell summarized their position in his book reflecting on his own participation in these events: "The workers' militias and police-forces must be preserved in their present form and every effort to 'bourgeoisify' them must be resisted. If the workers do not control the armed forces, the armed forces will control the workers. The war and the revolution are inseparable."[42] One may, of course, also refer to Orwell's statement earlier in the book, in which he wrote what remains one of my most-loved statements ever composed in the English language: "I have no particular love for the idealized 'worker' as he appears in the bourgeois Communist's mind, but when I see an actual flesh-and-blood worker in conflict with his natural enemy, the policeman, I do not have to ask myself which side I am on."[43]

Sadly, many of the CNT's position holders were struggling with the question that Orwell apparently did not. Taken by surprise, anarchist ministers Juan García Oliver and Federica Montseny rushed to Barcelona to urge a stand down. García Oliver's doubt spread to the town of Barbastro, where the troops of the Durruti Division, now known as the 26th, were preparing to march on Barcelona. His pleas to stand down caused them to delay, but there was no such doubt in the POUM and Ortiz columns. However, before they could begin their march, the Republic's air force threatened that they would be bombed if they did.

Left without support in Barcelona, the workers of the CNT-FAI held tight to their barricades as a symbol of the worker power so many of them had died to build. The police began to fire on them, killing Ascaso's brother Domingo—who had left the front in opposition to the militarization of his unit—among others. Anarchists and Assault Guards attacked each other's headquarters, and once again the streets of the city filled with gun smoke and the screams of the dying. On top of union buildings and collectivized workplaces, workers anxiously waited with their rifles and bombs ready. Orwell found himself on the roof of the Poliorama Theater, defending the POUM headquarters.

Taking advantage of the situation in the city, a group of police and socialists wearing red armbands and plain clothes abducted and murdered much-loved anarchist writers Camillo Berneri and Francesco Barbieri, presumably on the orders of the NKVD (Soviet secret police). Emma Goldman called Berneri "that most gentle of anarchists" in her piece on political oppression in the Republic, but the state's actions that day were anything but gentle. Across Catalonia, in Tarragona, Vic, and Tortosa, police assaulted collectivized telephone exchanges, and workers tried to defend themselves from the same state that had, less than a year before, relied on them for its defense.

Despite the pleas of the ministers, the libertarians who held onto the ideal of the revolution chose to die fighting rather than submit to the world they had escaped the previous summer. When García Oliver begged them on the radio to step down, Libertarian Youth shot their radios. They also transported a 75 mm cannon from the coast and turned it on the police. The government sent 5,000 Assault Guards, all well armed and equipped, rapidly rushing further from the front lines, where they could have turned their weapons on fascists. Instead, they turned them on the workers, and their overwhelming force allowed them to rapidly win the day. This, in turn, facilitated the purging of the POUM and the radical anarchists.

In Madrid, the crisis would soon force Largo Caballero to stand down. For all his faults, he had not been a pawn of the Soviets, despite his nickname "the Spanish Lenin." With Soviet influence growing, the Stalinists and their allies wasted no time taking advantage of the situation Juan Negrín was installed as prime minister and became a much more Moscow-friendly governor.

Orwell concluded, "The Barcelona fighting had given the government the long-wanted excuse to assume fuller control of Catalonia. The workers' militias were to be broken up and redistributed among the Popular Army."[44] He saw the conflict as a "triangular" struggle between the fascists, the state, and the revolution, echoing the concept of the "three-way fight" that is often raised in contemporary anarchist discussions.[45]

The plan of the Friends of Durruti, while heroic, would have been difficult to execute. Even if the Friends of Durruti had succeeded in installing a revolutionary government, they would have faced attack from less revolutionary parts of the Republic immediately. The popular fervor of the previous summer had dwindled, and now the staunchly anti-anarchist USSR held the Republic's gold and its only chance of buying the weapons that it needed to win the war. Even if the anarchists had succeeded in fomenting revolution all over the Republic and regaining the spirit of July 1936, matching the weapons output of fascist Italy and Nazi Germany would have been an extremely steep uphill struggle even for collectivized workers.

Historians, and those who present themselves as historians, have rushed to condemn the actions of the May Days as misguided. The academe far too often fails to consider perspectives outside of those of the state. As historians, we might be tempted to see revolutions as organized and requiring certain conditions, because economic data and individuals are easier to write books about. However, I suspect I have attended more revolutions than many of my academic colleagues, and the truth is that a large part of any revolution relies on spontaneity and spirit, fraternal love, joy, and a tenacious refusal to back down even if it means death. Anarchists had seen their spirit send soldiers running from them in the streets, and they had seen it carry them through Valencia. What held them back was not a lack of people to salute but a lack of weapons. A crucial error made in Spain was to not secure those weapons by any means, and instead to trust that the state would provide them. The modern Soviet weapons sent to Spain never made it to the anarchists, and when anarchists saw them, it was when they were turned against them by the police.

For the Friends of Durruti and other anarchists who opposed integration into the state, there was no reason to placate the Stalinists. They had no interest in the system of global alliances, nonintervention, and international aid because it had no interest in them and had shown them none of its value. They knew the state, which had swung from left to right over the past six years, had met them with violence no matter what ideology was used to justify it. They knew solidarity, and they knew it was the only thing that had never let them down, we can't blame them for deciding to fight for a society based on it.

The death of Durruti, the militarization of the columns, and the disbandment of collectives signaled in many ways the end of the Spanish Revolution. But the revolution had many afterlives. Eight years and one month after the Spanish Civil War began, members of the 9th Company of the Régiment de Marche du Tchad of the Free French Army were the first unit to enter Paris, which they did in their half tracks. The vehicles had each been given names like Teruel, Madrid, and Guernica. The anarchists in La Nueve, as the unit was known, had wanted to name their vehicle Durruti, but French officers refused to allow them to do so. La Nueve went on to fight their way through France, capturing the Eagle's Nest where Nazi officials took their holidays.[46] While it's true that Spanish anarchists buried Durruti and their revolution, it's fitting that in the end they also buried fascism.

3

Myanmar

The first time I spoke to Zaw Lin Htun, he was holding a rifle in one hand and a puppy in the other. He and his friends were on the front lines in a house riddled with bullet holes, and they'd found the dog wandering through the warzone and decided to take care of it. A few months before, he didn't have a rifle or a dog. His only experience of war had been playing war games like PUBG on his phone, and he was living the happy life of a recently graduated education student. Speaking through a translator on an encrypted messaging app from a base in the jungle, he told me and a colleague that he'd been a driver. Every day, our translator said, "He woke up, did what he needed. He got breakfast and he went out to go drive, he came back and then he took a shower, and then he talked on the phone with the girl he loves and then played video games." His existence before the coup, he said, was "not that special, not that different from others."

Our translator struggled to pick up the exact words over a staticky connection, and Zaw's video of the jungle base cut in and out. Sometimes it hung up over the giant teddy bear—which was the size of an actual bear—that they'd set up in a deckchair like it was keeping watch. We'd been planning to talk to Zaw the day before, but the military had cut off all internet access. But late on a Friday night, Zaw called me on my phone, and I picked up and was able to see and hear him. We'd been chatting for a while, exchanging texts and calls, and developing the trust that's necessary for a teenage guerrilla to share his life story with a thirtysomething British journalist. While I waited for my colleague and our translator to log on, I showed Zaw around my house, and he showed me around his base. He laughed at my chickens, and I marveled at the bamboo sleeping platforms his unit had built in the few short months they'd been in the jungle. He was an objectively good-looking young man, with his hair dyed blonde and an easy smile that flashed across his face between his camouflage cap and the grenades on his chest as I stumbled through some basic Burmese.[1] His friends waved at the camera, and I returned the three-fingered salute that the People's Defense Forces (PDF) of Myanmar use when they flashed it at me.

Most soldiers are kids, some not yet old enough to vote or drink legally in the US but old enough to kill and die at the behest of politicians. For every grizzled sergeant major in their thirties I meet, there are a dozen or more teenagers who I sometimes feel compelled to remind to call their mothers. In some respects, they grow up fast, but looking at Zaw and his friends goofing around for the camera reminded me of how young they were and what an intrusion this war was at a time in their lives when they should be doing almost anything else. At least they didn't have officers to tell them to behave.

Despite living a peaceful life, one he described as unremarkable, Zaw had inherited a long history of struggle. He was part of a student union that, on the August 8, 1988, had participated in a national uprising against the Burma Socialist Program Party, the country's governing military junta that was attempting to pave a Burmese road to socialism with the blood of its people (in 1977 it had earned the unenviable title of being the first state to send a visitor to Phnom Penh after the Khmer Rouge took power). The cycle of protests began at the Rangoon Institute of Technology and peaked on 8/8/88, the date which gave the movement its name. That day, thousands of people around the country flooded into the streets to resist the decades of tyranny that had stripped them of their dreams and their futures. At rallies weeks later, they heard from Aung San Suu Kyi, the daughter of Second World War partisan and Burmese independence hero Aung San and a staunch advocate for nonviolent protest.[2] Soon she became a figurehead for their movement and allied it with contemporary visions of neoliberal feminism and nonviolent resistance in the west.

Even with Aung San Suu Kyi at its helm, the 8888 uprising ultimately

---

1. A note on "Burma" and "Myanmar": both words in English are derived from the same Burmese word, with the latter being the more formal version. The US government continues to use "Burma," and in practice, many English-speaking Burmese use the unofficial name as a small act of resistance against the junta that imposed the name change in 1989. However, younger generations use both words, and the conflict has largely been covered under the hashtag #whatshappeninginmyanmar.

2. A note on Burmese names: it is not traditional to have a first and last name in Burma; rather one simply has a name. During colonial times, it became common to incorporate one's parents' names into one's name in some cases. This format is not universal.

failed, leading to a coup and the installation of a body that called itself the State Law and Order Restoration Council in government. Thousands of students, workers, and even monks took to the streets of one of the most impoverished countries on earth, and, in the months after the shift in military rule, thousands were killed. As many as 10,000 of the students fled to the mountains, where they joined the dozens of armed groups from the more than 53 different ethnicities that are excluded from the junta's concept of Burmese identity. These groups, known as ethnic revolutionary organizations or EROs, had been fighting for decades. Postcolonial Burma discarded ethnic autonomy, while attacking ethnic civilians, who found themselves excluded from the power, patronage, and profit that Bamar leaders—from the nation's majority ethnic group that controls most institutions of the state—kept for themselves in Mandalay and Rangoon.

In the months after the 1988 coup, the junta changed the official English version of the country's name to Myanmar, and Rangoon became Yangon. While the name of the country changed, the junta continued to rule over the people it had suppressed using violence and fear. Since 1948 when it was formed, the Burmese government has mostly represented the Bamar or Burman majority ethnic group. Following the Second World War and British colonial rule coming to an end in 1948, an agreement was reached at Panglong between the various ethnic groups who had fought fascism and colonialism. Previously, British colonial rulers had sought to divide the different ethnic and religious groups for more than a century, favoring some groups over others, while they were able to extract the country's teak, minerals, and labor. The Panglong meeting's agreement promised significant autonomy for many ethnic groups. Soon after it was signed, Aung San—Aung San Suu Kyi's father—was killed and the agreement never materialized. Instead, various flavors of unpopular authoritarian regimes attempted to subdue the multiple insurgencies that emerged after the abandonment of Panglong in 1948 and have been emerging ever since. These various ethnic revolutionary organizations that oppose the central government of Myanmar have a vast array of political and national aspirations, international backers, and military techniques. What they all share is a disagreement with the way the state is structured for the benefit of only some of its citizens.

For the next two decades after 1988, attempts at a democratic opening were rebuffed, while the army was built up and resource extraction by multinationals increased. Elections in 1990 returned a majority for Aung San Suu

Kyi's National League for Democracy (NLD), but the military refused to cede power. In 2007, high fuel prices and ongoing oppression sparked the Saffron Revolution, in which monks dressed in their saffron robes joined the demonstrations. Despite Buddhism being integral to the military's vision of the Burmese nation, the soldiers showed little hesitation in killing monks and storming pagodas. International words of condemnation did little to unseat the junta, nor did their incredibly incompetent response to Cyclone Nargis the following year, which included blocking foreign aid, amid more than 200,000 deaths largely from the tidal surge.

For decades many of the groups opposing junta rule had been Marxist-Leninist or in some cases Maoist. The first rebellion against the new Burmese state, in 1948, came from the communists, and they quickly gained steam as whole units of the nation's military defected to their cause. The Communist Party of Burma forged alliances with other ethnic revolutionary organizations including the Karen National Union (KNU), and it chose the Chinese side of the Sino-Soviet split in the 1950s. For several decades, it remained adherent to Maoist thought, even conducting its own cultural revolution and purges in the 1960s. In the 1970s, the ethnic makeup of the party began to shift as the majority Bamar senior leadership was purged and replaced with ethnic Kachin and Wa cadres.[3] The party's adherence to a Maoist style of organizing left it ill prepared to take advantage of the 8888 uprising, as it had continued to focus on rural organizing and the revolution in the cities was not one it had planned for. Shortly after this, a coup within the party caused it to fracture, with the bulk of the party becoming the CCP-aligned (more commercially than politically) United Wa State Army, and some splinter groups forming the Myanmar National Democratic Alliance and the associated Myanmar National Democratic Alliance Army (MNDAA). Others fled to China, from where they reentered Myanmar after the 2021 coup and began establishing an insurgency that did not focus on spreading their ideology so much as on forging alliances and, in a rather uniquely Burmese twist, repurposing hundreds of elephants the junta was forcing to labor in its forestry enterprises.

Explicit anarchist organizing in Myanmar has been rare. Since approximately 2000, anarchists in Myanmar have been concentrated in the punk music scene and Food Not Bombs groups. The band Rebel Riot, formed after

---

3. In recent statements, their spokesman Zhou Min has told me, "We never adopted a policy or rule to put the Bamar leaders at high levels."

the Saffron Revolution in 2007, explicitly identify as anarchist and explicitly state that they are as much an organizing community as a band. Their fans and members have some overlap with Food Not Bombs, which has several chapters across the country. In the beginning of the revolution, there was a short-lived attempt to establish an explicitly anarchist "Black Army" in Karen territory, but this failed. Some anarchists subsequently joined PDF units and Underground Groups, others fled the country. Anarchist slogans and symbols are consistently present in Yangon demonstrations and other areas.

Of course, more conservative leftists and the military have both used "anarchist" as a slur and see punks as evidence of Western lifestyles corrupting their youth. Certainly, it is true that in the cities in the 2010s, there were signs of change as money from the Global North flooded into Nay Pyi Taw and Yangon. With Myanmar's much-heralded "opening" came visits from Hillary Clinton and Barack Obama and the associated skyrocketing rent, with little in the way of material changes for working people. The process began with elections that barred major opposition parties and continued in 2015 with a multiparty election for the first time in decades. But even with this limited progress the country's long-standing interethnic differences were far from resolved, and the Bamar majority military had not allowed itself to be subject to any form of civilian-led accountability. While conflicts between the military and ethnic revolutionary organizations ebbed and flowed, so did interpersonal ones in the capital (Nay Pyi Taw). The political opening of the system led not so much to competition between ideologies and alternative futures as it did competition between individuals hungry to position themselves at the helm of a new vehicle for Western investment and ideology. The National League for Democracy—Aung San Suu Kyi's party—won the 2015 election, obtaining more than the 67 percent supermajority required to outvote appointed and elected pro-military legislators. However, they did not have enough votes to amend the constitution, which barred Aung San Suu Kyi from holding the presidency because her children had foreign citizenships. Under General Min Aung Hlaing, the military held steadfast in its refusal to allow the figurehead of the pro-democracy movement to assume the presidency, and instead she installed an old school friend while making no secret of her intent to be head of state in all but name. The country courted foreign investors, rents in the capital skyrocketed along with a boom in car ownership that gridlocked the once walkable city, and thousands of column inches celebrated the role Aung San Suu Kyi had played in bringing democracy and prosperity to the people of Burma.

Meanwhile, in the southwest of the country, the opening was having entirely different consequences. As Burma opened up to the world,
ideas and information flooded in via the internet. For Burmese people,
arriving late to the online party, the internet became synonymous with
Facebook. Often the social media site was exempt from data limits on cell
phone accounts, and it became a replacement for email, search engines,
and real-life discussion. It was largely on Facebook that the beginnings of a
nativist movement formed, which claimed falsely that Muslims in Rakhine
State were undocumented migrants from Bangladesh. At the time, few had
heard the word "Rohingya," which is the name of a majority-Muslim ethnic group in Rakhine State. A rumor spread that their presence was part
of a sort of top-down push to appear diverse, a forced multiculturalism
that occurred as a result of increased Western influence. The historical
record refutes this; Rohingya people have lived in the region for centuries.
Nonetheless, some Burmese people increased the use of the slur "Kalar" to
refer to Rohingya people. The word was associated with a dark skin color
and contained obvious racist undertones. At the same time as the hatred
towards the Rohingya was growing online in Myanmar, South Korean cultural influences—also a product of the internet age in Myanmar—moved
pop culture towards a lighter-skinned ideal of beauty heavily influenced by
K-pop and Korean soap operas.

In July 2014, a Facebook rumor began to spread that a Muslim Mandalay
tea shop owner had raped a Buddhist employee. Soon the anger moved from
the comment section to the streets, and a mob began throwing stones at the
tea shop. Putting their EU-funded crowd control training to use, the police
dispersed the mob this time. But online the hate continued as ultra-nationalist
monks like Ashin Wirathu peddled the bigoted lie of an Islamic scheme to
displace Buddhism in Myanmar and called for ethnic cleansing and a ban on
mixed-faith marriage.[4] That night, ministers scrambled to request content
moderation from Facebook but were unable to contact a human representative of the company.[5] It was only when they blocked access to the site entirely

---

4. Wirathu, and the 969 movement of which he was a part, expressed admiration
for white nationalist groups like the English Defence League peddling their own version
of the "great replacement" theory and frequently incited violence.

5. At the time there was just one Burmese-speaking moderator and approximately 18 million Burmese-speaking users on the platform.

that Facebook got in touch, seemingly more concerned with the loss of advertising revenue than of human life.

With the 2015 elections came a new round of conspiracies.[6] Wirathu and others began calling Buddhists to defend the so-called "western gate" on the border with Bangladesh. It was in this atmosphere that an attack on a Burmese border outpost by a small rebel group called the Arakan Rohingya Salvation Army (ARSA). The group had begun recruiting men in the Rakhine State region following riots in 2012, but it was not until 2016 that they began a more serious insurgency campaign. The decision in October 2016 to attack the border outpost from the Bangladeshi side resulted in nine deaths and gave the pretext for thousands more.

Across Facebook, and in their press conferences, pro-military voices started to accuse the ARSA, without evidence, of being affiliated with and trained by global jihadist movements such as the Islamic State of Iraq and al-Sham (ISIS) to kill Burmese Buddhists. Anti-Rohingya hatred spread like wildfire across Burmese Facebook pages. Very soon the website became an "anti-Rohingya echo chamber" according to Amnesty International. Facebook algorithms put more hateful content in the phones and minds of people across the country because doing so increased the time they spent on the social media site and thus boosted advertising revenue. In 2017, General Min Aung Hlaing, a regular poster who logged on multiple times a day to share his comings, goings, and musings, posted to his Facebook page: "We openly declare that absolutely, our country has no Rohingya race."[1]

Very quickly, this genocidal rhetoric led to genocidal actions. In the year following the attack on the border outpost, Rohingya people were systematically murdered, raped, and driven out of the country by the military and associated militias. The military claimed they were undocumented migrants from Bangladesh, and as many as 700,000 Rohingya fled there. For most, it was their first time leaving Myanmar. Those unlucky enough not to make it out in time saw their villages burned, their people murdered, and rape used systematically by the Burmese military and its affiliated Buddhist militias. All the while, Aung San Suu Kyi and the NLD denied the crimes and sought to deflect the growing international concern.

---

6. This moment also coincided with the first census in thirty years, which was implemented with help from the UN but failed to include insights from other genocides the UN has witnessed and allow for a more fluid and less zero-sum concept of ethnicity.

At the time, most of the rebels fighting in the jungle were too young to notice the genocide being committed in their name, but looking back on it has allowed many of them to see the state for what it is and reject ideas of revolution that replace the junta with another state apparatus. Zaw was Bamar, the same ethnicity as the majority of the military and political leaders. Before the coup, he looked down on other ethnicities like the Rohingya, seeing them as bandits at best and terrorists at worst. "We thought they were rabble rousing, causing trouble," he said. "That's the language the military used all the time, and we believed it, at least a bit, so we were scared of them."

Speaking to me from the jungle, fighting the same people who had perpetrated the Rohingya genocide, he said the same words were now used to describe him and his comrades in arms. "We understand it now because we had to face it ourselves. And then they're gonna call us terrorists. And however much they tell us [that], we know that we are fighting for human rights, and we know that each person deserves these basic things." This is a story I have heard from every young Bamar fighter I have spoken to. They all had concerns about leaving their cities to join the ethnic revolutionary organizations, but they all tell me that they were misled by the state into hating people who in fact share their struggle against arbitrary authority and state violence. The same divide-and-conquer methods of rule that the British Empire deployed in Burma are now deployed by the Burmese military to control its own empire.

The state did, at the beginning of its democratic opening, have an opportunity to improve the relations between ethnicities. In 2016, it convened a conference called "21st century Panglong." But the conference chose to enshrine, rather than question, the ethnic identities and armed groups representing them. The rigid identity categories that divided people across Burma were not up for debate, and neither was the nature of the brutal extractive capitalism that caused people across the country to work themselves into an early grave pulling jade from the ground or teak from the jungle just to feed their families. The leadership of the ethnic revolutionary organizations had popular support, though some were corrupt and shored up resource deals. They gained leverage by continuing their armed resistance, which the military would not accept—any agreement required the disarming of all these organizations and would subject them to command from Nay Pyi Taw—the capital that the military built for itself. Three ethnic revolutionary organizations, the Arakan Army (AA), the Myanmar National Democratic Alliance Army, and the Ta'ang National Liberation Army did not attend, and the most powerful ERO, the United Wa State Army, attended only as an observer and then left. By August 2020, the government had reached a limited agreement with some of the ethnic revolutionary organizations who were present.

Within a year, all semblance of peace had collapsed, and Zaw's journey to the jungle had begun. By the time he left Yangon, he was joining a no-holds-barred war between the government and the people that began on February 1, 2021, when the country's military turned on its government. In a narrative that will sound all too familiar to US readers, the military had lost seats in the November 2020 election and decided to fabricate allegations of massive voter fraud. While the vote was not, by many standards, free or fair, it did reflect a massive lack of support for the military's political role and a preference—especially on the part of Bamar people—for the NLD.

The news of the coup made front pages around the world through March but then coverage slowed; after all, it was less than a month since a much more bungled attempt at the same thing had taken place in Washington DC. Where the coup did register, it was through a video of Khing Hnin Wai, a physical education teacher in Nay Pyi Taw who was making a video for an aerobics contest and inadvertently caught the opening moments of the coup in her backdrop. As she shimmied left and right in her neon yellow outfit, vehicles full of troops followed an armored personnel carrier toward the city's parliament. Soon the internet and TV networks were turned off and people nervously snuck outside to purchase enough food to wait in their homes until it was clear what was going to happen next.

In the following days, Min Aung Hlaing established the State Administration Council (SAC) and installed himself at its head. President Win Myint was jailed for waving at an NLD convoy and thus apparently violating rules regarding campaigning in the pandemic. Aung San Suu Kyi, who was barred from holding the presidency but held the office of state counselor and de facto leader, was arrested on charges of breaking import laws by bringing in radios for her security team. For Andy, my fixer, friend, and guide to all things Burmese, the lack of leadership was at first a crisis before it became an opportunity. "They arrested Aung San Suu Kyi and all the big leaders right at the top," he said. "So we were like, okay, is someone going to tell us what to do?" In the following days, weeks, and years after they lost their leaders, the young people of Myanmar would find that nobody was coming and that they already had all the leadership they needed.

The day after the coup, healthcare workers launched a massive campaign of national civil disobedience that would become the Civil Disobedience Movement. Their position at the forefront of the revolution was remarkable, given that many of the doctors were established and enjoyed a high status that would be relatively unchallenged by a change in government. But looking back at this moment from today, four years into the revolution and with many of these doctors treating patients in hospitals in the jungle, there can be no doubting their commitment. Dr. Wonder was one of the doctors who pinned on the movement's red ribbon and walked off the job. He told me he felt he owed it to future and past generations to take a stand. "We have always been fighting for democracy," Wonder said. This was his generation's turn, he said. The people who participated in the 1988 uprising had raised his generation on tales of blood in the streets and comrades who disappeared in the night. This time, he said, his generation wasn't going to let the military win again.

Having just completed a twenty-four hour shift on February 1, Dr. Wonder went home to sleep. He woke up to numerous phone messages about the coup. "I saw the news, that really, really bad news," he told us a year later in a crowded hotel room that we were using to conduct interviews. "They broke our future."

He quickly convened a meeting with his colleagues, with whom there was some debate about what should be done. "Who governs our country is not our concern," one senior doctor told the group. "No," Dr. Wonder and his colleagues replied; the government sending them patients with bullet wounds was absolutely their concern. Wonder was old enough to have been a child at the time of 8888, and he knew that backing down now might mean another generation living in fear. "This should be the last time," he told his colleagues. The older doctors in the room had likely been practicing in 1988; they'd seen the protesters in the streets and had later seen them in the morgue. They'd seen soldiers and police barge in and arrest their patients, and they knew what was coming. Eventually, the senior doctors conceded to Dr. Wonder and his fellow residents. "Our generation has already passed through these difficulties before," one of the senior doctors told the residents. "Your generation shouldn't accept that."

Within days, it became clear that the Gen Z and millennial people of Myanmar were not going to accept the coup either. On February 4, thirty people gathered at the University of Medicine in Mandalay to protest the coup; six of them were arrested by plainclothes police. The junta quickly enacted a plan to block Facebook, Twitter, and Instagram access. But citizens moved quicker to download VPNs and encrypted messaging apps that let them work around the ban and organize in opposition to the coup. Two days after the university protest, 20,000 workers from fourteen unions flooded the streets of Mandalay, clad in red and carrying banners. They faced off with police blocking their way and raised their hands in a three-fingered salute of defiance.

That same week, Andy crossed the border from Thailand, where he had been living as a refugee, and returned to Myanmar to participate in what was fast becoming a revolution. Before the coup, he said, he had never conceived of himself as a revolutionary. "I'd never been to a protest. I'd never been involved in any of these things. And I never thought I would be." But the first time he felt the power of a mass of people standing up against the state in the streets of the border town of Myawaddy, he knew he had to be part of it. "When I went there, the first day I arrived, there were 200,000 people on the street protesting. And this big group of people walking street after street and everyone coming out of their house. We have this symbol, three fingers, from the *Hunger Games*, that's like our symbol for democracy now, or for our movement now, and everyone came out of their house doing that. And [they were] giving us water, food, everything. It was beautiful. It was something else. And then from that day, I was hooked." Andy was a passionate photographer and he decided that his role in the revolution would be to make photographs that showed the world what was happening, in the hope that it would care. "I was like, 'Okay, this is what I'm going to do now. I'm going to be a photographer in this and I'm going to take photos of these people and their stories and I'm going to share it. And that's my part, that's my role.'"

The salute Andy talks about came to the movement from the *Hunger Games*, a young adult novel and film in which the protagonists fight for their freedom against a dictatorship that has atomized their country into competing regions. It came via Thailand, where it was used in protests against a 2014 military coup. The *Hunger Games* films, with their themes of resistance against dictatorship and self-sacrifice for the greater good, resonated with the young protesters, who equipped themselves with flags and protest signs and faced down soldiers armed with machine guns.

In an attempt to gain the international support and solidarity that protesters in Hong Kong received—or, failing that, simply international attention—Burmese protesters used signs that reflected common online memes. One young protester who was an admin of the Burmese-language Cardi B fan page on Facebook, held a sign that read, "We Are Protesting Peacefully," a reference to the singer's hugely popular 2020 song "WAP." Another protester, a young man—presumably single—held a sign that said, "Say no to dictatorship, yes to relationship." He was joined in the streets by such memorable slogans as "Don't fuck my country, fuck my friend" and "It's so bad even introverts are here." Aside from the obvious sexual tension felt by young people after a year of coronavirus lockdowns, signs referenced the Doge, Pepe the frog, and the angry goose meme. These signs might be considered reactionary by US readers now, but in the Burmese context they just represented engagement with parts of the web the protesters hoped international audiences would recognize and so come to their aid as fellow citizens of the internet. The protesters/ politics were diverse, but often they used the language of anti-fascism to describe their shared opposition to the coup.

Sadly, despite their unimpeachable wit, the peaceful protesters in the streets of Yangon, Nay Pyi Taw, and Mandalay got very little other than a few retweets from the neoliberal core states who they had hoped would save them. Nor did they receive help from China, despite the efforts of pro-Chinese communist groups like the Leftist Youth Organization to spread Maoist thought and solidarity in the country. When humor didn't dislodge the junta or motivate the US, EU, or UN to act, the people of Myanmar remained in the streets anyway. The junta, having seen that the community of states was unconcerned with its seizure of power, began taking steps to quash the protest.

A week after protests began, a general strike had brought the country to a standstill. Railway workers, copper miners, teachers, civil servants, medical workers, and others walked off the job and into the streets. The military declared martial law, imposed an 8 p.m. to 4 a.m. curfew, and suspended many of the rights guaranteed to citizens under the constitution. By the next day, February 9, police across the country had begun to use chemical irritants, rubber bullets, and water cannons in a desperate attempt to reclaim the streets.

The states of the world failed to help the people of Myanmar, but the people of the world began to step up. The three-finger salute was just one of the many things those young Burmese protesters received from the Milk Tea Alliance, an online solidarity movement that joined their struggle with that of people fighting for freedom in China, Hong Kong, Thailand, Indonesia, and India. A few weeks later, when state violence increased and less-lethals, tear gas, and police baton charges became the norm, protesters airdropped infographics from Hong Kong, avoiding the metadata left by a text message. "There were so many infographics," Andy remembered. Each one detailed "how to be in the protest, how to do certain things, depending on the situation." Andy says that at the time the protests in Hong Kong had begun, he had seen them as a spectacle, something he would have liked to photograph, but he didn't know much about their politics. When the state in Myanmar began using violence to suppress its people, he said he cast his mind back to those protests, and after a few Google searches he found Hong Kongers expressing their solidarity on the internet. "It's not just us," he thought.

The Hong Kong infographics detailed the various roles that Hong Kongers had found to work, including a group of "shield soldiers" equipped with shields and helmets, followed by other "frontliners" with umbrellas to protect from water cannons, tear gas, and surveillance. Behind them stood people adopting the role of "light mages" with lasers to blind drones or police, and medics from the Civil Disobedience Movement stood ready to evacuate and treat casualties. Hong Kong also informed the aesthetic of Myanmar protests as hard hats, goggles, and heatproof gloves for throwing back tear gas canisters became de rigueur.

Zaw recounted a desperate scramble to buy PPE before shops closed or were closed by the junta. He and his friends dashed around the city trying to find goggles, hard hats, and any way to fight back. But soon it became clear that it was impossible for the people to go toe to toe with the state without the state causing casualties. On February 9, nineteen-year-old Mya Thwe Thwe Khaing joined one of the many protests around the country. In Nay Pyi Taw, where gatherings of more than five people were banned, she had joined a protest dozens of times larger than the five-person limit. Wearing her motorcycle helmet, she was taking shelter behind a bus stop and holding hands with her sister after the police opened fire with a water cannon. Then a police officer appeared in front of the police shield wall, took aim with an MA-13 submachine gun, and shot her in the head. Instantly she fell to the ground while her sister still held her hand. Quickly other protesters, including her sister, attempted to render aid, and transported her to hospital. Her twentieth birthday came and went while she was on life support. The next day, doctors tried and failed to remove the 9 mm round from her head. On Valentine's Day, her family made the difficult decision to turn off the life support machine and let her die, which she did a few days later.

Her funeral was attended by tens of thousands of people. All along the route of her procession they held up the three-fingered salute as the gold hearse drove past, flanked by hundreds of mopeds decorated with ribbons and flowers, with riders holding up her photo. Her sister, in addressing the press and the mourners, urged the crowd to keep fighting. "I will continue the revolution," she said. "I will continue to fight against the military dictatorship. To compensate for the suffering of my younger sister, I would like to urge all the people in the nation to continue to fight against the military dictatorship until it is rooted out."[2]

Within three weeks, an instinctive response to the military's seizure of power had morphed from a demand to return to the previous status quo into a self-declared "Spring Revolution." The young people of Myanmar had gone past demanding a return to the limited democracy of the NLD and the authoritarian rule of the junta, and instead dedicated themselves to a revolutionary ideal for which they were prepared to die and that was also worth dying for. The revolution changed from being about never going back to being about moving forward. In the years since Mya Thwe Thwe Khaing became one of the first revolutionary martyrs, the movement has gained coherence and a set of shared goals that were forged not in meeting rooms but in the streets, mountains, and jungles of Myanmar. Today their goal is a federated system where each community is able to choose its own future and its own social compact. Some no longer want to send representatives to Nay Pyi Taw; they want to see power closer to the people. Nor are they willing to allow the state to regain the monopoly on violence. "If we had a second amendment like the US," one PDF fighter told me, "the coup would have never happened."

The politics of the Spring Revolution are not the kind we can concisely summarize or point to a theorist for. These politics were, like those of all revolutions, forged in the flames of street-to-street battles with the state. They coalesced around a few guiding principles, though: a removal of the military from politics, the institution of community governance and a federalized national democracy, an end to the rigging and overturning of elections, equal rights for people regardless of ethnicity, and a voice for the youth. Myanmar's new generation of revolutionaries' demands went beyond the institutions and trappings of democracy that the country already had and instead demanded a democracy befitting a multiethnic polity. Over the course of their time in the streets, as the states of the world abandoned them, they began to reconceive of what democracy meant. What value was the liberal democracy of the US, they thought, if it was letting them die in the streets? Holding true to their core principles, they looked for something more consonant with their belief in solidarity and people power.

In the first month of that revolution, the movement took on many of the cultural trappings of the 8888 revolution. Although the generation in the streets in 2021 leaned more toward the music of Cardi B than toward the '70s rock band Kansas, it was a tune from the latter that became the revolution's anthem. Zaw was a student union member, and it was with his fellow students that he took to the streets. With them, they carried the legacy of their predecessors in 1988, which manifested itself not only in their red ribbons but also in their anthem. "Kabar Makyay Bu" ([We Won't Stop Fighting] Until the End of the World) was written by Naing Myanmar to the tune of Kansas's "Dust in the Wind." Naing Myanmar wrote the song by candlelight in the first days of the 1988 uprising and recorded it with friends on cassette tapes. "I was the oldest one in the group and the others were around twenty years old. No one had much money," Naing Myanmar told *The Irrawaddy*, a magazine in Myanmar. "We put together as much as we could, then went to the cheapest recording studio in the city."[3]

From the cassette tapes they made in the studio, the song quickly spread around the country in 1988, recorded and re-recorded and passed from hand to hand and voice to voice at protests and meetings. More than three decades later, in 2021, the song returned to the streets and was sung by thousands at protests around the country. In early 2022, on a reporting trip, I sat in a small shipping container home as Andy and his brothers passed around an acoustic guitar and sang the same song that their parents' generation had sung in the streets of Yangon decades before. The words Naing Myanmar wrote hung particularly heavy in the little home as we sat among the wrappers and discarded bandages that we had accumulated after spending the last hour going over how to use the items in the trauma kits that we all carried. Every time my colleague or I mentioned an injury, the boys looked at us and nodded as they tried to brush away a traumatic memory of seeing a friend or a stranger suffering just such a wound and being unable to help.

The song's chorus ends with the line "This is the land of martyrs." Since people began singing "Kabar Makyay Bu," there have been many more martyrs. I've seen the song sung by young fighters all across the country as they gathered around funeral pyres in the mountains to bid farewell to their friends in a traditional Buddhist cremation (or Christian or Muslim funeral). As they say goodbye to their fallen friends, they reaffirm their commitment to continue fighting for autonomy and dignity their brothers and sister in arms won't live to see with the chorus "(We'll keep fighting) until the end of the world."

Fighting was what Zaw and his friends resolved to do after the military began killing them in the streets. At first, they scrambled to turn trashcans into shields, find gas masks to filter the tear gas out of the air, and to equip themselves with gear that allowed them to pick up tear gas grenades and return them to the police. The student protesters' aesthetic was one that had traveled the world in the previous two years, from Hong Kong to Portland and now back to Myanmar. I've worn the same equipment myself, seen countless thousands of others don the same de facto uniform, and can appreciate how the pink gas mask filters and yellow hard hats became the de facto uniform of people resisting state violence, binding us together in our struggles against the state.

Sadly, there is little that a respirator or a hard hat can do to stop a bullet, and on Armed Forces Day, March 27, 2021, the military took advantage of this. In a single day, they murdered more than 114 protesters, including a thirteen-year-old girl. Across the country, police and soldiers fired into crowds, into houses, and into the bodies of the people they were supposedly sworn to protect. Across the nation people picked up bricks, set fire to tires, and fashioned Molotov cocktails as they struggled to respond. In a single day it became clear that no matter how abhorrent and inhumane the junta's treatment of its people was, the "international community" was not going to send anything more than a strongly worded tweet.

The rest of the world sat on its hands, and foreign embassies in the capital issued condemnations from the safety of their compounds. Almost every protester I have spoken to since then has told me the same thing, that they thought the sheer brutality of the junta would compel the world to act under the principle of responsibility to protect.[7] But their signs and their faith in the myth of a rules-based world order were no match for the junta's bullets, and the UN stood by as more and more people died. At the time, Andy told me, this belief in intervention was expressed with a grim acceptance that not everyone would live to see the blue helmets of UN troops come riding to their rescue. "To the UN, people were saying, how many dead people do you need for you to take action? And there are people saying, if you need one more, I'll

---

7. The "responsibility to protect" principle (R2P principle) passed the UN General Assembly in 2005, and it essentially holds that where a state fails to protect its population from genocide, war crimes, or crimes against humanity, the international community ought to intervene.

be that person I'll just fucking die. I'll just get killed by the military so that you will come in and fix it and change the situation in the country." Over time, the people would realize that the rules-based world order wasn't real, at least not for people like them. This didn't dull their desire to fight, but it changed what they were fighting for.

"It took about month and a half for us to finally say, fuck the peaceful protest, fuck the international community, they're not coming," Andy told me. "If they would've come, they would've come a long time ago, and we started fighting back." It was at this moment that Andy and thousands of others took their future into their own hands. The states of the world weren't coming to save them, but that was fine, they were building a new world in the streets and the mountains where states didn't matter and people did.

But by the end of April, six hundred protesters had died, their deaths did nothing to compel action, and the best the people of Myanmar got was a statement posted online and a few official condemnations. "Words of condemnation or concern are frankly ringing hollow to the people of Myanmar while the military junta commits mass murder against them," said Tom Andrews, a UN special rapporteur for Myanmar.[4] But after months in the streets and hundreds of deaths, it became very clear to Zaw, Andy, and everyone else that words of condemnation were all they were going to get.

Speaking to the state in the language it used to communicate with them, which was violence, meant facing up to the fact that they could die. Andy told me they were ready for this: "The most fucked-up thing that we had to plan was, what if someone gets shot?" he said. "If someone gets shot and if all five of us [Andy and his four brothers] go running in there, there's more targets, you know what I mean? So then if someone with less weight gets shot, then this person goes, if someone heavier gets shot, these two people go, something like that." Shooting was not their only concern, though; being arrested might be far worse. The military would arrest, torture, and kill civilians and then call their families to collect their mangled corpses. "There were so many fucking bodies that returned back from the military after torture, with no organs inside," Andy told me. "They poured fucking acid in your mouth." The military thought doing this would dissuade people from protesting; in fact it succeeded in showing protesters that it was better to die than to fall into the hands of the police.

Andy and his brothers had a plan for that as well. "We're not going to get fucking arrested," he told me. They lived in a single room, all five of them, with a single roll-up warehouse-style door that they spent every night worrying about hearing a knock on. Andy's crew had only "a sword, Molotovs, and a useless taser." What they resolved to do was take as many soldiers to the grave with them as they could. "Our plan was literally just to burn that fucking door down, so then it would be difficult for them to come in. . . . We'll do what we can with the weapons we have. But we weren't going to make it out."

This embrace of violence wasn't so much motivated by a desire for revenge as one for justice. Andy told me a year later that "we didn't even want to kill them. We just want to be like, 'You can't do these things and not feel any consequences of that. We are not animals, you can't just come in and kill one of our friends and think that we're not going to do anything back.' If we let that happen, then they're never going to stop."

Protests began to peter out as the military made people pay in blood for opposing their seizure of power. Not only would they shoot protesters, they would also force other civilians to clear protest barricades at gunpoint, and they would hold civilians in any neighborhood responsible for protests in their area even if they were not involved. "The military controls them with fear," Andy told me. "So then, the next time that we tried to build something, people were like, 'Not near my house, please.' What do you say? Okay, fine. By the end of March, there was no more protest."

Moving on from making signs and banners, protesters built weapons. These began with huge catapults powered by surgical tubing that could fire rocks or paint-filled balloons at the police. They evolved into air rifles made using plastic piping as the barrel and a can of lighter gas as the propellant. The strikers from cheap lighters served as triggers, igniting the gas and sending a marble or a ball bearing from a bicycle wheel in the general direction of the police. A year after these weapons were first used, some rebels showed one to a colleague and me. We fired steel bearings into a pond with a satisfying pop. Although errant, they were reasonably powerful and might serve well to keep a cop's head down for long enough for people to escape.

Some groups took to making explosives and bombs. These are the time-honored tools of underground urban fighting, but not many of the young people of Myanmar had spent much time fighting in the streets, and sometimes this showed in their tactics. Andy told me of a time when, after seeing a fellow protester shot in the head, they decided it was time to strike back against a police station. "I'm like, 'Fuck yeah. Okay, let's do it,'" he said. Unfortunately, they were not well prepared. "We didn't have enough Molotovs and anything like that," he said. Despite their lack of weapons or plans, they soon had a group of willing volunteers. "We went to one of the police stations. . . . We had a whole speech, and I was like, we're not killing anyone, that's not our goal here. . . . There could be kids in there, there could be women, just innocent people that weren't involved in this. We weren't trying to attack people, we were trying to attack the police, the military."

Even after seeing their friends die, they clung onto what separated them from the people they were fighting, their respect for innocent life. As they approached the police station, cops started throwing stun grenades at the group. "Everyone ran away," Andy told me. "We we're like, what the fuck? It's just a sound grenade!" Eventually, a few people returned and tried to throw the Molotovs, but, out of fear and a lack of familiarity, they all missed. "I didn't want to," Andy told me, "but I took the Molotov, and I threw it. . . . And then the police ran out . . . because it started burning!" With the cops on the back foot, the rest of the group was quickly inspired to take up the offensive. "When the police started running, these guys would fire stones with slingshots . . . and then someone from another street started hearing what's going on here, and they shot this huge firework pointing at the police station. So there was a burning and there were all these people on this side throwing rocks at them, that was our group. And then there was another street shooting these fireworks at them, they were so confused, man!"

As every guerrilla fighter knows, it's very difficult to hold territory against the state and the best tactic is generally to strike a blow and then disappear. About forty-five minutes later, Andy and his friends did exactly that when a special team arrived as backup. "Those are the ones that will fuck you up so bad," Andy said. "As we were running, we were saying, 'We burned the dogs down!'[8] And people came out of their houses, it was probably midnight or one in the morning, and the whole street . . . was clapping at us." But their moment of elation was cut short. A police car rounded the corner behind them. "They started following us, and they were shooting; it was a fucking machine gun, it wasn't rubber bullets, they were trying to fucking kill us." When they turned to run the other way, they were met by another police vehicle, leaving them trapped. With their victory rapidly turning to a disaster, they found their salvation in the people for whose freedom they were fighting.

8. "Dogs" is a common derogatory term in Myanmar. Police and soldiers are called dogs by revolutionaries, and they in turn are called dogs by the police.

"I [heard] someone say 'Come in, come in,'" Andy recalled. "That was one of the neighborhood people we didn't even know these people. . . . They were like, 'Okay, we'll let you hide.'"

Andy and his friends hid for two hours, hearing gunshots outside. Andy was separated from his brothers and friends, "I'm like, fuck, are they dead?" he recalled. "We couldn't call them, it was very fucked up." Eventually they were safely reunited, but they began to realize that they couldn't survive many more of these urban missions before someone sold them out to the military for a few kyats or just for the chance to stay alive. "After that, we got more paranoid," Andy said. "There were so many nights that we didn't sleep [after that]."

It was around the same time that Andy decided to leave for the mountains. His friend had been arrested and had acid poured in his mouth, and now the authorities had a phone with contact information for Andy and his comrades. The military had found their group. For three nervous days, they hid in their home with the lights off. Then they caught a ride to Karen State. Two days later, the military kicked in the door to their empty home.

Like Andy, Zaw had also given up on the international community, and he'd seen how risky urban operations were. After a peaceful protest failed, and his friends died, Zaw had to make a difficult decision. "There are two paths, right?" he told me over a video call. "We can be normal. We can go on the streets, we can ask for the people's power back." But Zaw knew that wasn't going to work. The military was gunning for them, he said, so "the only path that's left for us is to take those guns for ourselves."

The path that Zaw took was the one that led him to the jungle, where he joined with the Karenni people in eastern Myanmar. The Karenni are one of the groups Zaw had been raised to see as terrorists and troublemakers. Now he was one too. "What we were calling rebels are what we kind of became," he laughed on the phone, unusually reflective for such a young man. "But we know why we are now rebels, that's because of their [the junta's] terrorism, their oppressive regime, and their violation of human rights." As it turned out, Zaw was very good at being a rebel. "So around the end of May, we started entering training school," he told me. It was a long walk, and most of the students were more used to working on a computer in the city than scrambling up and down the steep slopes in the mountains. "It was very tiring," Zaw said, "We had to go up and down a lot of hills, it was two days of walking to get there." Once there, they began training, men and women side by side. As they spent more time in the jungle, they grew as fighters and changed as people.

Zaw said that undergoing the training and seeing the growth in their capacity to fight back only deepened his resolve. He was not alone in this sentiment, and by June 19 youth from the cities and the mountains had come together to form the Karenni Nationalities Defense Force (KNDF). Within it was Zaw's unit, the Karenni Generation Z Army (KGZA). The same thing happened all across the country: young people took up arms against the state, and those who could not afford arms picked up stretchers and bandages, ready to serve as casualty evacuation teams.

In our conversation, Zaw kept using the same adjective to describe his group, one that translates to "tech-savvy" but might be closer to "highly online." It was this same quality that, as I will cover in a later chapter, allowed young Burmese rebels to find a solution to the state's regulation of firearms by using a $300 3D printer and Reddit. I remember one photo of Zaw and his friends—who also happened to be in his platoon—lying on the ground like young people spending a lazy summer afternoon in the park. Young men and women lay together, holding their phones up between them and the sky and laughing at whatever they saw on their screens. It would be an unremarkable picture if it weren't for the assortment of rifles, grenades, and tactical gear that adorned all of them.

The guns Zaw and his friends took up were, to someone so accustomed to seeing AK47s and M16s all over the world, comically incapable of the task at hand. Their homemade .22 rifles resembled the one my parents gave me on my eleventh birthday. It was a perfect weapon for a young person to spend long days crawling around hedgerows shooting rabbits, as I did when I was a child in rural England. However, a .22 is entirely inappropriate for taking on a military with fighter jets, tanks, and machine guns. Nonetheless, it was with their single-shot .22 rifles in hand that they took on an army patrol outside Demoso.

When I first began talking with Zaw, it was because of his habit of livestreaming firefights on a chest-mounted phone camera. Phone mounts for bulletproof vests exist so that well-funded state militaries can use high-tech friend-or-foe identifiers on a virtual map to place all their colleagues on the battlefield, call in precision airstrikes, and avoid friendly fire. Zaw used a replica phone mount (designed to give the aesthetic of a US Special Forces soldier to Thai airsoft enthusiasts across the border) to share his fighting with his online community. While much had changed in the few months since the coup, the commitment to Facebook among young Burmese people had not, and Zaw and his unit would regularly post their fights, calls for donations, and receipts for the weapons, ammunition, and food they purchased with help from their supporters.

The battle the KGZA fought in Demoso didn't make it onto Facebook, but many of their subsequent firefights did. Over a few weeks, I saw Zaw and his friends mature as soldiers. They obtained better weapons from donations and from soldiers they killed or captured. They learned the difference between cover, which will stop the full-power rifle rounds the military use against them, and concealment, which might hide them from sight but won't protect them from a rifle round that could pass through most of the thin-walled buildings of the area. They never lost some of their more endearing tactical quirks, such as smack-talking their enemies while reloading or before sending a few rounds in their direction.

In combat, Zaw's team supported one another and exhibited a great degree of composure under fire. Often they would pass a single rifle equipped with a telescopic sight along the firing line to the person in the best position to make a long shot, or throw magazines to a friend who had run out of ammunition before stepping out, unarmed, to smack-talk the poorly trained junta fighters, whose inaccurate rifles and inadequate training would make a hit at greater than fifty yards more a question of luck than skill. They learned to fire, move, and communicate as a squad and to not defer to the leadership of any one individual. "When we make decisions in our group," Zaw told me, "There's no master and student, there's no teacher." Instead, he said, they discuss things in a group and listen to their more experienced friends. "There are people who are good. They're older people who are more trained, and then there are new recruits, new people who just came in. So, of course, the people who are there for longer and know more about the situation have more voice when we discuss." Some of the founding members of the group tried to establish larger-scale strategic plans, operating on a form of consensus decision making that allowed any of them to veto a decision. "We don't really vote," Zaw said. Instead, they rely on a member proposing an idea and others either endorsing it or refusing to go along with it, until they arrive at a plan that nobody has objections to, rather than one the majority approves but the minority may dislike.

Not having a leader doesn't mean there was a lack of leadership in the KGZA. While they may have lacked a distinct authority structure, they summed up their approach in a perfectly Gen Z fashion, using a meme they shared on their Facebook page. A "boss" is depicted sitting on a chair in a cart with the word "mission" written on it and ordering their employees to pull it. A "leader" (the words are in English) is seen at the front of the line, pulling the same cart alongside their comrades without the boss in place. The model of consensus organizing and leadership that they used wasn't derived from a background in theory or an ideological commitment; it was merely what made sense to them in the moment. They were rebelling against the arbitrary authority of the junta and saw no need to replicate such authority in their own structures.

As the war intensified, any luster that armed rebellion once had wore off as they saw their siblings in arms fall. Still, they continued to try to build a better world even as they fought against the one they were leaving behind. "We don't have to really discuss forever and talk like all politicians. We trust each other," Zaw told me. The distinction between *some* and *all* politicians was one I didn't miss. Zaw's revolution wasn't the same as the 8888 movement; for him democracy seemed to mean more than elections.

On their Facebook page the KNDF shared videos of fighters running, doing pushups, training with their M16 rifles, and standing in formation. They accompanied these with music videos that they shot and sang themselves, depicting their fallen friends and footage from their battles. It was the first days of what they now called the Spring Revolution, and while they didn't have a name for their ideology, it's one that anthropologist James C. Scott would surely have argued we can understand using the "anarchist squint."[5]

Zaw and his friends were among many who had left the cities for the mountains in the hope that they would one day return to liberate their homes from the junta. By the summer of 2021, the National Unity Government (NUG) had formed, which drew heavily on the NLD but also included ministers from ethnic nationalities, including the Rohingya. On May 5, it declared an armed wing called the People's Defense Force (PDF). In theory, the PDF was subsidiary to the NUG's ministry of defense and shared a code of conduct and a commitment to a federal democratic Myanmar (though not all PDFs were aligned with the NUG). Before sharing meals, members of the PDF pledge allegiance to the people of Myanmar. In practice they fought side by side with ethnic revolutionary organizations, and that summer the Chin, Karen, and other ethnic revolutionary organizations ended ceasefires and began attacking junta outposts.

The exact ideological outlook of different units within the revolution and even groups within units is very diverse. The Black Army in Karen territory, was explicitly anarchist, but it did not last long. Some groups, like KNDF, have committed to removing themselves from politics once the war is over, others hold a Marxist perspective but seem to hint that their route to power might eschew vanguardism in favor of the ballot box. Ethnonationalist and separatist groups also exist, and in some areas these dominate the revolution. There exists a religious tendency that one could call anarchist-adjacent in Venerable Nyar Na's Present Karma Buddhism, but it is far from a majority position.

Rebels are all united by a commitment to "federal democracy," but explanations of this concept I have heard range from a US-type system to one more akin to the democratic confederalism of Abdullah Öcalan. Some explanations draw on the dissident communist Minn Latt Yekhaun's "Irra-Lwin" model, named for the two principal rivers that would unite the many statelets that would participate in his vision of a federated Myanmar. EROs tend to be less libertarian in their politics, but they have nonetheless trained, armed, and fought side by side with PDFs. Other groups, like the KGZA, fight in federation with larger formations but retain relative autonomy.

Rebels funded their new PDF units with crowdfunding, including an ingenious scheme that garnered ad revenue by directing millions of pro-democracy Burmese to click on advertisements in YouTube videos via Telegram channels. With many advertisements paying on a per-click basis, the PDF collected the thousands of dollars in revenue from the clicks these ads generated. By September, the NUG claimed 1,700 junta troops had been killed, most of them forced conscripts whose families were essentially held hostage to prevent them from defecting.

Across the country civilians were displaced by the fighting, and the military pulled back from the small arms and close-quarters battles in villages and jungles, only to take advantage of their access to artillery and air support by bombing the PDF and ERO fighters. Often junta mortars in one position were targeted at another of its positions, allowing the junta to target its own position if it was at risk of capture. Where the junta took losses, they turned to the most brutal suppression, burning houses and killing civilians, holding the family members of those who they suspected had helped or joined the resistance. In cities, underground groups responded with bombings, moped-mounted drive-by shootings of police and military leaders, and targeted assassinations of the junta's leadership. In the dry season, the PDF and ethnic revolutionary organizations attacked military outposts around the country, ambushing convoys and making travel for the junta's troops almost impossible and always unsafe.

From the outside, I was following the war through the incredible volume of content, which began as live streams and later became slick videos with opening graphics, crunchy guitar soundtracks, and overhead drone shots. Every morning I'd make coffee and watch Burmese soldiers die on my phone as kids who were delivering pizza a year before dropped grenades from hobby drones. I'd marvel at their rifles that had been kicking around the region since the US initially deployed them in Vietnam, all their black parts worn to a shiny chromed finish by decades of use. I had signed a contract with a major podcasting company and was working on an audio documentary with a colleague about their struggles. Many American listeners had substantially changed their view of the state since they confronted it in the streets in 2020. The war in Myanmar offered a vision of what might have happened if the conspiracy theories that led Trump supporters to storm Congress on January 6, 2021, had had support among the military. Oddly, the war also offered hope. People in Myanmar with virtually no state support came together, stood up against the state and forced it back.

Like many in the US, I purchased more guns in 2020. Data from the NIH suggests that 7.5 million people in the US became new gun owners that year and that 21.8 million guns were sold, both record highs. In my office, above the desk where I am writing this, there's a rifle that was made in Russia, shipped to Spain in violation of the non-intervention agreement, and used to fight fascism there in the Civil War before being brought to the US by a returning fighter. I've spent hours restoring it to the condition it would have been in when it last helped people defend themselves against the coercive power of the state. I don't shoot it often. I have other guns for that, but I keep it around to remind me that even the most totalitarian state's power is not insurmountable. It reminds me of a line that another volunteer who fought in Spain, George Orwell, wrote in the *Evening Standard*. "The totalitarian states can do great things," Orwell wrote. "But there is one thing they cannot do: they cannot give the factory-worker a rifle and tell him to take it home and keep it in his bedroom. That rifle hanging on the wall of the working class flat or labourer's cottage is the symbol of democracy. It is our job to see that it stays there."[6]

What I saw in Myanmar, often from young people with similar vintage rifles, which they call "tumi," reinforced that belief that the state cannot rule a people who refuse to grant it a monopoly on legitimate violence. Even in the age of the jet fighter and remote-controlled drone, the people in arms were more than standing their ground against the state. The conflict in Myanmar became a sort of daily reminder to me that, as I watched totalitarianism on the rise around the world, there was still hope. The conflict got so little coverage that even other reporters would be shocked to hear about the kids with homemade guns taking on the state. They were even more shocked to see them sending professional soldiers into panicked retreat. I was so enthused by a rare instance of the good guys winning against the odds that I overlooked the realities of war, which I am all too familiar with.

I find that my strength and weakness as a journalist is that my sources are my friends, and therefore my friends are my sources. Quite often, I would call or text Zaw and his unit, along with other Burmese friends I'd made on social media. Most of this chatting was not for work but rather to check in and share some news or a funny photo, and to reach out and vicariously feel the freedom they had fought to achieve. I'd worked for months on a scripted podcast about the conflict in Myanmar, and it had begun airing in March 2022. I sent a few messages to the various young fighters in it to let them know it was being well received; most of them responded to say they were happy to see the world standing in solidarity with them. Zaw never got back to me, but that wasn't unusual; he had a war to win and couldn't always be on his phone. The night before the final episode, I was trying to squeeze in some exercise in my back garden after a busy day. While I was resting, I flicked open one of the Burmese Telegram channels I check pretty often. I don't think I even really thought about it; it was the sort of muscle memory cell phone use I am not too proud of. I glanced down at my phone and saw a body that was unmistakably Zaw's, with a massive head wound. He was dead.

Dealing with this kind of thing is part of my job, but I rarely invest as much in topics I cover as I have in the revolution in Myanmar. Seeing the body of someone whose against-the-odds story I had just shared with tens of thousands of listeners, all of whom were waiting for an update tomorrow, felt like a punch in the gut. Already out of breath from working out, and now even more so from the shock, I sat on my back lawn for ten minutes, checking again and again that it was really Zaw in the photo, and remembering one of the realities of war: however liberatory the struggle, none of us are bulletproof.

A few weeks before, the KGZA had detained two journalists who were traveling in their area of operations without press passes. It's an incident I still don't have a clear timeline of events for. The journalists were detained and later released. On their release, they complained about their treatment to deputy minister Ei Thinzar Maung, of the National Unity Government, who herself had emerged as a protest leader since the coup. Ei Thinzar Maung, allegedly without contacting the KGZA, then made a post on Facebook urging people to stop donating to the KGZA. In the post, she included Zaw's photo. Nine days later, he was dead. Soon after, the post was deleted. Rumors spread quickly, and Ei Thinzar Maung didn't address them or apologize. Zaw's funeral, attended by his sobbing girlfriend, comrades, and family, was filled with hate for the deputy minister, whom they blamed for his death.

Zaw's comrades, after they buried him and said their goodbyes, took to the mountains once more and continued their fight. Just like other units, they struggled with arms and ammunition shortages and a lack of heavy weapons. A few months later, a PDF fighter I spoke to on a crackling encrypted line told me he'd left Myanmar and come to Bangkok to live as a refugee and to try to raise awareness of their struggle with their neighbors. I asked him how it felt to go from being a fighter to being a refugee. Due to the lack of ammunition, even as fighters they had been "just refugees with uniforms," he said.

Despite the shortages, Zaw's unit continued to repurpose drones and experiment with homemade rocket artillery and bombs to try to bridge some of these gaps, and they had remarkable success. Like other PDFs and the anti-junta resistance as a whole, they sought to deny the junta the ability to safely travel between its bases and strongholds, ambushing junta soldiers on jungle roads and stealing whatever weapons they could. The junta responded by bombing cities and civilian targets, trying to make the population reject the rebels, and, in the process, creating more hatred for their cruel and tyrannical regime. Rebel units increasingly became the providers of medical care. Doctors who fled the junta's control of their hospitals began providing medical care to fighters and civilians in jungle hospitals.

In April 2022, a few weeks after Zaw died, I was sitting on a rooftop in Mae Sot, Thailand, looking across the wide and muddy Moei River and into the emerald rainforest above Myawaddy. The International Friendship Bridge No. 2, which connected Thailand and Myanmar, looked far from friendly, with huge coils of razor wire separating my colleague and me from Myanmar, and Myanmar from the world. A colleague and I were waiting to meet a source from the PDF, and meanwhile we were killing time at a going away party for an NGO volunteer by drinking terrible whiskey and testing Andy and his brothers on their first aid skills. Every fifteen minutes or so, one of us would shout "bang" before pointing to a body part on ourselves or one of the boys and pretending to have been shot. The boys would then spring into action, applying pressure and a bandage or wrapping the limb with a tourniquet before carrying their brother or friend to safety. We were not, perhaps, the best party guests, but we were having fun and also having more of that terrible whiskey than one should while at work.

After several of these drills, I'd gone to refill my plastic cup and was standing over a table when, for a brief moment, the sky across the river lit up with a huge yellow flash. As everyone spun around, the boom from the explosion—the sound traveling slower than the light—reached our little rooftop. Having assessed that we were comfortably distant from the blast, and that nobody needed our well-honed first aid skills, we all rushed to take up viewing positions for what we assumed would be a series of air strikes on positions of Karen National Union—one of the EROs— just across the river. But all we heard was a flurry of gunfire, followed by a cascade of Facebook notifications. A large car bomb had been detonated at the bridge, and nobody had claimed responsibility. A government building had been destroyed and the bridge itself damaged.

Myawaddy, the city across the river, seemed an impossibly big target for the resistance. It's a large city with a significant border crossing that clears more than a billion dollars in trade annually. A Chinese-funded casino sits on the Burmese bank of the Moei River, one of eighteen in the city. Most of these facilities are run with Chinese money tied to transnational crime organizations, and they operate in a sort of legal no-go zone for the Burmese state. Many of them are the home to online scams of the type known as "pig butchering." These scams involve young women (or men posing as women), often forced to work there, who gradually gain the trust of wealthy older men before swindling them out of their money.

The Myawaddy border area is controlled in large part by a Border Guard Force (BGF). The BGFs are a number of military–co-opted militias that span Myanmar's border regions. This BGF had once been known as the Democratic Karen Buddhist Army (not to be confused with the Democratic Karen Benevolent Army, one of its offshoots). The primary loyalty of most BGF units is to crime and corruption rather than to any explicit politics. In 2022, the junta allowed the BGF to keep running casinos and scam compounds for transnational criminal organizations, and so the BGF remained loyal to the junta. The combined government and BGF forces seemed insurmountable, and indeed Myawaddy had not seen fighting in the seventy-five years that the Karen National Union had fought its war against the Burmese government.

But in the months after I stood on that rooftop, the situation had massively shifted in favor of the resistance. By late 2024, Myawaddy was one of dozens of cities that had fallen to the broad alliance of ethnic revolutionary organizations and PDFs that make up Myanmar's resistance movement.[9] Beginning in October 2023, fighters across the country had swept the junta's army out of much of the colonial periphery.

Although "Operation 1027" officially launched on October 27, 2023, the preparations for this offensive took nearly a year, according to my sources. The operation itself was a coordinated offensive between the Arakan Army (AA), Myanmar National Democratic Alliance Army, and the Ta'ang National Liberation Army, collectively known as the Three Brotherhood Alliance. With their forces concentrated in Shan and Rakhine States, the Alliance's troops remained largely quiet for the first weeks after the coup, with the Ta'ang engaging in February before widespread opposition to the junta in March 2021.[10] The groups took advantage of the junta withdrawing troops from some of their areas to reinforce areas with more fighting and used the time to arm and equip PDF units of mainly ethnic Bamar fighters, like the Mandalay PDF who joined the Ta'ang rebels in the mountains in July 2021 after peaceful protest and urban sabotage failed. The Alliance also provided weapons, training, and support to independent groups of other ethnicities, like the KNDF, as they fought the junta in other parts of Myanmar.

In October 2023, the Three Brotherhood Alliance entered the conflict in full force. Their offensive was preceded by a series of junta atrocities, including the shelling of a camp for internally displaced persons (IDPs) and the massacre of people attempting to escape forced labor in a casino. The latter included the many Chinese citizens, who were held and forced to work against their will in online scams run from the casinos. Many have speculated the junta killings of these Chinese citizens resulted in China's backing the ERO offensive.

9. Myawaddy was subsequently recaptured by the junta.

10. The AA signed a ceasefire with the junta in late 2022, but this only lasted a year.

Whether the Alliance fighters were motivated by outrage at the atrocities they'd witnessed or simply by a desire to execute a plan that had been years in the making doesn't matter much. What does matter is that the offensive swept through Shan State, seized over two hundred junta positions, and forced the junta to withdraw its troops from much of the region.

Stating their goals as protecting civilian life, self-defense, control of their territory, preventing the growth of scam compounds, and destroying the junta, the Alliance stuck decisively in the predawn hours of October 27. They were joined by Bamar majority groups like Mandalay PDF and the Bamar People's Liberation Army (BPLA).[11]

In just four days, this alliance of ethnic revolutionary organizations and PDFs swept through junta defenses and fought off airborne assaults. The Kachin Independence Army remained in the fight, as they had been, as junta positions across the north of the country came under attack from small arms and homemade drones dropping grenades and mortar bombs. In Tabayin, the junta's troops used twenty refugees as human shields. In Laukkai, five hundred foreigners who had recently been liberated from forced labor in online scam operations were captured by junta troops. Rather than being repatriated, they were forced to dig bunkers and trenches and distributed around frontline positions as human shields. Some were tortured, others sexually assaulted. Rather than changing its ways as it began to lose control of the areas it had long treated as its colonial periphery, the junta stepped up its brutality.

With the junta on the back foot, other actors across the country rose up to take advantage of its weakness. In the north, the Kachin swept towns and border crossings. In the west, the Arakan Army—known as an oppressive force against the Rohingya people—pushed back the junta and sank its riverboats. In Karenni State, where Zaw had fought and died, rebels seized most of the capital city of Loikaw, including its university campus where some of them had been studying when the coup happened. In one video, numerically superior KNDF forces can be seen shouting out to junta soldiers to surrender. "I gave them 30 minutes to surrender or face a lethal attack," said Deputy

---

11. The BPLA copied the naming conventions and aesthetic of other ethnic revolutionary organizations and was led by Maung Saung Khaa, a prominent Bamar poet. Unlike other EROs, the BPLA specifically seeks to reduce the dominance of its ethnic group in national affairs, and it fights alongside other ethnic groups for a federal Myanmar.

Commander-in-Chief Maui in an interview with *The Irrawaddy*, an English-and Burmese-language newspaper. "They shouted that they would surrender. I told them to leave their weapons behind and come out one by one. These are the rules of engagement; they are what good soldiers should do. We have not taken up arms out of cruelty."[7] The KNDF also captured a pilot when they managed to shoot down a fighter jet using heavy machine guns, a first for the group and a serious blow to the junta, who had previously been able to bomb rebel positions with relative impunity.

This surrender was not remarkable—thousands of junta soldiers surrendered in the last months of 2023. In the city of Laukkai, 2,389 junta personnel and about 1,600 of their family members surrendered in January 2024. In a deal brokered with the junta, they were sent back to regime territory. Their commanders were punished by the junta and the troops redeployed. Some of them surrendered a second time three months later in Myawaddy, indicating the desperation of the regime.

These gains were not without losses. One of the casualties was Sayar Richard, a KNDF fighter who had previously read aloud a statement of solidarity to the Rojava revolution. His death was mourned not just among his comrades but also in Rojava, where the local press carried news of his passing to his fellow revolutionaries half a world away. My friends in the Syrian Democratic Forces (SDF) sent messages in solidarity and support, using the Kurdish slogan *şehîd namirin*, which means "martyrs never die."

By early 2024 most of Karenni State was liberated, as was much of western Shan State to the north, where the Ta'ang and Kokang advances were. More ethnic revolutionary organizations had joined the conflict, and the combined forces of the Karen National Liberation Army (KNLA), its associated PDFs, and the Karen National Union's civilian leadership stood poised to seize the border town of Myawaddy. For weeks, they had fought their way along a chain of military bases along the Moei River, capturing 600 troops. Now only Light Infantry Battalion 275 (LIB 275), remained. The battalion was offered a chance to surrender, but instead many of the soldiers chose to slip away with the help of Border Guard Forces and hide under the bridge between Myanmar and Thailand, figuring the Karen fighters would not risk fighting so close to the border lest a stray bullet or bomb hit a Thai soldier.

For a few days, the Karen forces stayed outside the city, BGF units patrolled inside the city, LIB 275 stayed under the bridge, and Thai forces stayed on the other side of it, refusing to let the soldiers claim asylum while they were still armed. The Border Guard Force in Myawaddy had declared itself neutral in the fight between the government and the revolutionaries, and in March 2024 it was rebranded as the Karen National Army (KNA). When the KNLA and the PDF entered the town, the KNA did not participate in the fighting. However, after the battle was over it began secretly cooperating with the junta, and it brought LIB 275 soldiers back to their base to reclaim it. The KNLA, unwilling to fight the KNA and the junta, elected to withdraw from the city and focus on a column of troops that the junta had sent to reinforce the city. Once again, as it had in Spain, the state showed its ability to buy the loyalty of groups not committed to its destruction.

In Rakhine State, the scene of the Rohingya genocide that has been more or less ongoing since 2017, the Arakan Army saw huge gains in early 2024. The junta's response was a classic of colonial government, the divide and rule strategy. In this instance, the junta began to forcibly recruit Rohingya youth, who just a few years before it had been forcibly expelling to Bangladesh. It also began to strike alliances with armed Rohingya Islamist groups. The junta's soldiers forced Rohingya civilians to protest against the Arakan Army, and they used new recruits as little more than human shields and cannon fodder, paying their villages with a few bags of rice for each son they lost. Other recruits were forced to burn down the homes of ethnic Rakhine people, further stoking tensions between the two ethnic groups.

The Arakan Army, particularly its chief Twan Mrat Naing, responded as the junta surely hoped they would. Twan Mrat Naing tweeted several times, calling the Rohingya "Bengalis" and accusing them of "selfish grumpiness and sabotaging, dragging the struggle in the wrong direction" (@TwanMrat, May 19, 2024). These were not just idle words, and soon accusations of massacres, the burning of Rohingya houses, and illegal abductions also became too frequent and too credible to disregard. It was one of the most public tests of the Spring Revolution's aspirations for a future in which Myanmar was for everyone, not just certain religious or ethnic groups.

In response, 195 organizations, both armed and civil society, issued a statement. They condemned the junta's manipulation of the Rohingya people, saying, "In addition to the fact that the military junta is working to create such ethnic conflict, the revolutionary forces and the public need to be especially prudent, aware, and understanding that the Rohingya people . . . are being forced into patterns that the terrorist military junta wants to portray." They were not bashful in condemning the AA's burning of Buthidaung, home to many Rohingya civilians, saying, "This incident is a war crime and a crime against humanity."[8]

However, many of the organizations drafting the statement were outside Myanmar, with notable exceptions such as the Karen Women's Organization, and of those who did sign openly only a few were actual armed PDF groups. Exactly who burned Budithang remains, for most Burmese, unclear. The AA blamed the junta and published videos of their troops helping internally displaced Rohingya people. Twan Mrat Naing called the allegations "distorted [and] misleading craps [sic]" (@TwanMrat, May 18, 2024). Since then, there have been other well-documented drone attacks on Rohingya IDPs, killing dozens of civilians who were fleeing the conflict.

It is certainly true that the military has set up fake Telegram channels and used photos of other incidents, many of which they committed, to stoke the conflict between the AA and the Rohingya people. Many of these have then appeared in local press articles and have been demonstrably proved to be false. The NUG, which had previously spoken out, backtracked on its condemnation of the AA, and many online supporters of the revolution totally dismissed accusations of wrongdoing by the undoubtedly powerful group.

It is clear that the junta set a trap for the AA in May 2024, and it's also clear that the AA's rhetoric did not help it overcome allegations that it walked right into that trap. What the AA did in early 2024 will not change the fact that the overwhelming bulk of atrocities, including those against Rohingya people, were committed by the junta. But the knee-jerk return to exclusionary language on the part of the AA and the rush to deny and distract from any possible complicity by many groups offer a worrying omen for the future of Myanmar as the AA sweeps through Rakhine State, and, at the time of this writing, the AA has recently captured the military headquarters for the region. In private, young fighters have shared with me that a "liberation" of Rakhine that does not include the Rohingya people isn't really liberation at all, but the failure of more established stakeholders like EROs and the NUG to make clear and unequivocal statements only serves to illustrate Orwell's point, that they must not disarm even once the junta is gone if they wish to ensure meaningful liberation. Meanwhile from refugee camps in Bangladesh, young Rohingya men told me that "the only way forward is together, as a nation of brothers," and they told me of their plans to facilitate anti-genocide training for PDFs.

Elsewhere, ethnic revolutionary organizations have repeatedly proven their critics wrong with regard to the extent of their goals. A consistent critique from self-appointed expert analysts outside the revolution has been that ethnic revolutionary organizations will only support the revolution until they have liberated their own territory and that after they have used their young Bamar allies to regain their territory they will abandon them. This has not happened. Even after the successes of Operation 1027, the ethnic revolutionary organizations responsible for the operation have continued their fight against the junta, launching "operation 1027 part 2" in the summer of 2024. In doing so they have not only increased the areas under their control but also drawn junta resources away from the PDFs. This has allowed Mandalay PDF to sweep across the country's drier lowlands, often facing disorganized conscripts or pro-junta militias. The junta's resulting attempt to draft young people has left those young people with a choice between fighting for the revolution or against it, and, unsurprisingly, rebel numbers have grown.

The rebels set out to change their country, but in doing so they changed the world. Including all the anti-coup fighters in Myanmar among the anarchists is a stretch; they encompass a huge variety of political positions, from state-communist to liberal statist, and their ethnic revolutionary organization allies include some ethno-nationalists. Explicit anarchist organizations in Myanmar tend to exist mostly in the punk scene and in mutual aid. But some pro-democracy fighters' methods, often conceived without much in the way of the study of ideologies but simply created out of a sense of equality and fairness, are aligned with the way anarchists might organize, as are their DIY supply chains.

They organize based on democratic and horizontal tendencies, they recognize that gender and racial hierarchies only divide them from their common interests, and they seek not to seize power but instead to share it among all the people they liberate. Between rotations on the front, units gather to sing and dance without the dour self-seriousness that makes so many revolutionaries so lamentably dull. Since the revolution began, trans women have fought as women, women have been incorporated in positions that had previously been closed to them, and LGBTQIA people have been embraced in a country whose government had been at best indifferent to their existence before. Muslim people, who were murdered by the state a decade ago, now fight side by side with their Buddhist, Christian, and atheist or agnostic comrades, and in the fires of conflict they have forged a solidarity that ensures they keep their rifles in their hands until all of them are free.

Moreover, the analysis of the young rebels changed, centering on the existence of the Burmese state, a colonial construct, as part of the problem. I remember a night in a bar on the Thai-Burmese border, playing pool and talking with Andy and his brothers. Andy asked who I had voted for, and I told him I didn't always vote. I explained my position on voting and the legitimacy it transfers to institutions that I don't believe reflect or respond to the will of the people they claim to govern. At best, I told him, it's a harm reduction tool. I understand that for someone who has seen people die for the right to vote, this seems a strange stance, but I tried to explain that democracy for me should mean something more than a tick in a box every four years.

Over the next few months I watched Andy and other members of Myanmar's resistance movement become aware of the revolution in Rojava, and the possibility of a politics without a state that pits each group against the other. I heard from them that they were pushing back against a "revolution of too many organizations" and too much hierarchy. Over the years I have covered this conflict I have watched whole units in Chinland and Karenni State make statements of solidarity with people in Rojava and reject political solutions that rely on centralized power and the sort of democracy that only offers two bad choices every four years. I've seen them put on keffiyehs and stand for a free Palestine and send love and solidarity to their comrades in Ukraine. I have seen people work to translate the works of Öcalan, Graeber, and Debbie Bookchin into Burmese. In the four years I have been observing this revolution, the internationalism of capital has crumbled thanks to tariffs and a right-wing electoral surge around the Global North, but Myanmar has shown a vision of the future in which the internationalism of peoples can flourish.

In 2021, many young people in Myanmar, raised to trust the rules-based world order and those who selectively enforce those rules, took to the streets, village lanes and fields in the days after the coup. Now, with four years of war behind them, many are dead, while those who survive have been disabused of the notion that abstract rules have any power in a system that presumes the rights and longevity of states over those of individuals. In late 2023, the United Nations Food Program director for Southeast Asia, Pio Smith, posted several Tweets from Nay Pyi Taw, in which Smith appeared to be meeting officials from the junta. For many in the international community, this seemed to contradict the UN's mission and goals. But if we see the conflict in Myanmar as not one *against* the state but *about* the state, this makes perfect sense. The

United Nations, China, and the Association of Southeast Asian Nations (ASEAN) have all repeatedly shown a willingness to treat the junta as the legitimate and unquestioned government of the country in practical terms, even while they issue public hand-wringing about that government's abuses of its own citizens.

The revolution today finds itself at a juncture. Some tendencies within it wish to centralize power, either in Nay Pyi Taw or in a series of statelets. The leaders of EROs who have been subjected to state violence want a monopoly on violence in their areas. Well-meaning Bamar politicians want a central government that is strong enough to prevent future interethnic tensions. But re-creating the structures that allowed a genocide and a coup to happen will not prevent future genocides and coups. As Dr. Wonder told us, this should be the last generation of Burmese young people who must fight for their freedom, and the only way to ensure this is the case is to do away with the structures that allowed so much repression for so long. If the revolution is to be worth all the death and violence, it must devolve power to the people, reject any monopoly on violence, and embrace a Myanmar in which every ethnic group including the Rohingya have a right to self-determination and peaceful coexistence. The model that Zaw and revolutionary armorer Myauk articulated to me, one Myauk called "equality leadership," has allowed them to liberate more than half the country. There's no reason the same horizontal approach cannot allow the whole country to live in peace once the war is over.

Today's PDF fighters, joining to avoid conscription by the junta, are entering a very different force from the one Zaw and his friends created. According to training documents provided to me by Mandalay PDF, they undertake basic training lasting forty-five to ninety days, in which they learn the basics of a federal democratic system and the importance of "respect [for] the religion, ideology of each public, culture, political opinions, racial identities and sexual perceptions." The PDF fighters must adhere to a code of conduct and agree to treat prisoners and civilians with decency. While these rules haven't been universally accepted, and abuses of civilians have been documented, in comparison to those documented and shared with great pride by the professional army of Israel in the same time period, the PDF's ad hoc code of conduct seems to have been significantly more closely adhered to.

Like Zaw, many of the young people who left the cities for the mountains—or the young already living in mountainous or rural regions—and picked up rusted old muskets or handmade .22 rifles to fight for freedom won't ever live to see it, and thousands of them have already given their lives in the struggle. I still wake up to the horrible sight of Burmese mothers burying their children more often than I'd like. But every fighter, including the fallen, experienced freedom among their comrades in the mountains. They have shown that they can live without gods or masters and with no need for misogyny and ethnic division. In their small groups in the jungle, they've shown the world and each other that they can organize without the support of capital or the state and still thrive. Even if nothing remains of them but the ashes left behind from their cremation, a burial site, or the photos their friends post on Facebook every year to remember their deaths, their ability to stand alone against the state and force a modern military into retreat has moved the world tangibly closer to freedom and made state violence a risk to the state's continued existence, and for that reason they should give all of us a great deal of hope.

4

Rojava

And always remember that "every storm begins with a single raindrop."
Make sure you're that raindrop.

—Tekoşer Piling (Lorenzo Orsetti)

In the gray light between dawn and sunrise in Qamişlo, the first sounds of the Fajr prayer woke up the cats outside my window. They'd barely gotten back to sleep since the last ambulance flew past in a cacophony of noise and light. Recognizing neither god nor master, the cats mewed their disapproval and returned to their hunt for mice and affection. I'd been awake for hours, or it felt like hours. Readjusting to a place where death drops from the night sky makes minutes last for hours, and hours last for seconds. Last night seemed like a week, and I wasn't even anywhere near the front lines. Turkish drones had buzzed overhead, as they had every night for a week, on their way to destroy the attempt to build a society without a state here, and in the process had destroyed some poor mother's whole life. The drones weren't coming after me, but every day everyone in Rojava plays a game of chance with their lives, and every night this week someone had lost. So instead of sleeping I'd spent my night being anxious about friends in Gaza who hadn't returned my messages, playing a game I'd downloaded on my phone called Farm Simulator, and seeking the affection of Western Kurdistan's communally cared-for cats.

Two calls to prayer later that day, after I'd completed my daily lap of the market, during which I drank between three and five cups of tea with strangers who mostly laughed at my attempts to speak Kurdish and asked me about America, we set off to a place my fixer Khabat and her brother Diwar wanted me to see. It was a cemetery that, if you didn't know what it was for, would strike you as little more than a well-kept and orderly place where people laid their loved ones to rest and brought them flowers and candles on special days when they wanted to feel close to them. The white graves sit in little rows, white granite headstones atop gray tombs, each of which has a small area of dirt in the middle where grieving families can plant a tree or some flowers so that the remains of their loved one can give something a new life. Small cypress trees mark the paths in between the graves. When you walk into the cemetery, you see pictures of the deceased incorporated into the front of the tombs, with the yellow and green flags of the People's Protection Units and the Women's Protection Units (better known by their Kurdish initials as the YPG and the YPJ) in the background. Each gravestone, as you walk along the rows, follows a similar pattern, listing the deceased's name, the place and date of their birth, and their place and date of death. At the top, they all say the same thing: "şehîd" and the deceased's first name. Şehîd means martyr, and the cemetery is full of them. Every little white stone represents a grieving family and a life that ended too soon, another young person whose life has been cut short by the state, be it Syrian, Turkish, or Islamic.

The martyrs' cemetery is a profoundly impactful place. I'm no stranger to conflict, and I'm well aware of the tragic cost of war even for the victors. In the tiny English village that I grew up in, a stone obelisk adjacent to the only shop and the pub lists the names of young people who died in the First and Second World Wars; it's always struck me how many names there were, given the few hundred people who lived there. Since then, I've had sources and friends die, I've seen strangers die, and I've wondered what happened to friends who disappeared one day without the closure of a funeral or a grave. As I got closer to one end of the martyrs' cemetery, open holes awaited the latest martyrs, who had died the night before in the drone strikes that had battered the surrounding countryside. Looking at the last row of graves, for fighters killed in Deir Ez-Zor or civilians killed by drone strikes, I did the depressing operation of subtracting the year of their birth from the year of their death. Many of them were barely older than high school age, and their graves were adorned with fresh flowers from grieving parents.

Before I visited the cemetery, I'd been talking to the mother of one of its newer residents. Şehîd Aheng Hisen was just fourteen when he died, his mother, Mafusa, told me after serving us tea. We sat in the main room of their home on cushions on the floor, his portrait and one of those calendars that companies give out as promotional items at hardware stores in the region were the only things decorating the walls. Aheng had been a goalkeeper, she said, and had loved nothing more than football. Mafusa showed me a photo of him in his jersey, smiling and excited about the life that lay ahead of him, waving his giant gloves and looking like he might even grow into them one day. He looked like so many of my friends' children, but an accident of birth had placed him in a place where people tried to build democracy without the state, and every day the Turkish state took a few innocent lives while US troops, safe in their bases a few kilometers away, looked the other way and said nothing to the mother who had lost her baby.

One summer day, during his school holidays, Aheng came home for lunch after a morning of working as a mechanic. He ate his lunch, just like any other day, and then he went back to the workshop just a few hundred meters from the house. That afternoon, Mafusa told me through Diwar, who was translating, she heard an ear-splitting woosh followed by an explosion. Mafusa and her husband knew the explosion was in the industrial area where Aheng worked. "We were so worried," Mafusa told me, as she wiped away the tears. "We knew that our son was there. We hoped he was okay. And we got there as soon as possible."

There, lying face down on the ground, was Aheng. Next to him were his friends Ahmed and Shamim. Aheng's father picked him up, thinking he could at least hold his son in their last moments together. He felt a pulse, albeit a faint one, in his son's neck. "He didn't give up hope," my translator Diwar told me as he deciphered Mafusa's words between her tearful sniffs. As we spoke, Aheng's father was outside. I already felt bad enough about Mafusa going through this horrific experience again, and I was happy to leave him unmolested as he fed a pet budgerigar some sunflower seeds. On the day of the drone attack, the hands that were now gently feeding seeds to the little yellow bird had been holding Aheng as the parents rushed to the hospital with all three of their boys. "As soon as they got there, they saw the hospital was very crowded," Diwar told me. It had been the same on the morning of our interview: I'd heard ambulances tearing through the streets after drone strikes, and the night before, I had heard appeals for blood donations as I spent every sleepless, anxious moment wondering if every flashing streetlight was a bomb.

The doctors told Mafusa that there was no hope for Aheng, and not long afterward he died right there in front of the hospital, surrounded by his loving parents, his dying friends, and dozens of other people trying to get treatment. I offered Mafusa my condolences, but there wasn't much I could say to make it better. Her son's absence had left a gaping hole in her life that my words weren't going to fill. In Rojava, my fixer Khabat told me, they say, "Şehîd *namirin*." It means "Martyrs never die."

Martyrs are everywhere in Rojava. They were the first thing I noticed as I stepped into the office of the Asayish (internal security) officer assigned to the border between Rojava and the more neoliberal vision of Kurdish identity in Iraqi Kurdistan. Dominating one wall of the room opposite his desk was a large plant, decorated like a Christmas tree with little yellow and green cards. Each of the cards contained a photo of a young person, smiling and looking at the camera in military fatigues. The officer noticed me looking at the plant. "Şehîd," he said. The officer offered me a cigarette and went around the tree naming cousins, siblings, and childhood friends who had given their lives. Within half an hour, we were out of the office and driving down a winding road filled with potholes and discussing the bombings that had happened the night before. We hoped to be in Qamişlo before nightfall, when the bombing would begin again and someone would earn a new plot in the martyrs' cemetery.

That's how the war is in Kurdistan now. Every day, and every night, there's a chance that death will come for you out of the sky, and you'll be immortalized on the little portraits that cover the roundabouts in Qamişlo, and on the wall of your home, and in the hearts of your friends. There's not much you can do to avoid it, and just for the crime of existing outside of the state, the people of the Autonomous Administration of North and East Syria (AANES), sometimes known as Rojava, pay with their children's lives. In this revolution, the absent feel very present. Their portraits are everywhere. Alongside them are photos of Abdullah Öcalan, the movement's thought leader who has been imprisoned by Turkey since 1999 and who is known here as "Apo," which is the vocative form of the Kurdish word for a paternal uncle. Reber Apo (leader Apo) is everywhere in Rojava, and, admittedly, as a middle-aged anarchist I am always a little concerned about a much-venerated mustachioed man staring at me from the walls. However, unlike so many other men on the left, over his lifetime of political thought Öcalan has moved further and further from centralizing power. Certainly, it's unusual to recount the history of a movement that moved from a state communist outlook to a libertarian one at the behest of its dear leader. However, most of the faces smiling at me from the cemetery in Qamişlo are of people who were born, lived, and died in the time since Rojava's revolution embraced the libertarian left; it was all they'd known, and it was what they'd died for. Öcalan is important in starting this journey, but the people on the ground played just as important a role in defending and deepening the revolution.

Today's SDF and AANES politics is probably best understood in terms of tendencies. Within both the movement and society there exists a strong tendency that favors the model outlined by Öcalan, which is generally referred to as democratic confederalism. But there also exists a tendency which, as much as it would not like to admit it, has not fully reformed its thinking from the top-down Marxist-nationalist model that was previously the dominant paradigm in the movement. There is also a tendency that is closer to anarchism, particularly among women and the youth, which sees Öcalan as having shown the movement the way but no longer hangs on his every word or sees the need for a leader. There is an unreconstructed ethnonationalist tendency as well. The SDF is somewhat similar, with a distinction between cadre, who have pledged their life to the struggle and left their homes to commit to it, and local "heremi" units who are not cadre. There now exist "heremei cadre" who can make a pledge but remain at home, so this distinction is somewhat outdated.

In society in Rojava, there also exists a tendency—mostly among men, and particularly older men—to grumble in private about the women's liberation that has occurred as part of the revolution, as well as a tendency to see the left libertarian politics of the AANES as a means to the end of a Kurdish state. All these tendencies existing in parallel might be seen as a problem for the revolution, and in cases where the more authoritarian tendency has prevailed it is, but in others it shows the plurality of thought and perspectives that we can find in any community where people don't fear to speak their minds.

There was a US base not far from where Aheng was killed, you won't see any portraits of Apo there, but the US has been allied with the YPG in its fight against the Islamic State for nearly a decade. Allies, though, are not friends, and all my interviews in Rojava began with my interviewee imploring me to share their suffering with the Americans and wondering why their so-called allies were letting them die. But the project in Rojava isn't what the US is supporting with the Humvees and helicopters I saw occasionally in my time there, and people here know that. The US allied with the Syrian Democratic Forces, the armed forces of the AANES, only in their battle against the so-called Islamic State, who are called by their Arabic acronym, "DAESH," in this part of the world. The SDF, a multiethnic force that is now majority Arab, is often mistakenly referred to as "the Kurds" in legacy media. The Kurdish units within the SDF are the YPG and YPJ, but they fight alongside Assyrian, Armenian, and Arab units as well as international volunteer groups including Tekoşîna Anarşîst (Anarchist Struggle). US Special Forces, regular forces, and air support deployed to Syria as part of Operation Inherent Resolve provide them with training, artillery, and air support in their fight against the Islamic State but not in their fight against the better-equipped Turkish state. The US may share a common enemy with the people of Rojava, but it does not share the revolutionary aims of the democratic confederalist movement that allowed these people to build a revolution in the midst of a civil war that had been raging for more than a decade, as evidenced by the rows and rows of graves in that Qamişlo cemetery.

Many histories of the Rojava revolution will begin in 2012 when a civil war in Syria between the Ba'athist government and the people began in earnest following protests and insurgencies the previous year. Across the region, the Arab Spring had brought people into the streets demanding change, and in Syria the regime had met them with bullets, bombs, and secret police raids. In response, large swaths of the state's military defected, creating the Free Syrian Army (FSA) and fighting for secular democracy, which in some cases embraced neighborhood councils as the basic unit of organization, and Islamists of various factions took up arms against the government and in favor of theocracy. And one of the most vicious conflicts of the century began.

In the northeast of the country, President Bashar al-Assad elected to withdraw his troops, and a largely bloodless withdrawal of the state occurred. The YPG, the armed wing of the Öcalan-inspired Democratic Union Party (or PYD by its Kurdish initials), emerged as the major military force in the area, and the PYD joined with the Kurdish National Council to form the Kurdish Supreme Committee to govern the area. This makes sense as a starting point for a history of the AANES if one is studying it from the perspective of the Syrian Civil War, but to understand how the PYD was able to step in as the state stepped back we must look at how it built a movement that was strong enough to contest the state. My Kurdish friends would use the analogy of a mushroom here, which has a whole web of spores but bursts forth only in the place and time when conditions are right.

The Kurdistan Workers Party is better known by its initials, the PKK. It began its life in the 1970s as, like many national liberation movements of the Cold War, a Marxist-Leninist organization, in this case seeking an independent Kurdish nation. To learn about the history of the movement and how it evolved from statist to libertarian and from Marxist to radically feminist,

I would need to travel across Kurdistan to the mountains that had so often offered refuge to Kurdish people in a time when the four different states that divide their homeland are trying to kill them.

In the shadow of those mountains, I met Zagros Hiwa. Hiwa is a spokesperson for the Kurdistan Communities Union (KCK), the umbrella group that unites the various elements of the Kurdish freedom movement inspired by Abdullah Öcalan's political thought. Being divided into the Iranian, Syrian, Iraqi, and Iranian states, the Kurdish freedom movement took on slightly different characteristics in all four areas, and the KCK plays a coordinating role between them.

"When the movement started, at first, the struggle was not armed," Hiwa told me in a small park in the middle of a big city. He'd smuggled himself out of the mountains to meet me because, he said, it wasn't safe for me to come up there. At first, he said, the movement was "organizing the students, the working class, the women, and so many strata of the society." At this time the movement took on a more nationalist character, and it was not until later that it evolved into the internationalist movement I saw in Rojava.

"The main way of the struggle was democratic, organizing people through syndicates, through unions, through, let's say, building up parties," Hiwa told me. After that, Hiwa explained, there was a coup. During the 1980 Turkish coup, Hiwa told me, "About 10,000 PKK members went into prison," where torture was common. Soon after, the Kurdish language was banned by the coup regime, as were all expressions of Kurdish culture. Turkish nationalism sees Kurdish identity and the Turkish nation as mutually exclusive, and so any manifestation of Kurdish liberty, anywhere, is an existential threat to the national vision of the Turkish state and so it must be fought and destroyed. The government, Hiwa told me, had "zero tolerance for the rights of Kurdish people, of women, of the working class." Indeed, the state denied the existence of Kurds, calling them "mountain Turks." In this scenario, Hiwa said, "Military struggle was a way to prove that you exist." For the Kurdish movement, "it was the only way left."[1]

At this time, Hiwa said, the movement had the "nation-state mentality." It was not until later that they decided to "change the paradigm" and move

---

1. It should be noted that, before the coup, the PKK made assassination attempts on Kurdish politicians who it saw as collaborating with the Turkish state in the oppression of the Kurdish people but did not attempt an insurgency as it would later.

away from the idea of liberation taking the form of a separate Kurdish state and instead began to see the absence of the state as necessary for true liberation. In a revolution, Hiwa said, "you open a space for society," but when the revolution is over "you should not return to the same model . . . society should be able to defend itself against the state." It followed that this liberation could not be complete if it was only for Kurdish people; it had to include all the parts of society in the liberated area. This gave rise to what is referred to as the "democratic nation" model.

From the beginning of the armed struggle, women have been part of the struggle. "You cannot hand over your liberation struggle to others to liberate you," Hiwa explained. "Now you are fighting for freedom," he went on. Freedom, Hiwa says, must consider all oppressed groups: "When we go far back in history, we know that the first class that was repressed was women. The first nations that were repressed were women, and the first gender that was repressed [was] women. So if you are going to liberate the society, you have to address this issue, this deep issue."

This analysis, that women's liberation was crucial in society's liberation, is at the core of Öcalan's evolved political thought. In 2013, Öcalan's book *Liberating Life* (the Kurdish word for woman, *jin*, is derived from the word for life, *jiyan*) laid out the analysis in straightforward terms: "The extent to which society can be thoroughly transformed is determined by the extent of the transformation attained by women. Similarly, the level of woman's freedom and equality determines the freedom and equality of all sections of society."[1] Arising from the centrality of feminism in the Rojava revolution is the study of women and their liberation, called jineoloji. This unique brand of feminism is distinct from the "lean in" neoliberal feminism that became so popular in the US at the same time as Kurdish women were liberating themselves. Where former Facebook CEO Cheryl Sandberg told women to liberate themselves alone by fighting to climb higher up the ladder of oppression, jineoloji held that women and society must liberate themselves together and that without a fundamental change in the way men and women see the world and each other, neither could ever be free.

In Rojava, I met with Rihan Loqo, a spokeswoman for Kongra Star, the Kurdish women's confederation, who explained to me that oppression of women had come from the regime, society, and the family and that they must change all three in order to achieve liberation. The women's revolution was not something that happened after the political revolution, she said, or something that they could put aside until the exigencies of war were gone. In Cuba and Vietnam, she told me, the revolution had used women as fighters and then sent them home once things were done. This wouldn't be possible in Rojava, she said, because women had built the revolution, fought for it, and were integral to it. They could not be sent home because without them there was no revolution.

Jineoloji is one of what Hiwa called the three pillars of the movement: "democracy, ecology, in the sense of environmentalism, and the emancipation of women." Öcalan has not always placed these pillars at the center of his thought, and indeed much of his ideological development has happened since his incarceration by the Turkish state in 1999. For the quarter of a century since then, the Kurdish freedom movement's ideological North Star has been locked up, for long periods totally incommunicado and unable to leave the island where he has largely been unable to talk to anyone, or meet with his lawyers. Today he is considered the honorary leader, but as with all other institutions of the Kurdish freedom movement, the KCK is led by two co-chairs, one man and one woman, to ensure that the institution does not replicate patriarchal power structures.

In the years before he was incarcerated, Öcalan spent much of his time in exile. Ba'athist Syria, despite its own oppressive policies toward Kurdish people and their culture, allowed him to escape Turkey there. The Syrian state saw the PKK as a useful tool and allowed the PKK to train in the Beqaa Valley, in Syrian-controlled Lebanon, and later in Damascus. During this time Kurds fought and died for a free Palestine as Israel attacked the Democratic Front for the Liberation of Palestine, with whom the Kurds were training. Meanwhile in Syria, the regime stripped citizenship from tens of thousands of Kurds, making it impossible for them to access schools or hospitals, and it tried to install "Arab belts" as part of an attempt at demographic change in Kurdish areas. In 1998, following threats from Turkey, the Syrian government ejected the PKK. Militants moved their training ground into the rugged peaks of northern Iraq, which I could see in the background as Hiwa and I sat in our little cast iron chairs and I tried not to jump out of my skin when a motorcycle backfired in the alleyway behind us.

Turkish aggression, which is what had me nervously gazing at the sky after a week of nightly drone bombings of people exactly like the ones I was sharing my afternoon with, has been a constant in the history of the Kurdish freedom movement. At times, from 1999 to 2004 and from 2013 to

2015, there have been ceasefires, and at times the nominal goal of the movement has been autonomy and equality for all groups within the state rather than liberation from it, but the Turkish state has remained steadfast in its position that the PKK is a terrorist group, that the PYD is part of the PKK, and that even demands for Kurdish-language education represent support for the group and therefore cannot, under any circumstances, be permitted. This constant state violence has impacted the group's ideology. Indeed, Kurdish people, who have not had a state of their own for centuries and were again denied one by the colonial powers on their post–World War I withdrawal, are well placed to understand an anarchist critique of the state and its incompatibility with democracy in any substantive sense that allows people and communities, not capital and remote state governance, to determine their own outcomes.

One of the first topics I discussed with Hiwa was society without the state. The state, he said "camouflages itself, it hides itself as something as the building block of society as the spinal cord of the society." He sees the state as "the organization which represents the interests of the higher class." Ever since the Ottoman and Persian empires divided them, Kurds have not had a state in their control. It's easy to see how this experience could lead to a desire for a state of one's own, but Hiwa says this is no longer the goal of the movement. "There have been a lot of liberation struggles, national liberation struggles, [in] which they have toppled one state, but at the place of the state they have erected another state. . . . The problem with liberty, with freedom, is not to replace one state with another state." Using the means of the state, he said, leads to the same kind of oppression, perhaps by another group. "So, for freedom movements, for the people, for women, for the working class who, who have a problem with oppression of the state, they have to build another mechanism for administration other than the state."

Hiwa continued as I frantically tried to take notes in my illegible shorthand: "So you defend yourself and you are establishing your own society as you are defending it. Because if you defend yourself, and if you don't develop an alternative model to the state, even if you succeed, after that, you will end up with the same system against which you have waged struggle." These, he said were the insights Apo had after many years of struggling both against the Turkish state and for a Kurdish one. All these ideas, and much more context that I haven't the space to include here, were conceived of before Bashar al-Assad decided to remove his troops from Kurdish areas of Syria, and without this journey that Öcalan and the movement took, I probably wouldn't have visited those areas.

Öcalan's political journey towards a libertarian leftism started after he was incarcerated. He had been arrested after a brief tour of Europe that saw him bounce from Russia to Greece and Italy before attempting to resolve his situation at the Hague. Eventually he flew to Nairobi at the invitation of Greek diplomats. Not long after his arrival in Kenya's capital, he was captured by Turkish intelligence agents with the help of the CIA. Öcalan had been hoping to return to Europe to face allegations of terrorism, but instead he would face a death penalty trial in Turkey. Protests erupted all over Kurdistan and its diaspora. In Berlin, they stormed the Israeli consulate, and security guards killed three protesters. Greek ambassadors' residences and embassies were stormed, and in Vienna both Greek and Kenyan embassies were occupied by protesters.

After he was transported to Turkey, lawyers from the Netherlands were detained for attempting to visit Öcalan and represent him. Throughout his trial, he had little to no access to lawyers, and his witnesses were not allowed to speak. When Turkey removed its death penalty in 2002, his sentence was commuted to life and, despite rulings in his favor by the European Court of Human Rights, he has been unable to appeal. Instead, he has remained imprisoned on the island of İmralı, guarded by up to one thousand troops. For years at a time, he has not been allowed to see his lawyers or visitors. While detained, Öcalan has spent his time reading social theory, including that of Murray Bookchin, with whom he corresponded and from whose libertarian municipalism Öcalan began rebuilding his own ideology.

I first became familiar with Bookchin during my PhD research, through his historical work on Spanish anarchism, but he is much better known for his work on anarchist theory. It was one of these theoretical works, *The Ecology of Freedom*, and his thoughts on the text and discussion of it with Bookchin that prompted Öcalan to write a "Declaration of Democratic Confederalism in Kurdistan," in 2005. It was in this way that the incarcerated leader of a movement of stateless people made the shift from state socialism to a more libertarian leftism. Öcalan's evolved thinking, which rooted power in local assemblies and sought to build democracy without the state, spread through the movement and became the ideology of the PYD. And so when the Syrian Arab Army (SAA) withdrew from Kurdish cities, the largest party in the region did not attempt to set up its own state in the space left behind.

Hiwa described the change in the movement as follows:

[Öcalan] said the farewell to an ideology that believes freedom, peace, and democracy comes through the state and the nation state. Instead, he developed a communitarian, let's say, community-based, paradigm which foresees bringing about freedom and peace and democracy by organizing people in villages, cities, neighborhoods, and provinces through common assemblies, congresses, and other forms of confederate units and unions. . . . Through his prison writings, Öcalan shared this new paradigm with his movement, the Kurdish people and all the other oppressed peoples in the world. Instead of nation-state, he developed the concept of a democratic nation, and, instead of a state, he developed the concept of democratic confederalism. So the Kurdish freedom movement adopted these, this new paradigm, and regrouped and reorganized itself to achieve this aim. . . . According to the new line of struggle, the Kurds can reach freedom and build their own democracy without necessarily building a separate state of their own. They can achieve this through democratic self rule.

Of course, Kurdish people were well disposed by their history to see the folly of the nation-state. In a follow-up interview conducted using encrypted messages as Turkey continued to bomb the mountains where he lives, Hiwa expounded on this. "As you know, Kurdistan is a land, the ancestral land of the Kurds being divided between four countries, Turkey, Iraq, Iran, and Syria. Divided by borders. People from one side of the border are Kurdish, on the other side of the border they are Kurdish," he told me. Often Kurdish cities, villages, and communities are split by the borders, and their arbitrary nature is obvious to even a casual observer.

Each morning in Qamişlo, in express contravention of the advice of the one risk management professional I have spoken with in my entire career, I'd walk around the market to buy some breakfast. In Syria it's hard not to notice that the schools, hospitals, and other state buildings are all fortified. Some of those strongpoints in Qamişlo still had regime soldiers guarding them, and Assad's troops had not left the airport either at that time. This gave my morning stroll a hint of danger, which made up for the lackluster instant coffee. More than once I turned down a street only to find myself staring at concrete barricades and mounted heavy machine guns. Seeing my predicament, strangers on the street would take my hand and quickly hustle me away from the barrel that was pivoting in our direction. Using a combination of French, English, Kurmanji, and Google Translate, they'd tell me these were Syrian Arab Army soldiers and that not so long ago these same troops had enforced a ban on the language we were speaking and killed their compatriots for demanding equal recognition by the state. As one of them emphatically told me, "Assad is a bad man!" Now Assad's troops remained in an uneasy truce with the SDF in these cities and in open conflict in other areas.

Sometimes the SDF is accused of collaborating with the Assad regime, and it should be noted that it was the Kurds who, in 2004, first rose up against the regime that had stripped many of them of their citizenship and forced many of them out of their homes. Violence erupted at a football game in Qamişlo, where security forces killed Kurdish fans; in response, Kurds burned the local Ba'ath Party headquarters and toppled a statue of Hafez al-Assad, father and predecessor of dictator Bashar al-Assad. The Assad regime acted with its predictable violence, and dozens were killed and thousands arrested.

So recent and complete is the change in Qamişlo that a generation that grew up speaking Kurdish at home but using Arabic at school has yet to standardize the spelling of certain words. Vowels are often swapped out, and despite the switch to a Roman alphabet, this makes using any form of map an absolute nightmare. Luckily, it's not hard to find a willing helper in Rojava, and more than once I arrived at a place like a sort of reverse pied piper, guided by a retinue of small children to whom I dispensed the tiny tchotchkes I always bring with me on such trips as a means of expressing my gratitude. "They speak better Kurdish than us," Khabat told me over lunch one day, laughing at my arrival with a gaggle of preteen kids, "because they learn it in school now."

Before children could safely learn Kurdish in school, the administration of the north and east of the country needed to be established. Syrian Kurds, Assyrians, and other groups beyond the Arab majority had joined the protests against the regime in 2011. The revolution began to take form after Mohamed Bouazizi, a fruit seller, set himself alight in protest at constant regime harassment in Tunisia, and people across the Arab world followed his light into the streets and raised their voices against the regimes that oppressed them. In Syria, the regime scrambled to try to buy off the Kurds, offering passports to thousands whom it had previously stripped of their Syrian citizenship, but the gesture had little impact on a people who had been oppressed by every iteration of the Syrian state for centuries.

As the conflict in Syria moved from one fought with words to one fought with weapons, the Syrian opposition began to coalesce. However, it decided to host its early meetings in Turkey, which de facto excluded Kurds. Around this same time, the YPG (which formed in 2007) entered the conflict in Syria. Siyamend Ali was a student then. "I didn't have any thought or any expectation that then one day I will join the military," he told me eleven years later in a small apartment in Hasakah, where he'd agreed to meet me despite the nightly drone strikes. It was hard to imagine the gray-haired man draped in the digital camouflage favored by the YPG with a pistol on his hip and a kind disposition hiding in his smile as anything else than a fighter. "Back at that time, it [the situation] was imposed on me or forced me to choose the life of being a soldier," he said. After just fifteen days of training, he was ready to fight, or as ready as he was going to get. The rest he would learn on the front lines.

As fighting both against the government and against the growing numbers of foreign jihadist fighters who had flooded into Syria continued, the social revolution began in Rojava. The YPG already contained mixed-gender units, but by the spring of 2013, it established the YPJ, an all-women's formation that stood alongside the men of the YPG as equals. Loqo told me that this represented a huge leap forward from the very patriarchal society that existed under the Assad regime. From a young age, women in Kurdistan had been told that even to go out and meet a relative they ought to take their little brother with them for safety. As she translated, Khabat offered her own example of this: "I was going to the shops, and my father asked me to take Diwar with me, even when he was little. I said 'He's so young! How he will fight this thief, he's so little!'" We all laughed at the thought of baby Diwar fighting off a thief, but this illustrated Loqo's point well. Loqo said they had to do away with this mentality, which taught women they needed men to be safe, and they did away with it on the battlefield. "This form of womanhood gave itself a big proof in the front or in the battlefields," Diwar translated for me. "Also, she had a leading role in her neighborhood, and also in her nation as well."

To cement those rights, an interim constitution was established, and three "cantons" were declared and established a system that transferred power as far as possible to local neighborhood, village, and city councils. These councils, composed of Kurds Arabs, Assyrians, Chechens, Turkmens, and Armenians elected co-chairs and representatives from the ethnic groups in the areas they administered. The constitution enshrined rights for women, minority groups, and workers. It established women's houses in every community, where women could escape gender-based violence, and it established a system of restorative justice, one that Tekoşîna Anarşîst—an explicitly anarchist formation within the SDF—was keen to remind me, when we spoke in late 2024, had its roots in queer and Black communities.

In the absence of the Syrian state, the so-called Islamic State of Iraq and al-Sham (an Arabic term for the greater Syria region) had risen to prominence among the jihadist groups in Syria. Known in the region by its Arabic acronym, DAESH, the group styled itself as a caliphate. Its interpretation of Sunni Islam saw all other faiths and all other branches of Islam as heretical and deserving of capital punishment.

Under the black banner it flew, the group attracted many foreign fighters and imposed its totalitarian-Islamist rule on a growing area. As it grew, it dropped the "Iraq and al Sham" from its name and proclaimed itself a global caliphate, the Islamic State (IS). In 2014 IS forces swept through Mosul, Fallujah, and much of Iraq as well as Aleppo and Deir ez-Zor in Syria. It also began its genocide of those it called nonbelievers, including the Yezidis.

The Yezidis are an ethnic group indigenous to the area that is today northwestern Iraq. Their monotheistic faith predates Zoroastrianism and Islam and is centered around a benevolent angel who appears in the form of a peacock. The Islamic State considered their faith tantamount to devil worship.

In August 2014, IS fighters took Shengal, a town that was under the control of Iraq's Kurdistan Regional Government (KRG) but which was primarily populated by Yezidis. As they took the town, the IS fighters began summarily murdering its inhabitants, burying some alive. Men in each Yezidi village fought bravely to give their families a chance to escape. Those who were captured faced execution and torture, but their families faced the arguably worse fate of being sold as slaves. The Yezidis held their ground for as long as they could, but they were little more than a hastily assembled militia armed with rusting Kalashnikovs and a few magazines each. When KRG's Peshmerga elected to pull out, the Yezidis were hopelessly outgunned. IS fighters swept through Yezidi villages, and this prompted a mass exodus to Mount Sinjar, where the world watched in horror as of thousands of Yezidis were trapped on the summit, surrounded by the black flags and genocidal fighters of the Islamic State. The older, younger, and sicker members of the community died of dehydration and hunger. The only way off the mountain was the occasional helicopter, which could take twelve people at a time. Twelve people per flight is not enough to meaningfully impact the thousands of people on the mountain, but it was enough to cause a panicked stampede for every flight and for parents to throw their children on board and hope to see them again one day or at least hope that someone would live to tell their stories.

In Rojava, Siyamend Ali was watching the same footage we were. "At that time we were in defense positions against ISIS," he said. "Daily, we lost a village or two to ISIS." On seeing the genocide of their neighbors unfolding, Ali says he and the other fighters gathered and voted on what to do. "We had suggested to our higher ranks or to our commanders that we must go there even when we were busy with fighting with ISIS," he remembered. Their commander permitted them to leave, and so Ali and his friends set off on the eighty-kilometer journey to Shengal.

"I felt sorry," Ali told me, "that there were international forces there and also the Iraqi soldiers, yet all of them have left the Shengal people there alone and exposed to ISIS's knives. About 60,000 people were exposed to an inevitable death." This, he says, is why his group of men and women fighters set off in their unarmored pickup trucks to face thousands of jihadists and open up a corridor to allow the Yezidis to flee. At this time, he said, "we were only about thirty people," Ali said. Pausing, cupping his hands together, he added: "All the countries of the world . . . They didn't support us."[2]

Their small group joined up with other fighters from the Yezidi community, likely members of the YBŞ (Yekîneyên Berxwedana Şengalê, or Sinjar Resistance Units), who formed the military arm of the democratic confederalist movement in Sinjar that was founded in 2007. "Our fight was on three levels," Ali told me. They wanted to first open a corridor, rescue civilians, and protect those who stayed there. "We were like about thirty or forty. They were like, so many . . . maybe thousands."

"I was fighting three days straight to open the corridor," Ali continued. "I don't even remember in those three days that I ever ate anything or drank water." His voice grew animated as he described the battle in detail, and I waited eagerly for Diwar to translate as they went back and forth. As Diwar translated, Ali pulled a packet of cigarettes from his fatigues and offered me one. The packet was a good sign; soldiers the world over like to smoke and tell their stories, and cigarettes are a universal currency. A few days later, I would

---

2.　US and UK special forces did participate in intelligence gathering, and the US sent airstrikes, but the evacuation and humanitarian corridor were solely opened by Ali and his comrades in arms.

be passing them out in a tense situation at a roadblock, and a few months later I'd hand them out at the border as I sat around a fire with Kurdish refugees who were sharing their stories. But this time I politely declined. I had already assaulted my body with a thirty-six-hour plane journey and the sort of energy drinks that are named after charismatic megafauna and that they only sell in truck stops in Iraq. These were the kinds of stories I'd come across the world to hear and I wanted to give them all my attention.

"ISIS were chasing them to kill them," Ali told me after recounting how the civilians fled the city for the mountains. "It was a great number of civilians," he said. His own troops had to move through the fleeing civilians in the opposite direction, towards the danger they were trying to escape. "We were coming from the top of the mountain, downwards. We were dressed up as civilians," Ali remembered. When they reached the gunfire they'd heard from above, they saw what the civilians were running from: "When we saw the ISIS members killing civilians, we killed them." Normally, dressing as civilians is considered dishonorable on the part of combatants, but in the case of the battle with the Islamic State, it didn't grant the Kurdish fighters any particular immunity from being targeted as ISIS killed without distinction. "We were hiding our weapons under our clothes," Ali said. "It was very crowded and very loud. And, like, even ISIS members couldn't differentiate who's a soldier who's undercover." To add to the chaos, daytime temperatures were above 113 Fahrenheit (45 Celsius), and there was very little water on the mountain aside from that being dropped by UK, US, and Iraqi military aircraft. So crowded was the mountaintop that the supplies fell directly onto desperate people, and some were killed by the supply drops.

Ali, Diwar, and I discussed how difficult this situation must have been with thousands of panicking civilians and no uniformed combatants. "ISIS members were coming in trucks, pickup trucks, filled with troops for support or attack," Ali said. The numbers of IS fighters were staggering, he said. "Those pickup trucks were filled with soldiers, and we were killing them all. When we killed them, another pickup truck would come, and we would keep killing them." The IS fighters continuing to dash towards the gunfire, which baffled Ali and his comrades. "Are they stupid to keep exposing themselves that easily?" he asked himself. "They didn't have any fear!" Later, he says he realized that they had faced little resistance up to that point, and "so they were very confident, they knew there was nothing to stop them." It was only later that the IS fighters began to act as if they might encounter determined opposition.

I asked Ali how his fighters were able to resupply. Killing that many people requires significant ammunition. Besides, guns overheat, jam, and get dirty with sustained use. And even if they don't, it's hard to carry enough ammunition to keep fighting for days at a time against a numerically superior enemy. It was, apparently, a good question. It's always good to indicate in these interviews that while I haven't fought in combat, I'm not a total novice to the practicalities of conflict. Ali said he and his friends were very careful and precise with their shots but they also found ammunition in the houses civilians had fled. At that time and still today, AK platform rifles were common in Iraq, and many homes would have a rifle and a few magazines. In most cases, these magazines and the 7.62 × 39 caliber ammunition they contained could be used without issue in the rifles Ali and his friends carried. When the need became desperate, they took magazines from the bodies of the ISIS fighters they killed, who also used the same weapons.

At a certain point, Ali continued, they captured a weapon that changed the course of the battle: "We reached a Peshmerga outpost and we found a 23 mm gun. It wasn't even used, it was just left by them when they fled. We seized it and placed it on the mountain, and it helped us to dominate the area." The gun they captured was almost certainly a ZU-23, a Soviet-era antiaircraft machine gun that is commonly used atop pickup trucks known as "technicals," where its devastating firepower can be used against ground targets. It fires bullets that weigh nearly half a pound (190g) and spits them out at a rate of 400 per minute with an effective range of one and a half miles (2.5 km).

Ali said that the autocannon turned the tide decisively and allowed them to repel the IS assault. "After we killed them [the IS fighters], we talked to the people [seeking refuge on the mountain], and we were telling them that we are here to protect them and we are YPG. Some of them didn't even know what the YPG was." They took the civilians to the top of the mountain, and slowly the civilians spread the news, and more of them gathered. Eventually, the YPG was able to evacuate around 35,000 people in the corridor they had opened. The US, UK, and Iraqi governments had previously dropped food for the people trapped on the mountain, and both British Special Air Service and US Marines and Special Forces were operating there at some point, but their respective governments did not reply to requests for comment about the battle.

Hiwa, speaking nearly a decade later, was more forthright in his condemnation of the state's actions in Sinjar. "So at the time of Sinjar, it was a time when a state failed." The failure of the state left a space for the community, he said. "It was the time for the community to speak and to act on it on its own. The state didn't feel responsibility at that time.... Had they felt a responsibility, they wouldn't have left Sinjar.... But when DAESH made that onslaught on Sinjar, they all ran away." In his account, there were just seven guerrillas embedded among the Yezidis defending them on the mountain; this group seized the anti-aircraft artillery and was later joined by others.

I've tried for over a year to speak to anyone else who was on that mountain. I've met Yezidi refugees in the mountains of Southern California, but none who were in Sinjar. I asked Hiwa to help me in my search for the fighters, but he said it was likely none of them survived a decade of war. The story Ali told me lines up with reporting at the time, but exact numbers and details beyond those he gave me are impossible to verify. Some stories have five fighters, others a dozen. What is apparent is that in their decision to fight IS on the Yezidis' sacred mountain, the YPG and YPJ illustrated the difference between a state society and a democratic one. For them, the need for solidarity and mutual aid overcame differences in politics or identity; they risked their lives to help. For the more statist vision of Kurdish identity in the KRG and the Iraqi state, it wasn't worth risking the lives of their soldiers for those of Yezidi civilians. The IS genocide of the Yezidis was one of its most heinous crimes, and the women sold into slavery are still being liberated a decade later, but without the intervention from Rojava, it would have been orders of magnitude worse.

The solidarity the YPG and YPJ showed to the Yezidis, who are sometimes regarded as ethnic Kurds but in many cases see themselves as a group apart, was not the only internationalism on display in Rojava. From the beginning of the conflict, Turkish leftists had made common cause with the people of Rojava and traveled across the border to fight with them against the By late 2014, as the world saw the horrors of theocratic fascism, the states of the neoliberal North hung back and refused to commit ground troops due to their concerns about public opinion after a decade of war in Iraq. Individuals from inside and outside the military felt they could not stand by while such horrors occurred.

At first, the volunteers came via a Facebook page called the Lions of Rojava; later they organized via other Facebook groups, Reddit, and other social networks, and a more formal structure was put in place. Volunteers traveled to Slemani, a town in northeastern Iraq near the mountain ranges where the KCK leadership has found refuge for decades. There, volunteers waited in safe houses and underwent a basic assessment. Some, including one who touted his combat experience from the video game *Call of Duty*, decided that Rojava was not for them after all and never made it past this point. Others, including several I spoke with for this book, then crossed through the mountains into Rojava, where their basic training at "the academy" began.

"They were all different types of volunteers," Sam, who was one of them, told me. "You know, some people were there primarily because of the military conflict, and others were there for the social movement." The crossing from the KRG to Rojava, one I made on a rickety bridge constructed out of plastic oil barrels, had been Sam's first taste of what was to come. "We had an arduous crossing, I would say," he laughed. "[We rode in] a number of trucks, we were smuggled through the mountains. And then we had to cross the river on an inflatable raft and then hike for about six hours through the desert." This was their introduction to the revolution.

At the academy, volunteers were fed and given cups of chai before their interviews. And then they discussed with academy cadres their reasons for coming, their knowledge of the revolution, and their hopes for their time in Rojava. After this, they began a course in Kurdish history, language skills, and jineoloji, and a day on each of the basic weapons as well as a week or so of tactical instruction. They were taught by experienced cadres, some international and some Kurdish, and they learned as much about the revolution in governance and gender as about the war against jihadism and Assadism. Even those who had come solely for a chance to fight ISIS appreciated the importance of the political discussions, Sam said. In many ways, he reflected, those volunteers who came for myriad nonpolitical reasons still became more accomplished revolutionaries than the anarchists who didn't visit Rojava but criticized it from afar.

This was a sentiment shared by Tekoşîna Anarşîst, who later established their anarchist formation under the SDF, not out of disagreement with the democratic confederalist system, but in order to bring together the anarchists in the Rojava revolution and to consolidate their experiences and learnings. The revolution in Rojava is not anarchist in the purest sense, but it is an attempt to create a society without the state. Anarchists often criticize the continued nationalism that plays a role in much of the support for the SDF if not the official stance of the AANES. They also criticize the leaderism of the Kurdish freedom movement, both in its adherence to Öcalan and in some of the formations in Rojava that appear like representative democracy. Some anarchists criticize the movement's devotion to its martyrs, saying they are incompatible with atheism. There is, of course, the issue of the incarceration of jihadist prisoners, and the alliance with the United States against the Islamic State. None of these disqualify the movement from support, and Tekoşîna Anarşîst attempts to provide an anarchist critique from a position of solidarity with the Rojava revolution, rather than one of condescension or misunderstanding, as has too often been the norm among leftists in the Global North.

Sam and others, after nearly two months in Kurdistan, asked their instructors if they could see the revolution they were training to fight for. Their instructors put together a weeklong tour at their request. This allowed him to witness what they were fighting to protect and to see that every village or town they liberated from the Islamic State had a chance to quickly become a more liberated and equal place. They saw young people working together to improve their communities, and they saw the challenges Rojava faced building a revolution in the middle of a war. "I was impressed," Sam said. "It's hard to tell from the outside, but there were anarchist groups doing work." He was especially taken with the Mala Jin, or women's houses, which offer a safe space for women in their communities. He was also shocked at the recovery of cities whose names are better known as battles. "To see Kobani being rebuilt in such a way, and they left the ISIS cages in place as a historical monument . . . I was impressed."

Some of the veterans from other militaries in Sam's class took it upon themselves to teach their comrades how to fight. "They were like, 'The shit they're teaching you, you're gonna get me killed,'" he recalled. So, the veterans set up their own classes, teaching how to break contact, how to clear buildings of enemy combatants or IEDs, and how to move and communicate as soldiers. The Kurdish fighters, he said, learned to fight at the front. Unlike their Western comrades, they didn't place much faith in equipment. "I had a friend that when he did six months in the mountains as well," Sam told me, "The first week, they threw his med pack into the river!" The Kurdish fighters told Sam's friend, "We have all the medicine we need in the plants that grow here." Ideology, self-sacrifice, and a desire to defend their communities were more important to local fighters, who learned the rest of their craft under fire.

Alongside his heavy bulletproof vest, Sam had brought a shovel and some Arabic-language permaculture leaflets. He loved gardening and had organized his classmates at the academy to tend the gardens. Once he finished his training, he met with the commanders. "We see your hard work here, with the plants," they said. "Maybe we'll send you to the youth organization in Kobani, because they're doing a big tree-planting campaign now. Or maybe we'll keep you here because you're, like, such a big motivator for the guys. But you're a revolutionary, right? You should see combat." Given what Sam knew of the revolution, he wanted to do whatever the people who had built it thought best. He and his team made their way to the front lines. At first, this was a shock. "I was, like, quite sure that they wouldn't send me to the front," Sam said. "I don't know anything about fighting. And there were all these other, like, actual military vets or active service guys that had gone AWOL to volunteer.[3] They were all really excited to be fighting, and I was, like, oh, yeah, just gonna, like, go to garden."

Sam and his friends would go on to fight their way through the core of the Islamic State and witness some of its final days. But in 2014, as Ali returned from Shengal to Rojava, IS's defeat was anything but certain. IS captured thousands of Yezidi and Christian women whom it sold as sex slaves. Several women who had been sexually assaulted by ISIS members jumped to their deaths from Mount Sinjar. People fled as IS advanced, running out into the desert to escape the horrific tortures of the Islamic State.

In Kobani, hundreds of kilometers to the west, the women of the YPJ fought to prevent other women and girls from suffering under IS like some Yezidi women had. The siege of Kobani, brought the world's attention to the fighters of the YPG and YPJ as they bravely held out in the town for more than six months. In Kobani, Free Syrian Army troops including the Northern Sun battalion that was led by Abu Layla—a fighter of mixed Kurdish and Arab descent who bucked misogynist naming conventions by taking the name of his daughter rather than his son—joined the YPG and YPJ in standing against the terror of the Islamic State. Even Iraqi Kurdish Peshmerga crossed into Kobani from Turkey to join the fight. With their backs to the Turkish

---

3. Hundreds of non-Syrian nationals volunteered over the course of the battle against IS. In the earlier part of the battle, many came to Rojava out of a desire to fight IS rather than a desire to support the revolution. This latter group of volunteers often included people who had trained in other militaries and either did not have a chance to fight during their time in uniform and wanted to see combat, or who had fought and felt compelled to continue fighting against IS. Several US military veterans were killed in the battle against IS.

border, the fighters fought at such close range that many preferred to carry several hand grenades instead of more rifle ammunition. Their resistance was nothing short of heroic, and it was at this time that the YPJ's sniper teams, hidden in the rubble and dust of the city, began to make a name for themselves. Urban warfare is, even for experienced soldiers, a game of chance, and, in the ruins of Kobani, ISIS fighters paid for every inch of ground with their lives. Khabat told me that the jihadists particularly feared being killed by women and so the YPJ would holler in high-pitched voices, hidden behind the rubble, to let them know that not only were they about to be engaged, but that it was women who were preparing to rid the world of their particular brand of misogyny.

Seeing the resistance of the fighters in Kobani, a coalition of states led by the United States lent their support to the fight, mostly in the form of airstrikes against Islamic State positions. These support missions, while vital to the defeat of the Islamic State, resulted in the deaths of thousands of civilians, including 1,600 in Raqqa alone according to Amnesty International.[2] The coalition was, with some exceptions from UK, French, and US Special Forces units, unwilling to fight on the ground against the Islamic State. Instead, the coalition relied on partner forces to target airstrikes, while its aircraft enjoyed almost total dominance of the skies. While the incredible firepower was certainly decisive in the eventual defeat of the Islamic State, the civilian death toll was enormous. Investigations into the apparently total lack of concern for civilian casualties in some incidents continue to create scandals in the US a decade later. However, at the time, US President Obama enjoyed high approval ratings and did not have to deal with the electoral consequences of a ground war. Instead, the costs of this new way of waging war were paid by the innocent people of Syria.

By 2015, the siege of Kobani had been lifted, and the YPG and YPJ, alongside their allies, had dealt a decisive blow to the Islamic State. Having swept across Iraq and Syria looting weapons and vehicles and murdering tens of thousands, the Islamic State seemed unstoppable. In Kobani, the world watched as the black flags of ISIS fell, and the yellow and green banners of the YPG and YPJ replaced them. In capital cities across the world, governments saw in the Kurdish forces a potential for solving the problem of the Islamic State, which by that time had fighters from around the world among its ranks, and to solve it without the electoral and societal consequences of a large-scale deployment. They put aside their political differences, closed their ears to Turkey's concerns about the commonalities between the PKK and the AANES, and entered into an alliance with the YPG and YPJ.

No sooner had the world recognized the fighting prowess of the people of Rojava than Turkey, fearing that the defeat of the Islamic State might lead to the establishment of a Kurdish one, began to organize against them. In the June 2015 Turkish elections, bombs went off in the Kurdish city of Diyarbakir, and two members of the leftist People's Democratic Party, who have long served as intermediaries between the Kurdish freedom movement and the Turkish government and run Kurdish candidates of their own, were killed. The PKK, who had been withdrawing their troops to Southern (Iraqi) Kurdistan since they signed a ceasefire agreement in 2013, urged their supporters to come out and protest against the Turkish government's detention of 260 YPG fighters who were crossing their borders to fight IS. More than thirty people involved in the protest were killed by police. Soon after, Turkey entered the battle against IS, but at the same time Turkish forces shelled and then bombed PKK positions inside Iraq, and the PKK responded with attacks of their own.

In late 2015, the coalition of Arab, Kurdish, Syriac, Turkmen, Armenian, and Chechen groups that had come together against IS formalized their alliance and began to operate under the banner of the Syrian Democratic Forces (SDF). The group included elements of the FSA who had fought in Kobani, the Assyrian Syriac Military Council—formed around a core of guerrillas who had fought alongside the PKK in the mountains since the 1990s and some of whom also shared the democratic confederalist ideology—and groups like Jayash al Thuwar who were multiethnic but had been rejected by the theocratic groups in the Syrian opposition for their atheist or anti-Islamist stances.

It was the SDF who launched a daring operation in 2015 to join the two islands of territory they controlled and fight their way across the pan-flat countryside toward Al-Hasakah. Years later, I drove through the area with Khabat and Diwar as they pointed out the huge concrete grain towers that had housed snipers. The Assad regime had decided Rojava would be the breadbasket of Syria, and it destroyed any trace of woodland, trees, or anything else that grew and couldn't be taxed. What it left was a terrain legible to the state, and a sniper's paradise, with the potential for shots so long that US troops deployed to the area reportedly requested newer sniper rifles to ensure they were able to overmatch the increasingly competent snipers of the Islamic State, many of whom had professional training from their service in state militaries, and high-level equipment according to the YPG fighters I spoke to who inspected their equipment after killing them.

As we drove across the plains of Hasakah, the scars of the battle were still obvious. Single-story adobe houses dotted the plains, as did the craters from the vehicle-borne IEDs that the Islamic State was so fond of building and using to breach SDF lines. They'd weld sheet metal across the front of the cars, leaving only a small slot for the driver to see through and making it nearly impossible for the SDF snipers to stop the vehicle. We drove across those same roads at night, with the dream catcher on Khabat's rearview mirror jumping up and down as the pockmarked road tested the car's aging suspension. In the back, Diwar and I curled up and watched clips from Sacha Baron Cohen's *Borat Subsequent Moviefilm*, and I tried in vain to explain QAnon and to not worry about the alarming regularity with which we encountered motorcycles coming towards us without headlights.

The big grain silos outside Hasakah have an equally big set of YPG and YPJ flags on them now, and Reber Apo looks on from a billboard across the road. The fighting was fierce here, with more than three hundred ISIS militants killed. The YPG and YPJ found themselves fighting alongside the regime against ISIS, and after capturing the town they were able to negotiate with the Syrian Arab Army to divide the city into areas of control. Less than a year later, the regime began attacking, bombing, and shelling YPG and Asayish (internal security forces) positions, and the YPG found itself facing its old enemy and brief ally. Despite the regime's airstrikes, to which the YPG could not respond, and the withdrawal of US Special Forces who had been embedded with them, the YPG was able to capture nearly all of the city by late August 2016. The remaining regime forces would only withdraw when the regime collapsed in late 2024. The territory gained included the building where I ate dinner with a family that had lost a husband and father to the fight against ISIS; his portrait still watched down on his child from the corner of his living room that, only a handful of years before, had been inside the territory of the Islamic State.

By late 2015, SDF forces had seized the Tishreen Dam and begun to fight west of the Euphrates River. Ironically, they were fighting in the very territory that saw the creation of the state millennia before. Despite both the US and the UK calling for an attack on Raqqa, neither was willing to commit significant ground forces to the assault. Turkey demanded that the YPG not be involved, but the US stressed that without the YPG and YPJ it was not possible to take Raqqa.

With the writing on the wall for the long-term future of their particularly egregious and violent vision of a theocratic state, IS fighters turned to suicide operations more often. These bombs and car bombs were often aimed at local civilians as well as SDF forces. Inside the city, things were even worse for civilians. Those suspected of talking to the foreign press could be beheaded, and their friends and neighbors forced to watch this spectacle of state cruelty. Airstrikes from both the regime and the coalition battered their houses and killed their neighbors in what appeared to be an indiscriminate use of the massive power of the states of the world against the Islamic State, with both parties indifferent to the suffering of thousands of civilians caught in the middle.

As the SDF advanced around the west of the city they made progress towards Tabqa Dam, where ISIS was hiding high profile hostages as a way to prevent airstrikes on the dam itself. The United States sent helicopters, which airlifted SDF fighters and a smaller number of US Special Operations Forces far behind enemy lines from where they fought their way to the dam. Airstrikes could not be used against the dam or in its vicinity, and, as the SDF fought for every yard and room in the dam, IS claimed that the dam was crumbling. Syrian and coalition engineers followed behind the fighters, assessing the integrity of the dam as the battle raged on not far ahead. Inside the control room for the dam, a dozen or so IS fighters held out without fresh air or electricity. After weeks of fighting the SDF was able to negotiate their surrender and the dismantling of any IEDs, and soon SDF forces were scaling the dam to remove the huge black ISIS banners and replace them with their own.

I asked Sam how it was seeing US troops, many of whom were expressly forbidden from direct small arms combat. "[They have a different] aesthetic," he laughed. "We'd be . . . going into the front, they'd be like, 'Oohrah! Get some!' You know? I'm like, 'I'm just gonna try to not get killed.'" The material differences were pretty clear, with US troops operating state of the art weapons and Sam and his friends using rifles essentially unchanged since their design in the 1940s. "We'd . . . trade stuff with them. . . . They were . . . jealous of us getting to go the front. . . . They want to bring the war trophies home, the ISIS flag or something like that. So we'd like trade them stuff . . . MREs, certain things like that."

By this time, about 80 percent of the SDF's fighters were Arabs, with a minority being Kurdish. Despite this, the whole SDF was often referred to as "Kurdish" in the legacy press. In fact, volunteers from around the world were fighting in the International Freedom Battalion, a formation of international volunteers that was formed as part of the YPG in 2015, as they encircled Raqqa and prepared to enter the maze of bombs, bullets, and blood that the Islamic State had laid for them in the city. Explicitly, they said their aims were global and that their politics were not confined to Rojava.

Among them were the Anarchist International Revolutionary People's Guerrilla Forces, an anarchist formation within the International Freedom Battalion that formed themselves during the Raqqa offensive and went on to fight extensively in it. They acknowledged in interviews that the revolution in Rojava was not purely anarchist in its form. "But that is why I am here," the IRPGF's Heval Sores told *Middle East Eye*. "To learn and provide critical solidarity and support."[3] Within the IRPGF, the Queer Insurrection and Liberation Army (TQILA) formed itself. Pronounced "tequila," the group was composed of "LGBT*QI+ comrades as well as others who seek to smash the gender binary and advance the women's revolution as well as the broader gender and sexual revolution," according to the IRPGF Twitter page.

Members of TQILA had watched from around the world as the Islamic State committed the most horrific crimes against people like them. "The images of gay men being thrown off roofs and stoned to death by DAESH [ISIS] was something we could not idly watch," one of them said. They went on to emphasize that the threat to queer people was global, not just local, and that they did not see such bigotry as inherent to any religion. They released a photo in which fighters held their flag, a Pride flag, and a homemade banner reading these fa**ots "kill fascists" TQILA-IRPGF (@IRPGF Jul24, 2017). They also released photos of the International Freedom Battalion commander holding a Pride flag with them in liberated Raqqa.

The Islamic State was less accepting, and in Raqqa it was now surrounded and under siege. Four thousand of its militants waited in the city, and outside ten times as many SDF troops including Arab, Kurdish, Yezidi, and international fighters were poised to attack. To begin the assault, US airstrikes pounded the city and its civilian population, which ISIS was using as shields. Despite this, the first attempts at attacks by the SDF were pushed back.

Civilian deaths were a goal for IS, who saw them as an excellent propaganda tool. They'd set up mortars or artillery pieces in civilian gardens and fire a few rounds every few days, hoping to receive counter-battery fire after they'd left. When civilians escaped, the SDF rescued them, sending boats across the Euphrates or troops to transport them back. IS saw this and began to hide among the civilians and then detonate suicide bombs or shoot SDF fighters.

This left the SDF in a very difficult position. The two dozen airstrikes a day that hit Raqqa have been rightly criticized for their massive civilian casualty rate. Seeing people's lives as expendable is not something one would associate with anarchism, an ideology that sees people as ends not means. But without much more than small arms, the SDF was not well equipped to take the city without this support and leaving it in the hands of IS would have been equally terrible for civilians.

At first, civilians were excited about the airstrikes. One local shopkeeper told the BBC that early on he'd gone to visit the site of one airstrike, where he saw the body of a French ISIS fighter. "He'd been consumed by flames in his own car," the shopkeeper said. "No one else was killed. There was no shrapnel damage to be seen. We were excited because we thought it was this technology that the US was bringing into the fight." Soon his opinion changed. "America is a superpower. It was supposed to use laser-guided bombs and precision munitions. What did we get instead? Massive bombs, mortar rounds, and countless artillery strikes. Is that how you liberate Raqqa?"[4]

As they fought their way across the city over four months of some of the most horrific fighting imaginable, the SDF began to converge on Al-Naim roundabout in the center of the city, known as the circle of hell. The roundabout is where fighters in the SDF, including Christian units, saw their friends crucified, beheaded, or whipped. For the roundabout to become safe, IS had to be removed. Eventually, the SDF negotiated for the IS remnants to remove themselves in a convoy containing a few hundred fighters and thousands of their families. Carrying their personal weapons, but without the black banners that had once struck fear into the armed forces of two different states, they drove through the desert and away from their capital. They were deposited in Islamic State territory, and Raqqa was freed. Allowing these fighters to leave doubtless saved many civilian lives not to mention those of SDF fighters, but it also set the scene for another battle in Deir ez-Zor.

All the while, the SDF also prepared for a battle on a different front, although not with entirely different characters. In January 2019, thousands of Turkish-backed Syrian National Army (SNA) fighters and Turkish troops crossed the Turkey-Syria border into Afrin. For many of them, this was not their first crossing of the border. Of the thousands of foreigners who joined IS, many had flown from European nations to Turkey and used a network of smugglers to cross the Turkey-Syria border to the Islamic State. Now, under the flags of a different state, some of them returned to exact vengeance on the Kurdish people, whom they blamed for the defeat of the Islamic State in Raqqa.

In Deir ez-Zor, SDF forces were not only pushing towards the last hold-outs of the Islamic State but also facing bombing from the Syrian state and its Russian allies. Despite having a common enemy in ISIS, the SDF and the Syrian Arab Army were still in conflict over the area. The SDF stated it would not allow the SAA to cross the Euphrates, the SAA responded by way of Russian bombers, and the SDF found itself at war with four different foes. In this struggle, the purported Anti-IS Coalition found itself divided, with Turkey and Russia now sending their military might against the people who just months before had captured the caliphate's capital.

The early Deir ez-Zor campaign met with great success, capturing both IS territory and prominent terrorists. But by March, the SDF had to halt its operations against the Islamic State to defend its people against the Turkish one. The coalition, which had been asking SDF fighters to die for four years in the battle against IS, offered no support as Turkey's rebadged jihadists poured over the border. "It was a big betrayal," Sam told me. "Promises were made, and they didn't hold up their side of the bargain. They still haven't, Turkey is still bombing. And it's totally within the means of the United States to just say, 'No, you can't do that anymore.'"

Turkish and SNA troops pushed into villages deep inside Syria, causing thousands of civilians to flee. Each village was fought for fiercely. In Hemman, YPJ fighter Avesta Habur blew herself up in an attack that destroyed a Turkish tank.[4] She was widely compared to Arîn Mirkan, a hero of the Kurdish wom-en's movement who similarly undertook a suicide attack during the Battle of Kobane. Her story appears later in this book.

In 2019, Turkey once again began demanding more land and concessions from the AANES, having faced no pushback for its actions the year before.

4. Choosing death over surrender is a common practice among the YPG and YPJ, and many fighters told me they kept a bullet in their pockets for just such a purpose. Previously the PKK has used suicide bombing as a tactic inside Turkey against security forces. During the Afrin offensive, Turkish-backed rebels gave a good illustration as to why many YPJ fighters don't feel they can surrender: the rebels filmed the mutilated corpse of Barin Kobani, a YPJ fighter, with her clothing pulled off to reveal her breasts and genitals, while fighters gathered around kicking, mutilating, and mocking her remains.

Under an agreement brokered by the US, the YPG and YPJ agreed to abandon their positions in a security corridor ranging from 5 to 14 kilometers deep, and joint US-Turkish patrols would monitor the area.

In the campaign against ISIS, the US's air and artillery support undoubtedly played a crucial role. You used to hear "Heval Trump" sometimes in Rojava when US jets were flying over and dropping bombs on the black flags of ISIS. But while states can be allies, it is not in their nature to be friends of movements like the one in Rojava. In a call with Erdoğan in late 2018, Trump asked, "If we withdraw our soldiers, can you clean up ISIS?," according to an unnamed Turkish official interviewed by Reuters. Erdoğan replied that Turkish forces were capable of the mission. "Then you do it," Trump told him, and he asked his national security adviser John Bolton to "start work for the withdrawal of U.S. troops from Syria." While administrators in DC reeled at the U-turn in policy, the Turkish state saw an opportunity and took full advantage of its free rein to attack the most effective fighters against IS, who had pushed the caliphate from thousands of kilometers of land across two countries to a small pocket in eastern Syria.

"They took down their defensive positions on the border because the United States asked them to. Very nice defensive positions," Sam told me. As states have so many times in the past, the US abandoned the Kurdish people when they most needed them. The US was happy to fly air support missions for the YPG and YPJ in Raqqa, allowing the ground forces to do the dusty, noisy, petrifying killing and dying that is necessary in urban warfare. But when those same ground forces needed support against another state, the US shrugged its shoulders and looked away. This is the nature of alliances with states, and the SDF would have been foolish to expect anything else. The US was never a supporter of the revolution in Rojava; it merely found an effective ally in the fight against IS. The SDF would likely have not succeeded in that fight without US support, and they can't really be blamed for accepting that support when it allowed the liberation of thousands of people. These are the sort of decisions that war forces onto movements, and the kind of betrayals they can expect.

With Trump's tacit approval, Turkey launched another offensive in 2019. This time the explicit goal was to establish a border "buffer zone" and resettle Arab refugees in previously majority Kurdish areas. Erdoğan openly expressed the sentiment that Kurdish people don't belong in North and East Syria, saying "These areas are not suitable for the lifestyle of Kurds . . . because these areas are virtually desert." In its military actions, Turkey also showed a disregard for human life, including using prohibited white phosphorus munitions that caused horrific burns. Its allied militias were worse, carrying out summary executions, kidnapping civilians for ransom, looting, and offering to transfer civilians to the AANES only to hand them over to Turkish intelligence and claim they were YPG.

Hiwa did not mince words about Turkey's 2019 operation, which was code-named Peace Spring. "I mean, forcing people to leave their lands and replacing those people with people which are not from that land, forcing people to leave their ancestral lands . . . It is a genocide." Hevrin Khalaf, a Kurdish politician, was captured by the SNA and dragged by her hair, beaten, and shot in the head by SNA rebels, who are so often painted as "moderate" in legacy media.

At the time the invasion was widely condemned, but words offer little help against bombs and bullets. The US did not take meaningful action and still hasn't. European leaders' criticisms were met with threats from Ankara to "flood" Europe with refugees if they called Erdoğan's invasion what it was.

After several days of heavy fighting, the US negotiated a ceasefire that largely conceded to Erdoğan. Turkey promptly violated the ceasefire and delayed medical aid from reaching the contested city of Ras al-Ayn. As if to further reinforce this point, US troops then reentered the AANES to guard oil fields, claiming they wanted to ensure IS did not have access to the oil.

In between saber-rattling states, the SDF still had to finish the battle against IS, which was now whittled down to its most dedicated surviving fighters and offered little hope of a negotiated settlement. Sam was with them as they restarted their campaign in Deir ez-Zor, pushing towards the heart of the Islamic State.

"The Kalash that I was assigned was an original 54," Sam told me. "Kalash" is the colloquial term for the dozens of AK variants in use in this part of the world. It's a term of some reverence; after all, the Kalashnikov has been part of many liberation struggles (and an equal number of oppressive regimes). Sam's Kalash "had been sitting in a box for sixty or seventy years," and over time the weight had caused parts of the weapon to compress, so that he had had to use a file to make it work. Nonetheless, it was this Cold War relic that he carried into battle against the Islamic State, while the largest armies in NATO either cheered from the sidelines or attacked his friends. Sam, who describes himself as an anarchist, wasn't too concerned with the inactivity of states, indeed he expected it. "We just did what needed to be done," he told me.

The difficulties the Rojava revolution faces are tremendous, and so is its potential. The revolutionaries have been forced into strange alliances and compromises—such as those made with tribal communities in Deir ez-Zor on women's rights. They have worked alongside the Russian, American, and Assadist regimes but only with the goal of furthering their own ability to carve out an island of liberty in a country racked by war and death.

The fighting in Deir ez-Zor was fierce, with the Islamic State relying heavily on suicide vehicle–borne improvised explosive devices. Every ISIS fighter wore a suicide vest, and every building the SDF took was riddled with IEDs that could kill anyone who put a foot wrong or opened the wrong door. In this fierce and deadly cauldron, the SDF took heavy casualties, and again their allies offered very little support other than airstrikes and artillery.[5]

As the SDF fought on, thousands of civilians fled the ISIS enclave, fearing the hellish ground combat and airstrikes that would accompany the collapse of the last pocket of the Islamic State. Although many of the remaining women and children in the pocket had taken up arms, there were also people who were not there of their own free will, including Yezidis. In one incident, on March 18, 2019, approximately fifty women and children were killed in an air strike. The operators of the drone, based in Qatar, had identified the crowd as civilians, and according to the New York Times they were shocked to see a jet flash across the drone's feed and then drop a 500-pound bomb on the crowd. As the group disappeared in a cloud of dust and death, the jet circled and dropped a 2,000-pound bomb on the survivors, and then another.[5]

Those sixty deaths were just some of the many that occurred in the dying days of the Islamic State. By March 2019, all that was left of the caliphate was a dirty field covered in bullet-riddled vehicles, bomb craters, tents, tarps, and hand-dug trenches and bunkers. It was an ignominious and undignified end to the Islamic State's reign of terror. On March 23, Mustafa Bali, the SDF's spokesman, tweeted, "Syrian Democratic Forces declare total elimination of

5. Colonel François-Régis Legrier, a French officer tasked with commanding the artillery support of the SDF, openly criticized the practice of refusing to commit ground troops in a piece for the Revue Défense Nationale. "By refusing ground engagement, we unnecessarily prolonged the conflict and thus contributed to increasing the number of casualties in the population," he wrote. "We have massively destroyed the infrastructure and given the population a disgusting image of what may be a Western-style liberation leaving behind the seeds of an imminent resurgence of a new adversary." In return for his concern for the lives of Syrian civilians, he was disciplined by the French military.

so-called caliphate and 100% territorial defeat of ISIS. On this unique day, we commemorate thousands of martyrs whose efforts made the victory possible. #SDFDefeatedISIS (@mustefabali).”

The war may have brought the territorial caliphate to an end, but the Islamic State remained a threat. Today more than 50,000 people remain detained in a hybrid refugee camp and prison at Al-Hawl, over half of them under the age of twelve. Although the SDF guards the camp, and it occasionally sends anti-terror forces into it to confiscate weapons, the interior of the camp is mostly administered by the women of the Islamic State. The SDF is very open about this being a problem; indeed, in my time there, almost everyone I met mentioned the need for more international help, including from the nations like the UK and Australia, who have refused to take back their citizens and charge them with any crimes they have committed. Instead, young children in the camp are radicalized almost from birth, sexual assault is common, and young men train with fake weapons for the return of a larger caliphate.

In 2022 more than one hundred ISIS sleeper cell fighters launched an attack on al-Sina’a prison, not far from where I’d shared dinner with Ali. They used three car bombs to blow open prison walls; simultaneously, prisoners rose up inside the prison, used smuggled weapons to overpower guards, and then stormed the armory. For ten days, fighting centered on the prison but spread to surrounding areas. The US-led coalition launched airstrikes that one fighter told me “obliterated buildings.” Civilians who refused to help the escaped ISIS fighters were killed, and others were taken hostage. The SDF gradually regained control of the prison, storming the basement cells where the last holdouts had entrenched themselves, but more than 150 SDF fighters were killed in the battle to retake the prison. While most of the ISIS fighters were re-detained or killed, some escaped and have still not been accounted for at the time of writing.

Undoubtedly, the incarceration of tens of thousands of children, many of whom were born after the end of the territorial caliphate, is not consistent with any version of libertarian left ideology. Nor is the mass detention without trial of those suspected of being enemy combatants, but it’s hard to see what good options the people of Rojava have in this scenario. It is also worth noting that Emma Goldman herself visited the Modelo prison in Catalonia in 1936 and found both fascists and priests there, suggesting this is not the first time such a situation has been faced and met with the same response. With Syrian citizens, the AANES has worked with the communities the incarcerated people came from to return them to those communities. A program has begun to remove children from the camps and educate them, not just in academic subjects but also in the basics of a diverse and accepting society.

While in Rojava, I found myself kicking a football around an old housing complex in Qamişlo while Khabat filtered the fuel for her car. The local kids, as kids do with adults everywhere, ran circles around me despite their significant handicap of being so young. Eventually, one of the girls scored a goal and I signaled for a high five in celebration. Instead, jokingly, she punched my hand. Fair enough, I hadn't been much help. Her punch was pretty ineffective; her wrist rolled downwards, and it looked like it hurt. So, without much else to do other than continue my humiliation, I set about showing her how to make a fist and throw a punch. Soon enough, I regretted my choices as she and her friends battered my palms, and Khabat came to rescue me from the gaggle of little kids now taking turns smashing my hands as hard as they could. We hopped in the car, where I rode in the back like the small child I'd shown myself to be, and Khabat told me these were the children of Islamists of the IS and other affiliated groups. A woman wearing a niqab, who I presumed was a mother of one or some of the kids, watched us as we left. I reflected on it much at the time. I find driving in Rojava occupies most of the available computing capacity in my brain even as a passenger, but later I realized that this small interaction showed how far the AANES had come. In the middle of one of the most savage wars of the twenty-first century, the AANES has built a world where a girl can leave one of the most misogynist societies in the world and become a young woman who has no qualms about approaching a stranger, humiliating him at football, and punching him as hard as she can.

The settlement the AANES has come to with Islamism is deeply imperfect. The AANES fought it into containment and now holds the Islamic State in a kind of Pandora's Box at Al-Hawl and other prisons across the region. The solution is repatriation, restorative justice where possible, and, for those who refuse to be reintegrated into society, an open and just process by which they are convicted. This is what the AANES has tried to do, but with the states of the world refusing to accept their citizens back, the AANES is hamstrung.

I had planned to conclude this chapter here. In December 2024, I was woken by a flood of encrypted messages as I had been in Rojava. This time, they were telling me that an offensive led by the Islamist group Hay'at Tahrir al-Sham (HTS) had successfully captured Aleppo. It was the start of one of those weeks where decades happen. From Aleppo, which had not seen a significant change in the front line in years, HTS pushed south to Hama on the road to Damascus. In the south, sleeper cells and more sectarian groups opposed to the regime rose up and began attacking the institutions of state control in Daraa and many other towns and villages.

Turkish proxy forces, seeing the weakness of the regime, made a push not against the dictatorship but against the AANES. The Turkish-backed Syrian National Army—a collection of Islamists who delight in war crimes—made quick advances as the regime's troops abandoned huge swaths of the west of the country. Within days, pockets of AANES control were surrounded in Aleppo and in Shehaba Canton, and refugees displaced once in 2018 were forced to flee again in the cold of the desert winter. As HTS and the Southern Front pushed toward Damascus, they met little resistance from Assad's Syrian Arab Army (SAA), which quickly lost any remaining morale as its Russian and Iranian backers fled the country. Russian soldiers, some of whom had paid bribes to avoid fighting in Ukraine, were killed in the HTS advance or stationed behind SAA units to fire on anyone retreating. Even these draconian measures failed, and the rebels advancing from the south captured Damascus at the end of a collapse that had lasted barely more than a week. Statues of Assad were toppled all over the country, and the regime's brutal prisons were thrown open and families reunited.

In Qamişlo too, the statues of Assad that still stood in the neutral areas of the city or in areas occupied by the regime were torn down. My friends sent videos of them smashed on the ground or set ablaze amid cheering crowds. But the end of the Assad regime was not the end of the war for Rojava or indeed for all of Syria. In a matter of hours, Israel and Turkey began bombing captured military equipment, with the former focusing on AANES territory.

The SNA, even as the Southern Operations Room forces and HTS swept towards Damascus, focused its energy on attacking the AANES. Just like in 2018, it was backed by Turkish drones and warplanes and conducted a grisly campaign of war crimes that it proudly shared on its Telegram channels. In Manbij, it attempted a thunder run into the city under a rolling barrage, a tactic that had worked against demoralized Assadists but which saw dozens of its fighters killed by the SDF's majority-Arab Manbij Military Council. But the city fell quickly, and soon videos surfaced of the SNA executing wounded SDF fighters, as well as looting and running the city more like an organized crime syndicate than a liberating army.

As I write this in early 2025, the SDF and SNA are fighting over the Tishreen Dam. Civilians in the AANES have mobilized to protest on the dam, in an active conflict zone, directly resulting in their deaths at the hands of SNA drones. The SDF and the Syrian interim government under HTS have signed an agreement, but it's too early for us to say what it will yield. Civilians continue to mobilize to the front lines and protest against the SNA's war crimes. It's far from a desirable outcome, and, while it shows the support of civilians for the SDF, it's hard to understand from a tactical perspective. Perhaps that's the wrong perspective from which to try to understand it.

On the battlefield, the SDF's use of modern drone technology has slowed the SNA advance, but Manbij remains in the hands of the SNA. Kobani, the city whose resistance began the end of the Islamic State, is under threat from Turkey. Once again, the SDF's allies have done little to help, and once again the AANES is about to be forced to contend with a Trump administration and its wildly unpredictable foreign policy. Meanwhile, behind the front lines, tens of thousands of refugees are being cared for after fleeing the SNA advance, and the revolution is continuing in advancing its civil society goals. Statements of solidarity from Myanmar, Western Sahara, and Uganda have shown the international impact of the women's revolution, and how much it is cherished as an example by women around the world.

When I got back from Kurdistan in late 2023, I stayed in touch with foreign volunteers from around the world. "The most important thing about Rojava," Sam told me "is that it exists." The details of the struggle, the revolution, the ideology, and the battles fought are less important than the fact that in an area that has been ravaged by war, terrorism, and dictatorship, people are living and thriving in a society based on mutual respect and without the state. This does not mean the revolution is above reproach or perfect, and, as I learned in Rojava, the most important form of solidarity can be the loving criticism given to help our friends become better.

Much of what I saw and learned in Rojava doesn't fit with the purest form of anarchism. It does not aspire to, but as it exists it brings power closer to the people and seeks to create a society without the state. What anarchists can take from the Rojava revolution is experience. Much of the left in the colonial core seems to perceive posting online as the primary form of praxis these days. David Graeber, in his writing on Rojava, called this the "loser left." The group, he said, is composed of those who are convinced a revolution can't really succeed and dedicate themselves to the criticism of those who do. Lorenzo

Orzetti, known by his nom de guerre Tekoşer Piling, an anarchist who died fighting in Rojava with Tekoşîna Anarşîst, had his own preferred term for them: "professional bullshitters." It's easy to offer critiques from behind the screen of a phone that costs as much as some people in Rojava make in a year. But people invested in building a world without the state can't engage in criticism of a project unless we first give it a chance to succeed, and the AANES should be seen as neither above reproach nor beneath contempt. Its chances of success, and of success in the way we would define it, are increased by our participation and solidarity.

While I walked with a friend to meet Zagros Hiwa, we spoke about the revolution in Myanmar. I'd been there not long before and seen the commitment and hope in the eyes of young people who had realized that together they could force the state back. "We'd like to learn more," the friend told me. "We don't have all the answers." Since then, there's been a significant exchange of solidarity between Rojava and Myanmar, one that invokes the internationalism that animated the best of the socialist and anticolonial movements. It's hard to return feeling hopeful after a week of sleepless nights and mornings that brought the news of more death and destruction, but somehow I did.

5

Discipline among the Anarchists

"Revolutionary" discipline depends on political consciousness—on an understanding of why orders must be obeyed; it takes time to diffuse this, but it also takes time to drill a man into an automaton on the barrack-square. The journalists who sneered at the militia-system seldom remembered that the militias had to hold the line while the Popular Army was training in the rear. And it is a tribute to the strength of "revolutionary" discipline that the militias stayed in the field-at all. For until about June 1937 there was nothing to keep them there, except class loyalty. Individual deserters could be shot—were shot, occasionally— but if a thousand men had decided to walk out of the line together there was no force to stop them.

—George Orwell, *Homage to Catalonia*

In a luxuriously carpeted living room in Hasakah, just a few kilometers from where Turkish drones had been dropping bombs the night before, Siyamend Ali, a spokesman for the Syrian Democratic Forces (SDF), quietly gave his considered answers to my questions via a translator, who also spoke in hushed tones. Ali, with a Glock on his hip, his hair slightly long for a soldier and gray but immaculately neat and dressed in his combat fatigues in the distinctive digital pattern used by the YPG and YPJ, leaned forward so we could hear him. Although the threat of drone strikes was very real, especially for a high-ranking fighter like Ali, that wasn't why he was speaking in whispers. All of us, the soldier, the translator (himself a former commando), and the war reporter, were trying our best to conduct our interview without waking the young boy sleeping on the sofa between us.

The thing that caught me most off guard about Ali, who had taken the risky trip into town to see me, was not the pistol on his hip, or the personal risk he'd shouldered without a word of complaint, but the easy familiarity with which he greeted me and my translators. Later, when we stopped our interview to share some food, I was again struck by Ali's felicity, the absence of any badges of rank, and the care and kindness with which he treated our host and her child. I've interviewed soldiers and spokespeople from all around the world, but rarely have I felt I was engaging in a conversation, let alone sharing a family meal. Indeed, most interviews feel rather more like a penalty shootout, in which the interviewee desperately dives left and right to prevent me from sending a shot past them and obtaining my goal of leaving the interview with a single piece of new or useful information. Ali, via my translator Diwar, casually batted topics back and forth with me, genuinely considering each response in a way that is deeply unusual for someone who has spent more than a decade at war and then been asked to talk to a visiting journalist at the height of a bombing campaign. It's not that there isn't a party line here—people will talk at the slightest opportunity about the value of ideology and Öcalan's thought—but at least I was getting responses to my actual questions and not statements that had been prepared beforehand regardless of what I asked.

On our way back from the interview we spotted a roadside cart with an espresso machine. Naturally, our driver spared no risk in transiting several lanes of nighttime traffic, most of which was not using headlights, to make sure we got some coffee that wasn't instant. Suitably caffeinated, we set off back to Qamişlo. As we sped across the plains dodging craters in the road and oncoming vehicles and livestock, I discussed the interview with Khabat and Diwar, who had both translated my conversation. "Heval means comrade," one of them said. "But it also means friend," the other butted in. Eventually, they both agreed that heval meant comrade and friend and something in between the two, and we continued on our over-caffeinated late-night journey across the plains of Rojava, wondering who the drones would kill that night. To distract ourselves and pass the time, Diwar and I curled up on the back seat watching films and sharing our favorite music on his smartphone like teenagers at a sleepover.

I'd become fast friends with Khabat and Diwar in just a couple of days. The kind of friendship that is forged in the stressful environment of conflict is hard to replicate elsewhere. Even the US military—which for recruitment relies heavily on abstract allegiance to the nation state and the inability of many young people to fund their own education or healthcare—cedes that it is not patriotism or financial obligation but "small unit cohesion" that sustains morale in combat. Indeed, the US Army's own research has shown that during sustained combat operations, troops feel less of a bond with abstract command structures and large units, and a greater fraternity with the handful of people they share stressful and life-changing experiences with.

This is not shocking news to anyone with even a passing familiarity with combat. But in a conventional military, this friendship must exist apart from, and is sometimes inhibited by, a complicated command structure. Officers and enlisted soldiers may share the same combat experiences but the former will always have theoretical authority over the latter, and each will have distinct career trajectories, entry requirements, and income. This system is seen as necessary to maintain the "discipline" of a conventional military. Officers, often required to be practicing a skilled profession or occasionally to be university graduates at the time of admission, retain some of the privileges of the aristocracy from which their status derives. Enlisted soldiers, some of whom also have university degrees and often more combat experience than the officers in their units, must call officers "sir" or "ma'am" and salute them. A salute in Rojava, the anarchists of Tekoşîna Anarşîst told me, is strictly a joke. This is not the case in most militaries, where even enlisted soldiers with years more experience and strong bonds with their team are, in theory, subordinate to a freshly minted officer of the lowest commissioned rank. While different conventional militaries may have different pathways from enlisted to officer, and different class performance expectations of officers, the binary distinction is almost universal and remains one of the more explicit examples of the enduring power of social class in a society that claims equality and equal access to opportunity. Rank is so important that it becomes a primary way of identifying a soldier, and it often replaces a first name.

So close is the tie between the officer corps and socioeconomic status outside of the military that for many a short period in service has become an important step in a planned career trajectory. In the past, some regiments of the British Army had such high uniform costs and mess bills (the costs of wining and dining at an officers-only social space) that officers needed a second income to support them. In short, military status is easily and totally convertible to social capital both inside and outside the military.

Emma Goldman, who visited the Aragon front in the autumn of 1936, asked Durruti how he addressed the question of order among his troops. He responded, "I've been an anarchist all my life and I hope to continue being one. It would be very unpleasant to suddenly convert myself into a general and command my comrades with senseless military discipline. The comrades who have come here have done so willingly and are ready to give their lives for the cause that they defend. I believe, as I have always believed, in liberty: liberty understood in the sense of responsibility. I consider discipline indispensable, but it should be self-discipline motivated by a common ideal and a strong feeling of camaraderie."[1]

The sine qua non of anarchism is that it believes that decent people will do the right thing without being compelled to do so by force or fear, but simply because they know it is the right thing to do. Thus, discipline among fighters in the anarchist columns in Spain relied heavily on a sense of duty rather than obedience. Plans were discussed, not sent down from above, and delegates were elected for each group of twenty-five, each group of one hundred, and each group of five hundred. All these numbers are approximate, but the system of electing a delegate and having committees of delegates at the centuria, group, and column levels was always adhered to. Transgressions, which might harm the collective or other individuals, were dealt with on a case-by-case basis rather than with a strict set of rules and punishments. Antoine Gimenez—a combatant in the international group of the Durruti Column—contrasted this approach with that of the POUM, who "were organized in the class style of every army in the world; rank meant everything."[2] This was not the approach of the anarchists according to Gimenez: "We have accepted a minimum discipline. We don't march in step, we don't salute our responsables, but we obey during the fighting."[3]

This "minimum discipline" might be a good description for the relations that members of Tekoşîna Anarşîst described to me in Rojava. "We know from experience that it is necessary to have military command and have someone with authority to make decisions for everyone in urgent and semi-urgent situations," they told me. "If there is more time, we will take more time to discuss." Most importantly, they said, Tekoşîna Anarşîst's command structure did not extend beyond strictly tactical matters.

The question of militarization—the implementation of systems of rank, the elimination of women fighters, and integration into the Republic's vertical command structure—was long debated among the anarchists in Spain. None of the anarchists wanted militarization, but some of them felt it was the only way for them to obtain the weapons, ammunition, and training that they needed to continue fighting. The question was not one of revolution or war, as it is often presented, but rather of what a revolutionary war must look like. The Iron Column in particular resisted militarization and the institution of a rank and command structure that comes with it. Others, including some from the Durruti Column and Cipriano Mera, who raised a column in Madrid that later became the 14th Division, were willing to comply to at least some degree. These decisions had to be made fast and under fire. While the model of the egalitarian guerrilla band had appealed to the anarchists, they were now fighting a conventional war against an organized military.

In Barcelona on March 9, 1937, militia members on leave organized an extraordinary meeting in the city to discuss militarization. There was, among many, a sentiment that discipline and better training were needed to meet their foes' increasing use of German and Italian weapons, practices, and tactics. Some felt this required accepting ranks and authority; others wanted technical delegates who could give advice but not orders.

Abel Paz only noted the last names of the discussants, making it hard to identify individuals. Styr-Nahir, according to Paz, argued that, in reality, the choice had been made for them: "The Spanish Anarchist organizations have preferred to come to an accommodation with the moderates instead of fighting them because this was the only feasible solution." He went on to say that "the spirit of the militia [was] unchanged" and that militarization was only a "formal concession."[4] The Durruti Column accepted a code, he said, and even though it was not widely used, it was a concession. Mera argued more stringently for militarization, citing battlefield defeats that he felt could have been avoided. In his memoirs, he wrote: "I explained my reasoning and the conclusion I had reached due to recent events, namely, the consequences of the lack of discipline, the defeats suffered for not following orders from military commanders, and the serious situation we were experiencing as a result of the prevailing disarray. Following this path, the loss of the war is certain and imminent. If we want to avoid it, there is no other solution, whether it pains us or not, than to militarize our militias and establish strong discipline."[5]

Despite their varied stances, they all agreed on the need to shelter comrades who had chosen to leave rather than submit to authority and were being prosecuted for desertion. Many comrades did leave, with some abandoning the fight altogether. Others joined the International Brigades, where they might better hide from purges, particularly those of suspected members of the FAI or POUM, and also enjoy the luxuries of relatively modern weaponry.

For Gimenez, the militarization of his unit signified the end of a revolution worth fighting for. "Now all that remained," he wrote, "was the war against fascism, the war between two forms of slavery."[6]

In the long decades after the war, with nothing but time to consider what went wrong for the most profound opening in libertarian politics of the twentieth century, Spain's exiled anarchists became rather critical of those who accepted militarization. Certainly this was not a universal position at the time. By 1938 one in three Spanish soldiers was an anarchist, according to José Peirats.[7] Even during the early months of the war, the anarchists adopted some of the aesthetic of militarism, with anarchist papers lauding the martyr heroes of the militia. Some of these aspects, like the celebration of physical fortitude among prominent anarchists, had always been present among the gunslinging anarchists. Ultimately the balance of what to take, aesthetically, tactically, and organizationally, from militaries organized along authoritarian lines is a debate that will continue among libertarian leftists in arms for decades to come, as it has since the Makhnovists integrated into the Red Army.[1]

In *Nosotros*, the publication of the FAI, the testimony of one of the Iron Column's "uncontrollables" was published in March 1937. The article reflected the feelings of many of the unnamed author's comrades as they saw their libertarian approach to combat slipping away, and the acceptance of by many of an authority system that they felt was unacceptable. "I am an escaped convict from San Miguel de los Reyes, that sinister prison, which the monarchy set up in order to bury alive those who, because they weren't cowards, would never submit to the infamous laws dictated by the powerful against the oppressed," the piece begins. "For eleven years I was subjected to the torment of not being a man, of being merely a thing, a number!"

The author goes on to explain that his column was not equipped by the state or reliant on it, saying: "The rifle that I hold and caress, which accompanies me since the day that I forsook the prison, is mine; it belongs to me.

---

1.   Nestor Makhno led the anarchist Revolutionary Insurgent Army of Ukraine, which was briefly absorbed into the Red Army during the Russian Civil War and Ukrainian War of Independence. The Makhnovists saw this alliance as purely military, and the Bolsheviks saw it as the Makhnovists submitting to their political control. This, along with antisemitic pogroms by Bolshevik units, quickly led to disagreements that resulted in Trotsky sending a detachment to arrest Makhno. The Mahknovists rescued the troops sent to arrest them when they became surrounded by the White Army, but thereafter the two groups parted ways and eventually fought one another.

I stripped it like a man from the hands of its former owner, and in the same manner, was obtained almost every other rifle held an owned by my comrades." The column, the author claims, had refused all discipline other than that of the individual: "Nobody could have behaved more properly towards the helpless and needy, towards those who had been robbed and persecuted all their lives, than us, the uncontrollables, outlaws, and escaped convicts." Despite this, and the column's bravery, the author suggests that a "black legend" has been spread about the column by those in the Republic who prioritize "bourgeois values" over the shared struggle. The author struggled, he writes, with a desire to fight not only the Francoists but also those on his side he knew were organizing against him.

"One day—a day that was mournful and overcast," the author continues, "the news that we must be militarized descended on the crests of the Sierra like an icy wind that penetrates the flesh." He laments that the man sleeping next to him will soon be a captain, the one keeping watch a lieutenant, and he will remain a peasant.

"Anybody, captive in prison or captive in the world, who has not understood the tragedy of men condemned to spend their lives blindly and silently obeying orders, can ever know the nether regions of pain or the terrible scar it leaves," the author continues. He laments that the brief moment of libertarian commonality and freedom that he had experienced at the front seemed to be ending. Instead, they would now be beset by what he calls a "caste" of professional officers. To reinforce the point the author gives the example of "battalions that call themselves proletarian, whose officers, having forgotten their humble origin, do not permit the militiamen on pain of terrible punishment to address them as 'thou.'"[2] This stood in sharp contrast to the anarchist system: "The delegate of a group or century was not imposed on us, he was elected by us. He did not regard himself as a lieutenant or as a captain but as a comrade."

Despite these hardships and indignities, the author goes on to say that the homogeneity of the column is of such importance that it must concede militarization if that is the only way. The column's withdrawal from the war or the breaking up of this bloc of fighting and fraternal anarchists would be worse even than accepting the unearned privilege of officers and the indignity

---

2. This refers to the familiar form of address "tu" in Spanish, which is used among friends and family as opposed to the more formal "usted."

of being given orders. "If our group of individuals presently making up our formation stays together, whether as a Column or a Battalion, the result will be the same." He writes, "When in combat, no one will be needed to imbue us with enthusiasm, and when at rest, no-one will tell us what to do, because it will not be tolerated. . . . Whatever we be called, Column, Battalion, or Division, the revolution, our anarchist and proletarian revolution, to which we have contributed glorious pages from the very first day, bids us not to surrender our arms and not to abandon the compact body we have constituted until now."[8]

And so, the uncontrollables submitted to at least nominal control. Post-militarization, the Durruti Column became the 26th Division, the Antonio Ortiz/Sur Ebro Column became the 24th, the Vivancos the 25th, and the Ascaso-Jover Column became the 28th, Mera's the 14th, and the Iron Column continued to fight fascism as the 83rd Mixed Brigade. In some cases, aside from the names, very little changed. The militias joked about the "little sardines" that appeared on uniforms to denote rank. Soon everyone wore them but treated them more like items of flair than a serious delineation of who commanded whom. So long as their units remained together, they remained reliant on camaraderie, not class. Over time, though, as the revolution and those who held it in their hearts died, so did the confederal atmosphere of the columns as they became divisions.

The anarchist companies continue to appear in histories earning the grudging respect of others. In Teruel, young anarchists pushed across frozen battlefields and into fierce machine gun fire, making their way into enemy trenches and the memories of those who fought alongside them. Even as the Republic crumbled, accounts of its last battles include authors of all political stripes noting the bravery, sacrifice, and success of anarchist formations.

Certainly, as the "uncontrollable" militant shared in *Nosotros*, this was not a happy arrangement:

[Before militarization] there is no hierarchy, there are no superiors, there are no harsh orders, but rather camaraderie, goodness and friendship among comrades, a joyful life amidst the disasters of war. And so, surrounded by comrades who believe that the struggle is for and about something, war seems gratifying, and even death is accepted with pleasure. But when you find yourself surrounded by officers and everything is hierarchy and orders; when in your hands you hold the wretched soldier's pay, scarcely enough to support your family in the rearguard, while the lieutenant, captain, commander, and colonel are all receiving three, four, ten times as much—without contributing one with more enthusiasm, knowledge or courage—life has a bitter taste to it, for you realize that this is no Revolution, but a few individuals taking advantage of an unfortunate situation at the expense of the people.[9]

Among the hevals of Rojava, there is an exceptionally strong camaraderie, but they have not yet begun wearing the "little sardines" that were forced upon the Iron Column. In the YPG and YPJ, there is no formal distinction between officer and enlisted, nor indeed any formal system of rank at all. Commanders exist, but they are not formally ranked. Ali, after more than a decade in the YPG, sat across from me in fatigues unadorned with symbols of rank. Without chevrons, bars, eagles, or stars to go by. Diwar simply greeted him as a friend, a heval, albeit a respected one. This, Ali explained, was exactly the point.

"If we ever meet someone, or whenever we see someone who's a higher rank, or maybe has higher duties than us," Ali told me animatedly through Diwar's translation, "we salute by listening to every word they say, and trying to be a friend and respecting them, paying them respect for their experience."[3]

Unsurprisingly, Ali says, this has sometimes made it difficult to work alongside more conventional militaries. While the small US Special Forces units often known as Green Berets who were embedded in Rojava might have a less strict rank structure, the need to form alliances beyond these small teams means that the hevals have to come up with some way of making Western generals feel they are meeting someone of equal importance. Ali says that at some point in the future, "the far future," they'll create some form of equivalency. "[We are aiming for] correspondence with the international military rank system. And at the same time, we trying to keep it balanced with our friendships all together. In other words, it is important not to let these ranks destroy our friendship ties." Nine decades after those

---

3. Diwar used "he" in my recording of this conversation. I feel "they" is more apt given that several examples were cited of women in command roles. Kurmanci Kurdish does have a gender-neutral pronoun, unlike other branches of the language, but I have often found that when translating into English people will use "he" even for objects with no gender, like a cup of coffee.

anarchists met in Barcelona to discuss military discipline, the democratic confederalists huddled in the corner of a sofa 3,000 miles away both nodded as Ali made his statement.

I asked one international volunteer what it looked like in practical terms to balance command and friendship, for example when someone's commander needs to ask them to conduct a mission. "Well, they would make requests of you," the volunteer said. "We'd go to the front. And, you know, we'd get down there we'd sit down with the commanders." He then described an example of how they'd converse rather than simply receive their orders. "They'd say, 'Well, this is our plan for the next week, week and a half, we'd like you to go here and here and try and clear these areas.'" The volunteers would then suggest they might take a certain route, or use terrain features to achieve that goal, and the commander would agree or suggest another approach. Commanders were comfortable letting fighters decide their own risk tolerance, with some being more willing to lead a push or enter a building and risk tripping a booby trap, and others preferring to take up other roles. "Sometimes they asked you to do something you don't want to do," the volunteer said, "you never have to do it."[4] Members of Tekoşîna Anarşîst agreed when I spoke to them: "The SDF approach us in a respectful way, there are not like orders of 'you have to do that,'" they told me on a call in 2024. "But if they ask us, it means it is important to them, so we will probably say yes."

I mentioned to Ali that in the British military it is customary and indeed obligatory to salute officers, not out of personal respect but because one is saluting the commission the officer holds and therefore indirectly the crown. Ali explained that in many ways, although the hevals do not salute, they don't lack respect for the people who have been selected to command positions. Indeed, their respect is for those people and their work rather than a badge or monarch. "It's more of like a moral salute," Diwar explained. "For example, when we see a commander. We pay so much respect," he said. The respect is not due to the person's rank or status but "because it requires so much sacrifice, so much experience, so much time" to attain the role of commander.

This does not mean that there are no consequences for actions that harm the collective. One foreign volunteer gave me an example of a case in which a member of their team had to leave right before an operation, too late for a

---

4. It's worth noting that the social pressure of being labeled a coward is still very much present.

replacement to be found. "There was an emergency with a family member. And he had to kind of like leave before the operation," the volunteer told me. "After the operation . . . we had a discussion about it. They wanted to . . . penalize him. And we discussed . . . including with him, what a proper penalty should be. We decided that he should go to jail for a week. . . . And he thought that that was an appropriate penalty for what he did because we were short handed and that was wrong for the team."

This system is not hugely distinct from that employed nearly a century before among the anarchists of Spain and Catalonia. In the beginning, most of the fighters in the CNT's columns were factory workers or other wage laborers, members of the syndicates that made up the CNT without military experience but with a deep-seated dislike of arbitrary authority. Over time, the structure of CNT formations emerged from discussions within them and drew heavily on the workplace anarcho-syndicalist organizing that many of the militia were familiar with rather than the accepted wisdom of military theorists at the time.

Durruti, the most notable of their commanders, took great care to not adorn himself with the badges of rank, nor to receive any special benefits from his leadership, often simply choosing the blue "mono" favored by factory workers and fighters alike. He ate with fighters, slept in their lodgings, and fought alongside them in combat. Emma Goldman, after a trip to meet, wrote:

> He had gained the confidence of the men and their affection because he had never played the part of a superior. He was one of them. He ate and slept as simply as they did. Often even denying himself his own portion for one weak or sick, and needing more than he. And he shared their danger in every battle. That was no doubt the secret of Durruti's success with his column. The men adored him. They not only carried out all his instructions, they were ready to follow him in the most perilous venture to repulse the fascist position.[10]

The military advisers attached to the Durruti Column objected to such an organization, fearing it would not stand the test of combat. However, several other military men, including officers, were already part of the formation as volunteers and were convinced anarchists. It was their help, regardless of their rank or social standing, that helped the column form itself into a formidable fighting force with a structure that allowed for decision making at a strategic level but still preserved significant individual autonomy. By the end of their summer campaign, the Durruti Column had earned the respect of both the bourgeois Catalan ERC and the Soviet ambassador for their discipline under fire and effectiveness in battle.

However, this autonomy could only extend to a certain degree and had to be prevented from harming the overall goals of the column. In an interview with *CNT* (the CNT's publication in Madrid), Durruti was open about the need for consequences for non-comradely action.

> Man! I'm very happy you brought this [discipline] up. People talk a lot about the topic but few hit the nail on the head. For me, discipline is nothing more than respect for your own responsibility and that of others. I'm against the discipline of the barracks, which only leads to stultification, hate, and automatism. But I also can't accept—indeed the necessities of war make it impossible—the so-called liberty that cowards turn to when they want to duck out of something. Our organization, the CNT, has the best discipline, and that's what enables the militants to trust the comrades occupying the posts in the Committees. They obey and carry out the organization's decisions. People have to obey the delegates in times of war; otherwise, it would be impossible to undertake any operation. If people disagree with them, there are meetings where they can suggest their replacement.

Durruti went on to explain to the interviewer how he would deal with lack of enthusiasm, desertion, and keeping up morale in difficult times: "I've seen all the tricks of the Great War in my Column: the dying mother, the pregnant compañera, the sick child, the swollen face, the bad eyes ... I have a magnificent health team. Anyone caught lying: a double shift with the pick and mattock! Discouraging letters from home? To the garbage!"

He continued: "When someone wants to return home, claiming that a volunteer can come and go, he must first hear my thoughts on the matter. After all, we rely on his strength. Afterwards, we'll let him leave, but only after we've taken his weapon—it belongs to the column—and he'll have to go on foot too because the cars also serve the war effort. It almost never comes to this. The militiaman's self-esteem quickly surfaces and, as a rule, with an attitude of 'No one will look down on me, not even the leader of the Column!' He returns to the battlefield, ready to fight heroically."[11]

Emma Goldman provided a similar analysis, recounting Durruti speaking to a comrade who wished to leave:

> "Don't you see comrade, the war you and I are waging is to safeguard our Revolution and the Revolution is to do away with the misery and suffering of the poor. We must conquer our fascist enemy. We must win the war. You are an essential part of it. Don't you see, comrade?" Durruti's comrades did see, they usually remained.
>
> Sometimes one would prove obdurate, and insist on leaving the front. "All right," Durruti tells him, "but you will go on foot, and by the time you reach your village, everybody will know that your courage had failed you, that you have run away, that you have shirked your self-imposed task." That worked like magic.[12]

While they may not have saluted, the anarchists did deal with transgressions. Elias Manzanera of the Iron Column describes an incident in which he and his comrades found people looting and claiming to be Iron Column soldiers. They were identified by victims and punished, albeit in a manner that is not mentioned.

Although punishment certainly occurred, it seems that anarchist columns heavily relied on self-discipline in Spain. Those who transgressed were subject to mostly social sanctions and the disappointment of their peers. In their publications, we see the war committee begging militians not to keep asking for leave, telling them that the time had come to renounce "domestic comforts" and "individual desires." In August 1936, the Durruti Column restructured itself to allow for clearer lines of command and organization. At this time, its newsletter, *El Frente*, reminded its members that "militians have to act in every moment as men of ideas, sensibility, conscience." It added, "In an unjust society, such things can be forgiven, but when we are laying the foundation of a nobler, more equitable social organization, acting in this way can not be tolerated. Brigandry is inexcusable in these circumstances, and, whoever does so, they will get what they deserve."[13]

By September, the tone had changed somewhat as the new structure settled in. "We are the army of Liberty," thundered *El Frente*, "and we must obey our delegates who have shouldered the responsibility of watching over our lives." However, an October article cleared up that what was being demanded was discipline, not obedience. "There are many colleagues who clearly lamentably confuse discipline with authority. The concept of authority, or authority itself, is clear and perfectly repudiated within our anarchist spaces. . . . Every war requires a military organization," it read. "This is a discipline. It ensures that individual efforts are coherently subordinated to the end that we are pursuing, that is: VICTORY. All of us are equal. There are, in fact, none of the old-fashioned superiors. There are, however, companions who have taken on the direction of the war, the military command." The passage was addressed to "those who, probably due to confusion of ideas between authority and discipline, put on a sour face and break down when you talk to them about it." It reminded them that anarchist self-discipline was an important form of organizing; "Organization, always. Then, discipline. Now more than ever DISCIPLINE!"[14]

Where shame, self-discipline, and social sanctions did not work, manual labor sometimes did. Those faking illness might find themselves "recovering" with a pickaxe in hand as they dug trenches. For more serious transgressions, militias could have their CNT cards revoked or even be expelled from the column. Roberto Martínez Catalan, author of an excellent history of the column, recounts an incident in which being expelled was exactly what some militias seemed to want: after having abandoned their positions, they were found drinking. Their actions infuriated Durruti, who sent them back from the front lines toward their column's rearguard positions without their trousers "so everyone would know that they are not anarchists, but vulgar rubbish!"[15] In another instance, he found some young militans deserting; he jumped out of his vehicle with his pistol drawn and ordered the deserters against a wall. As another fighter ambled past, Durruti offered the deserters' shoes to the man. "You can pick a pair if you like," said. "Why would we bury such good shoes and let them rot?"[16] The threat of execution was intended to show the deserters that their abandoning the front put not only their comrades' lives in danger but also their own. Durruti threatening execution nonetheless gave the appearance of arbitrary field executions, which are anything but libertarian in nature.

Actual capital punishment seems to have been a decision taken collectively. Two instances of it appear in Antoine Gimenez's memoirs. In the first, it is enemy prisoners who are executed. As a result, two members of the international group were excluded by vote because of their participation in the execution of prisoners, which the group disapproved of. In another incident, both the internationals and Durruti tried to stop the execution of a sixteen-year-old Falangist prisoner, Angel Caro Andrés, but militiamen whose own families had been executed by the Falange killed him. In other incidents, such as in the town of Alcarràs, the village committee protected local right-wing families from execution, risking their own lives in the process.

Gimenez does recount one instance of capital punishment of a fighter. In this case, an FAI delegate had taken jewelry that had been looted from a wealthy family and had given it to his partner, not the collective. When his partner showed up, festooned in stolen finery, she admitted the FAI delegate's wrongdoing. He was sentenced to be shot by a vote of the delegates, according to Gimenez.[17]

Gimenez recounts another incident, in which four peasants found sneaking into the camp with the intention of killing Durruti. They were captured and they made signs of the cross as they awaited their fate. The firing squad lined up, and the order was given to fire. Three of the peasants fell to the ground, while the fourth stood there apparently shocked but unharmed. Gimenez was appalled at the display of poor marksmanship until he saw another group step forward and throw buckets of water on the bodies, at which point they all began moving.[18] The rifles had been loaded with blanks, and the peasants were set free with an admonition for their ignorance of the true meaning of freedom and justice.

Indeed, just as Catholicism was used in Spain to keep the masses aligned with the interests of capital, so ultra-nationalist Buddhism is in Myanmar. Some of the worst atrocities of the war, including the barbaric roasting alive of two captured fighters, have been perpetrated by the Pyusawhti militias who fight on behalf of the junta. Undoubtedly, as in Spain, fighters in Myanmar are tempted to take revenge for the brutal murder of their comrades. This has occurred in some instances, but all the evidence I have seen in three years of war points to a more-humane-than-average treatment of prisoners of war.

I have interviewed several former junta soldiers who had stories of their forced conscription and reenlistment, and of the military's practice of holding soldiers' families hostage in order to ensure their loyalty. All the soldiers I interviewed had deserted to the rebels, bringing their weapons with them. For this, they received a bounty, with a small bonus for their weapons—larger bonuses are reserved for much-needed belt-fed machine guns and precision rifles—and an ongoing stipend to support their families. Indeed, rebel groups overwhelmed by the number of prisoners have sometimes returned them to the junta, where officers are punished, sometimes killed, and troops are often sent back to the front, resulting in some conscripts being captured twice. Rebel groups have also begun exploring concepts of restorative justice, reaching out across the world to the SDF to discuss this, in hopes that the scars created by the war will be healed as quickly as possible.

Discipline also means that within anarchist movements there must be mechanisms for accountability when norms and codes are violated. These mechanisms have, at times, been lacking in Myanmar, and young activists have rightly called attention to the willingness of the revolution at large to overlook actions by some ethnic revolutionary organizations that contradict the Geneva Convention and basic human decency. The movement is young and is finding its feet in terms of national coordination, but as long as there are voices being raised for accountability there's hope the revolution will continue in the largely positive direction it has begun. Finding ways to ensure that even the most powerful ethnic revolutionary organizations are accountable is difficult, but the fact that the work is being undertaken is a positive sign.

Young fighters have, at times, felt overwhelmed by the weight of the organizations that have appointed themselves in charge of the revolution. "[If] the country is united into one state but no one is safe," one fighter lamented, "what's the point?" He was worried that what began as a "community revolution" might become an "organizational revolution." "All the organizations," he said, "want the lands and authority. Not the system for the people." This imposition of authority on their spontaneous and horizontal revolution worried the fighter. He'd determined that the revolution had to be about more than changing the people in charge he told me, because "politicians [are] only interested in their own family or party."

Discipline among the soldiers in Myanmar takes a more military bent than that in revolutionary Spain or Rojava but varies widely from unit to unit. The KGZA, for example, did not have formal ranks and operated much like the Spanish and Kurdish groups, discussing plans and appointing leaders temporarily, not based on class or status. Other Karenni units rely on humor more than shouting or physical violence where their cadres can be seen training. The KNDF, for example, might learn to march in a regimented structure, but their passing-out parades that celebrate their graduation from basic training are as likely to include a freshly minted fighter rapping or playing guitar as they are about turns and inspection of troops by dignitaries. They're better known for their full unit dance parties than they are for marching around in formation. They certainly have not picked up the self-seriousness that characterizes military discipline in the Global North and often gather for huge concerts, dancing and singing in a way that would surely have warmed the heart of Emma Goldman, the anarchist writer and thinker who, in her book *Living My Life*, expressed disgust at being told dancing was unbecoming of an anarchist.

Some units in Myanmar have a more formal code of conduct. Mandalay PDF, whose drill instructors for new recruits are often young women, shared their written conduct documents with me in late 2023 when we met for a series of interviews via encrypted calls. The document outlined the formation of a court-martial and the punishments it could impose: "The battalion commander must decide for minor offenses either himself or by a battalion court-martial. The formation of a battalion court-martial shall be composed of the battalion commander, the lieutenant colonel officer, and two (2) other officers. Social punishment, physical fitness punishment, or imprisonment of not more than (2) weeks can be imposed depending on the type of crime." Only a court-martial composed of five to seven other soldiers can impose stricter penalties.

Certainly, some ethnic revolutionary organizations have more rigid structures, particularly those with a long history that dates back to the Second World War. Insurgent groups with a state communist lineage like the MNDAA enforce strict discipline on recruits and have been known to sentence fighters to death, with large public parades of the accused soldiers preceding their execution for embezzlement or corruption. Others, like the Karen National Liberation Army, seem more egalitarian in promotion practices but retain rank structures, according to one international volunteer who fought with them in the early 2000s. Mon soldiers, I am told, habitually talk back to their officers.

In Rojava, where international volunteers from all over the world have fought since the battle against the Islamic State began, discipline often takes the form of collective and self-criticism, a practice called *tekmil* in Kurmanji. Tekmil developed alongside the movement from Marxist-Leninism to democratic confederalism and was heavily influenced by the experience of women who wished to build their revolution without unaccountable male leaders. Tekoşîna Anarşîst provided an excellent reflection on the practice in a piece they shared in 2022. Although based on the authoritarian communist tradition, the practice of tekmil has remained integral to the revolution in Rojava even after it abandoned the statist concepts of Stalinist and Maoist thought. Crucially, Tekoşîna Anarşîst write, "Tekmil philosophy views criticism as a gift that comrades offer to one another with the best of intentions. From the perspective of such a philosophy, criticism is what allows us to grow as individuals, to work on our shortcomings—even though criticism can be very difficult to listen to and accept."[19]

Tekmil takes the physical form of a circle, with all participants standing or sitting respectfully and undistracted. Women's autonomous structures have their own tekmil, without men, to allow for a non-gendered dynamic to facilitate different insights on how to better challenge the patriarchal structures that persist both within individuals and the world at large. Tekmil at the front lines emphasizes brevity, whereas when more time is available it may take longer. A facilitator, often the commander in military spaces, will acknowledge those waiting to speak. The sequence begins with self-criticism and then criticism of others, offered in the third person. The facilitator ensures there is no repetition of criticisms, to prevent an individual from feeling singled out. Suggestions offered can then be discussed. The facilitator can then offer a summary and in, and in the case of the YPG and YPJ but not the Tekoşîna Anarşîst, a commander can adjudicate disputes. This practice, which has gradually become more egalitarian over time, is one that Tekoşîna Anarşîst have chosen to incorporate into their formation, which is an element of the SDF parallel to but not part of the YPG, because they feel it has great value.

Ali described tekmil as "a daily report or a daily small meeting." The literal translation of the word is "report," but it carries a very different meaning than the English sense. There are also less regular weekly or monthly meetings at which a commander can be criticized by their colleagues. In these instances, "if the criticism is repeated twice or three times, and if that person doesn't change, like, they give him a chance to change. If he doesn't change, they start to raise that suggestion to a higher rank of commander . . . and they decide what is to be done, like, to change him or to fix it."

Both tekmil and criticism of commanders work only because of the context of radical friendship and mutual respect between hevals in the movement. The desire for collective and self-improvement is the foundation of tekmil. The understanding that criticism comes from a place of love, both of the person being criticized and the cause both of you are fighting for, is the bedrock of the process. When I spoke to a Tekoşîna Anarşîst fighter about their fallen comrade Tekoşer Piling, some of their most cherished memories were of the way he kindly and constructively delivered criticism in tekmil, and in doing so helped them all to become better revolutionaries. In a sense, these criticisms were gifts he left with them that remained even after his death.

Discipline, for Tekoşîna Anarşîst, is something to understand, not to impose. "The main focus is on building discipline together, not imposing it," they told me. "It is a collective thing, when we set our collective standards, if we slip in them, we can then call ourselves back to collectively pay more attention." Despite these flexible approaches to rank and democratic approaches to discipline, much of which is very openly discussed by anarchist and anarchist-adjacent groups, the state seems incapable of comprehending. The logic of the state, and especially its military, holds that it is not possible to organize and deploy a military without strict adherence to a vertical power structure.

When Ali left our meeting in Hasakah, Diwar, Khabat, and I stayed behind for a few minutes. The young boy we'd been trying not to wake had stirred, and so I passed out some stickers and tiny glowsticks that I like to bring as gifts. Children don't get to choose where they grow up, and war can strip away some of the joys of childhood and leave them afraid of the dark. War had taken away this boy's father. I wasn't going to fix that with stickers and glowsticks, but I hope he had fun throwing them around with the lights off. I left the rest of the package with him, in case he needed them later.

Driving back across the countryside to Qamişlo, I wondered about the safety of that boy and that of the other people I had been meeting with. The precision of drone strikes lends itself to the killing of leaders. But, as I saw in my time in Rojava, the drone war has targeted civilian infrastructure, anti-narcotics agents, journalists like me, and a fourteen-year-old boy whose mother served me tea and wept as we sat on the floor of her house, and she shared with me memories of her son. The house I'd met Ali in, where the young boy was sleeping peacefully on the sofa, was also the home of someone who had been killed in combat, leaving his partner and young son behind.

Sadly, despite its advantages for organization and equality, the horizontal approach to military organizing does not mean that nobody is a target; instead, everybody is. States understand movements through the lens of the hierarchy they see as necessary. This means that individuals, perhaps those who are best loved or more often shown in propaganda materials, are often targeted by the state. For a movement drawn from and interwoven with community, this means everyone is a target and results in massive civilian casualties.

Many of us who are living our lives far from the front lines can learn from the concepts of minimum discipline and revolutionary criticism. Countless movements I have been part of could have been improved, and perhaps saved, by having an established process for criticism that centered our mutual desire to do the work and help each other do so in the best and kindest way. Likewise, in times of high stress, we sometimes need to rely on individuals to make decisions; this does not mean we ought to elevate them at other times. These lessons, learned on the front lines, can be applied in our own personal battles and collective struggles.

6

Arming the Anarchists

For years I have thought about making the revolution, but we had no
weapons, and now that we have them, do you think I'll leave it aside?
No! You know me!

—Buenaventura Durruti

US Special Forces deployed to Syria as part of Operation Inherent Resolve, an operation of a US-led global coalition containing troops from
twenty-seven states that began in 2014 and aimed to defeat IS by making
use of the coalition's overwhelming air superiority while relying on local
"partner forces" to do the ground fighting. At its peak, the coalition against
IS was active in Libya, Iraq, Afghanistan, Nigeria, and Syria. The US troops
deployed to Syria were—in theory—supposed to stay one "terrain feature"
from the front lines and were tasked with "training, advising, and assisting"
SDF forces. Unlike similar deployments to Iraq and Afghanistan, relatively
little media attention was paid to the American troops in Syrian Kurdistan,
not until Agence France Presse published photos of US troops wearing YPG
patches in May 2016.

Patches, either those that identify a unit or those that individual soldiers
wear for morale, are a common piece of military paraphernalia and are often
collected by soldiers and civilians alike. It's not uncommon for US Special
Forces soldiers to wear the patches of their partner units as a show of solidarity, and to avoid confusion on the battlefield. While writing this book, I
spoke to several US military veterans, all of whom had partner force patches
from their various deployments. However, Turkey, a member of the coalition
to defeat ISIS, didn't see the YPG as friendly troops at all, even though it was
the Kurds who shouldered the burden of doing the killing and the dying in
the battle with the Islamic State.

"It is unacceptable that an ally country is using the YPG insignia," Turkish foreign minister Mevlüt Çavuşoğlu said in an interview with a Turkish newspaper. "We reacted to it. It is impossible to accept it. This is a double standard and hypocrisy."[1] Certainly, Çavuşoğlu was correct that a double standard was being applied. The US maintains a line of demarcation between the YPG and YPJ, its valued allies, and the PKK, which it considers a terrorist group. But when PKK guerrillas crossed the border between Turkish Kurdistan and Syrian or Iraqi Kurdistan, they were instantly transformed into valued allies in the fight against terrorism.

The alliance of convenience that the US entered into with the Kurdish freedom movement (or with part of it) never signaled a shared political goal. In the years since the SDF lost 11,000 fighters battling ISIS, they have lost dozens every year to Turkish drone warfare. While I was visiting Rojava, a single drone strike killed thirty-nine anti-narcotics Asayish—internal security forces—in Derik, a town I'd traveled through just a couple of days before. A few days later, their families buried them in cities across Rojava, and I sat down for an interview with Rîhan Loqo, a spokeswoman for the women's movement in Rojava, Kongra Star. As with almost every conversation I had in Rojava, our talk began with a series of questions about why the US was not protecting its allies and why it refused to supply them with surface-to-air missiles, with which they might defend themselves against the Turkish drones, and F16 fighter jets (which the US sells to Turkey).

Young fighters in Myanmar asked me the same questions. Every single one of the people I met there had taken to the streets in the days after the coup with the genuine conviction that the US or the EU or the UN would step in to defend the country's people. One of them was my friend Andy. He told me that even after the police and army started shooting protesters, he and his comrades continued to show up in the streets because they felt that their deaths would command global attention and a response from the neoliberal democracies in the Global North. He recounted in detail the first time he and his brothers saw someone die and how quickly they became used to it.

Two and a half years and thousands of civilian deaths later, the multilateral organizations they'd hoped would help them have sent little more than a strongly worded letter to the people of Myanmar, though some economic sanctions have been put into place. Crucially for the thousands of young people who took to the mountains and jungles to fight back in the months after the coup, not one single state supported their struggle for democracy by sending them arms. A year after the coup in Myanmar, Russia's invasion of Ukraine saw almost every country in NATO send arms, ammunition, and supplies to Ukraine to allow its military to better fend off Russia's imperialist plans, but no such aid was sent to Myanmar, where Russian bombs continue to fall on innocent children. Shortly after Russia began its full-scale invasion of Ukraine, I traveled to the Thai-Burmese border to meet Burmese fighters. They expressed their solidarity and support with the people of Ukraine but wondered why the world had not done the same for Myanmar as it did for Ukraine.

This didn't stop Burmese rebels from trying to get weapons. PDF fighters I met told me that in the early days of the armed revolution they sold everything they owned to try to buy black market guns, and they made improvised weapons from whatever recipes they could find online.

Phyo Zeya Thaw, a former lawmaker for the National League for Democracy whose political career began as a hip-hop artist, was arrested for his alleged part in arms procurement. In a press release at the time of his arrest, the junta claimed that "due to the cooperation of the dutiful civilians who condemn the killing of civil service personnel and members of security forces, he was arrested together with two pistols, 48 rounds of 9 mm ammunition, one M16 gun, 74 rounds of 5.56 ammunition in Dagon Myothit (Seikkan) Township in Yangon." In the accompanying photo, Phyo Zeya Thaw's face is visibly swollen, presumably from abuse while detained.

Phyo Zeya Thaw came to prominence in the early 2000s with a hip-hop collective known as Generation Wave. While he claimed in a 2011 interview that "with hip-hop, we can express ourselves without fear,"[2] he had already been detained for several years by that point. Following his release, he switched his parachute pants for a fancy shirt and became an NLD lawmaker. The son of two middle-class parents, the rector of a dental academy and a dentist, he quickly became a favorite of Aung San Suu Kyi, and of her dog, who only calmed her incessant barking when comforted by Phyo Zeya Thaw.

While he may have once been associated with modern hip-hop trappings when he rapped under the name Nitric Acid, Phyo Zeya Thaw lived an austere life as a legislator, sleeping in a concrete dormitory and working long hours. But his passion was always for hip-hop, and in 2020 he stepped down from legislative work to return to his music. Sadly, the coup happened a few months later and he quickly left the studio and joined the people in the streets, just as he had in the Saffron Revolution more than a decade earlier.

Unlike the politicians who expressed their support from exile, Phyo Zeya Thaw expressed his desire for democracy by arming the people against the state, making a return to the old ways impossible. He was part of the underground resistance when three hundred junta troops descended on his home. After several months of detention, Phyo Zeya Thaw was publicly executed by hanging, along with several other high-profile pro-democracy activists with barely a harsh word from the governments of the world. A *New York Times* obituary quoted his mother, Khin Win May, as saying, "I will always be proud of my son because he gave his life for the country. He is a martyr who tried to bring democracy to Myanmar."[3]

Where states and the market had failed the people of Myanmar, communities didn't. When they went into the jungle, young Bamar rebels met more experienced fighters in ethnic revolutionary organizations who had been handmaking rifles for decades. In the early months of the conflict, Zaw would send me Facebook photos of bolt action rifles made with a lathe, a drill, a pipe, and a great deal of skill. These weapons, while impressive in their craftsmanship, were no match for the sustained rate of fire that modern automatic weapons are capable of, and while they allowed the rebels to ambush government troops, they would leave them seriously outgunned in a firefight.

The situation the rebels were in would not have been unfamiliar to the Catalan and Spanish anarchists of the 1930s. In the second republic, the anarchists tried to buy rifles from manufacturers in the Basque country but found their attempts frustrated by the government. However, through a combination of purchases, theft, and the collectivization of military stores taken in the first days of the revolution, they were able to amass thousands of rifles to take to the Aragon front. However, getting the rifles was only half the battle; ammunition soon became scarce, and detachments were dispatched to the rear to search for more by autumn 1936. These weapons were far from modern and often used different calibers of ammunition, making logistics a nightmare. The government was able to use this lack of ammunition and a shortage of reliable weapons as a cudgel against the anarchists later in the war in an attempt to force them to accept government oversight and militarization. Many dedicated anarchists found themselves arguing for rank, orders, and hierarchy just so they could access weapons to fight fascism.

At the start of the war, the arms manufacturing powerhouses of the Basqueland remained in Republican territory, and their reliable Astra 400 handguns were produced by the tens of thousands. The Astra 400 was known as the "mange tout" in France for its ability to digest numerous different types of 9 mm, 9 mm largo, 9 mm short, and other ammunition with the same bullet diameter, and as "el puro" in Spain due to its resemblance to the cigar of the same name. The weapons were a favorite of private citizens, bank robbers, and the gunslingers of the FAI. In the spring of 1937, Franco's forces swept northwards across the Basqueland supported by Italian and German fascists. The troops were also supported by Luftwaffe warplanes that infamously bombed the town of Guernica, where the Astra factory and its Republican-aligned employees were located. Republican efforts to arm the Basque militias were hampered by France's refusal to allow shipments to travel north of the Pyrenees.

The attack on Guernica forced the hand of the Republic, which was already desperate for arms. The strongest industrial area of Spain was in Catalonia, where migrants from across the country had found work in the decades before the war. This large, underpaid working class that was socially distinct from the Catalan bourgeoisie became the backbone of the strongest and most forthright anarcho-syndicalist area of the country. In Terrassa, just outside Barcelona, the Casa de Bach workshop at number 6 Sant Isidre Street was repurposed for the production of pistols under the auspices of the Industrias de Guerra de Cataluña. It used the Astra 400 model but differentiated its output with a different roll mark: a small oval on the barrel of the pistol bore the inscription "F. ASCASO. TARRASA. CATALUÑA."

Francisco Ascaso, of course, was a dear friend of Durruti and a hero of the Catalan revolution who had died in July 1936 on the revolution's second day, at age thirty-five. The first pistol bearing his name rolled off the production line just nine months later. Estimates of the total number of Astra pistols produced vary from five to eight thousand. Further south, in Alginet, Valencia, another factory was set up in an old fruit warehouse by the railway tracks. Beginning in January 1938, this factory produced Republica Española pistols, exact replicas of the Astra design, using union labor and expertise from Basques who had escaped the Francoist takeover in Guernica. More than 15,000 of these pistols were produced.

Eighty years later and half a world away, Kurdish freedom fighters would also take up their tools to create the means of defending their own revolution. Although their region was awash in small arms, they lacked anti-materiel rifles. The US, trying to appease Turkey, provided the Kurds with only minimal supplies and few of the heavy weapons systems they needed to defeat the Islamic State, which had outfitted itself from the arsenals of the Iraqi and Syrian militaries. Anti-materiel rifles allow a user to deliver a huge bullet with a reasonable degree of accuracy and range. In urban combat, their ability to shoot through cover, destroy vehicle engine blocks, and punch holes in walls is much sought after. In the battle against IS, they gave the SDF a way to stop suicide car bombs, which were a favorite tactic of the IS fighters when trying to breach SDF checkpoints and lines of defense.

Defending oneself against an oncoming car bomb is, even with the right weapons, no easy feat. One must engage a moving target and hit it in the right place to disable the engine or the driver before the vehicle gets close enough to kill everyone around it using the explosives packed inside. IS members grew very fond of these "suicide vehicle–borne improvised explosive devices," or SBVIEDs, and they frequently welded armor plates to the vehicles to prevent small arms fire from killing the driver before he made it to his target. Armed only with Kalashnikovs, and belt-fed and precision rifles, the SDF could not do much aside from firing at the vehicles and hoping to send a bullet through the slot drivers used to see where they were going. Ideally, an anti-tank missile would be used, and in some cases they were provided and fired by special forces from France or the US who were supporting the SDF, but these were in very short supply. Instead, the SDF turned to a solution that didn't leave them at the whims of politicians in the US or France.

Lacking the means to make their own anti-tank missiles, Kurdish gun-smiths looked for solutions in the weapons systems they did have access to. They took the barrel, bolt, and receiver from anti-aircraft machine guns, chiefly the infamous DSHK or "dushka," along with the trigger group from a rocket-propelled grenade launcher and mounted them to a rifle chassis. They then outfitted this weapon with a rifle scope recovered from the enemy or a cheap airsoft-grade replica scope that lasted only a few shots before rattling itself to death. The result was a fearsome weapon, both for the operator and the opposing force. They named this rifle the Zagros in the 12.7 × 108 mm DSHKA chambering and the Şer in the fearsome 14.5 × 114 mm KPV cartridge.

"You can clear buildings with that from a distance," one fighter familiar with the weapon told me. "If you put those into the room through the windows, they explode like hand grenades in the room. They'll break through concrete walls." These rifles made a significant difference in defeating the Islamic State in the house-to-house, street-to-street fighting in Raqqa, Kobani, and elsewhere in North and East Syria where high-rise concrete buildings are the norm and booby-trapped doors and stairwells make entering them a huge risk.

Until 2021, these and similar weapons used by the FSA and other Syrian rebel factions were some of the only mass-produced weapons not made for profit or by a corporation contracting with the government but rather by the people to fight for their own freedom. As someone with a perhaps overdeveloped affection for Catalan anarchism, I often look for Ascaso pistols in online auctions or in the estates of dead firearms collectors, and I monitor subreddits where such obscure firearms are discussed, hoping to find someone who doesn't know what they have and is selling one at a price I can afford.

It was on one of those subreddits that I first saw photos of the weapons being used by anti-junta rebels in Myanmar. With more willing fighters than weapons, young rebels had taken to using muzzle-loading muskets, home-made slamfire shotguns, and even swords and slingshots to fight back against a state intent on crushing them and their desire for liberty. Some of them told me they sold everything they owned to buy weapons, and the many who still could not afford them joined the fight as medics instead, rushing into gunfire unarmed to rescue their friends.

The rebels began arming themselves while they were still in the cities, as the military crackdown moved from tear gas to baton rounds to bullets. Protesters scrambled to keep up. The real point of inflection in the response to state violence with violence in self-defense came on March 27, 2021, when the state killed at least 110 people. The first time protesters armed themselves, it was with stones, rocks, and anything they could find. Then it was with catapults (made from surgical tubing), and slingshots. Soon, group chats emerged on various messaging apps using code words to describe the various weapons and armor that they might use to protect and defend themselves. To keep a degree of secrecy in case their chats were compromised, they called their suite of weapons "biryani," after the rice dish, and they shared a variety of "recipes" they found on YouTube.[4] One recipe, which seems to have come from a Filipino YouTuber, contained instructions for a rudimentary air rifle that used cans of propane designed for refilling cigarette lighters as a charge, plastic plumbing pipe as the barrel, and a cheap disposable lighter as the trigger and ignition system. They used it to fire marbles and bearings from bicycle wheels. It was accurate enough to harass large formations of police but nothing compared to even the most basic modern firearm that most people in the US could buy for under $100. Alongside the air rifles, the rebels used homemade smoke grenades, derived from household chemicals and fertilizer. With this rudimentary arsenal, they could not really stand toe to toe with the state, but they could create cover for a slightly safer retreat.

The government blamed "anarchic mobs" for the uptick in its violence towards its people, but it would be several months before Burmese anarchists began to organize at scale among the young people who were forging their new politics in the crucible of state violence and popular resistance. One protester I met in 2022 shared a video of themself making Molotov cocktails, a device that has been an ally of the people against the state for almost a century, ever since it was first used by Finnish partisans opposing an invasion by the USSR. These improvised incendiary devices are almost impossible to regulate, consisting of petrol, a glass container, and a fabric wick. When combined, these everyday items become the underdog's grenade and the menace of a tyrannical state. In Myanmar, Molotov cocktails flew through the windows of police stations, and into military bases, and into formations of troops as protesters attempted to use what they had to hand to stop the slaughter in the streets. Even as they first embraced violence as a tool in their struggle, the newly formed groups established a code of conduct. They would not attack schools or hospitals, they said, even when the junta occupied them.

While the Molotov cocktails had an impact, they were not enough to stop the slaughter. The desire for liberty, though, is much stronger than any state, and soon I was seeing more advanced homemade weapons popping up on the vintage and esoteric firearms subreddits. Homemade bolt action rifles became more common, but they were no match for the government-issued 5.56 NATO caliber assault rifles. However, a well-placed shot from concealment could net the rebels an assault rifle of their own once its previous owner ceased to need it.

These weapons were unusual but not entirely remarkable. I've seen their like in other conflict zones and in remote areas where people rely on firearms for hunting. Rudimentary single-shot shotguns and .22 rimfire rifles are common in such settings, as the lower pressures involved in their use make them much easier to manufacture and give them a lower likelihood of hurting the user. Rifles are much less common but not unheard of, and even the occasional artisanal Sten submachine gun or AK47 would not be entirely unique.

One evening while sitting on my sofa at home, I saw something much more surprising. In a 3D-printed firearms subreddit, I saw a poster asking questions about a type of firearm called the FGC9. The pistol caliber carbine, which derives its name from the sentiments of its creators (Fuck Gun Control) and the caliber (9 mm), was relatively unique in being made entirely of unregulated and easily accessible parts. The bulk of the gun is 3D-printed, and the rest is available in any hardware store. It requires a 3D printer and no other specialized tooling and can be manufactured by someone with no gunsmithing experience.

It was on that same subreddit that Ivan, one of the two designers of the FGC9, first became aware of its use in Myanmar.

Ivan first encountered in 3D printing in high school. "It was an old enough machine that it was known as a rapid prototype machine, and no one called it a 3D printer," he told me in a telephone interview in late 2023. "We designed little keychains and then printed them out on that machine, and I was enamored. But then, at this point in time, 3D printers were like $30,000 for anything pretty decent. So it was like, 'Oh, well, maybe one day I'll end up having one.' [I was] thinking like, way down the road, whenever I have a real job, I'll be able to afford one."

But technology progressed much faster than teenage Ivan had imagined. By the time he was in college, 3D printers were affordable. So much so that Ivan, who had two aging cars, "one was a '78. And one was an '85," purchased a small Prusa printer because it was cheaper for him to design and print the parts for the cars than it was to hunt them down online or buy reproduction parts from a dealer. "But having been a lifelong, by family upbringing, gun enthusiast, eventually the intrusive thoughts went out, and you go ahead and try to print a gun," he told me. "I don't think I've printed a [single] car part since."

Soon, Ivan began frequenting online groups that discussed the design and manufacture of 3D-printed guns. Many initial designs for printed guns relied on the easy availability of firearm parts, particularly barrels, for US consumers. Because firearms can be made from parts, most states pick a certain part and treat the purchasing of that part with the same scrutiny they would the purchase of a firearm. The logic of the state suggests that without this part, people cannot make a functioning firearm, so regulating a certain part prevents people from assembling a firearm from parts and avoiding a background check or ban on gun purchases. While much of the world regulates the pressure-bearing parts of a firearm, in the US only the part of the weapon that holds the trigger mechanism is legally regulated as the "firearm." This means that non-"firearm" gun parts, like the barrel, can be purchased without background checks. This quirk of US law played into the hands of home gunsmiths as trigger mechanism housings are relatively easy to replicate, whereas pressure-bearing components require more advanced techniques and materials.

It was in one such enthusiast group that Ivan met the FGC9's co-creator, who posted under the username JStark1809. Ivan lived in the US, where he could legally manufacture his guns as long as he adhered to some federal and state restrictions, and he could test them in the privacy of his yard. Although JStark took his pseudonym from Major-General John Stark, who fought for the US in the Revolutionary War and who coined the phrase "live free or die" in 1809, JStark lived in Germany where production and ownership of firearms are strictly controlled. JStark seems to have served briefly in a logistics unit of the Bundeswehr but had no access to firearms outside of this brief period. It was this strict control, Ivan says, that compelled JStark to design a weapon that would be accessible to anyone, anywhere.

Ivan says that both he and JStark were interested in 3D-printing guns but had grown disillusioned with the for-profit approach that groups like Cody Wilson's Defense Distributed took. Wilson, a right libertarian, had success-fully established in court the right to host gun printing files, but seemingly he saw the endeavor as more of a theoretical or profit-driven one than a chance to make a material contribution to liberation across the world. Wilson's design was for a single-shot pistol that was impractical at anything other than a short range and relied heavily on the element of surprise. Wilson would later go on to launch a right-wing crowdfunding website called Hatreon. JStark, Ivan said, was incensed that nobody had yet designed a gun that wasn't a single-shot range toy or a practical weapon that relied on firearms parts only available to US consumers. "He'd complain about Cody Wilson," Ivan said. JStark would say "[Wilson] has all this time and all this money, he had all these resources to make a 3D-printed gun that doesn't suck, and you know what he did? Nothing. He did none of that. He had all the people in the right places that he could have made it happen, and he didn't." JStark, Ivan said, "was mad about all of these people who came before him and wasted so much time making guns that didn't work."

In 2013, Wilson designed and demonstrated his single-shot pistol that could be made from scratch by a novice and used like the Liberator pistols of the Second World War for close-range shots that might aid in the acquisition of a better weapon from one's adversary. After Makerbot, a 3D printer ecosystem that hosted designs online, removed gun designs following the Sandy Hook school shooting, Wilson cofounded a website called DEFCAD to host his designs. For years DEFCAD was intermittently online and offline as it underwent a prolonged legal battle with the US State Department before agreeing in 2020 to charge would-be downloaders and confirm their location was in the United States, nullifying the value of the gun beyond being a novelty. Wilson also underwent his own legal challenges and was accused of paying a minor $500 for sex after meeting her on the website sugardaddymeet.com. Local news outlet KVUE reported that Wilson "pleaded guilty to a reduced charge of injury to a child in exchange for a recommended sentence." According to the same outlet, Wilson's plea bargain "requires him to be on probation for seven years, register as a sex offender, serve 475 hours of community service and pay $4,800 in restitution. It also requires him to have monitoring software installed on all his devices connected to the internet, have no unsupervised contact with minors and that he attends sexual offender treatment programs." After this period his case was dismissed, and Wilson appears to have retained his firearm rights.[5]

Understandably, Wilson's agreement to take payment and therefore de-anonymize downloaders seemed a betrayal to many in the 3D printing community, including Ivan and JStark—who, in the meantime, had set up their own free, open-source, decentralized platform. The platform was named Deterrence Dispensed, a name that played on Wilson's Defense Distributed. But Deterrence Dispensed was a decentralized endeavor with no central location, and the co-creators did not share their legal names or locations, making the platform much more resilient against legal attacks.

For JStark, who was Kurdish and not unfamiliar with state oppression given that his own parents had fled Turkey before he was born, Wilson's approach—both in charging for access to designs and in designing a gun that was impractical when a much better one could be made—was unacceptable. JStark "was just flabbergasted," Ivan told me, that it would fall to him to improve on Wilson's platform, when he was someone who "had limited—and really no—experience of owning guns on his own before that." JStark would rant, Ivan says, about the fact that it had to be him who showed the world that "we don't have to just make bad 3D-printed guns, or like little Funko Pops to put on our desk. We could actually make good guns with these things."

JStark and Ivan were very clear on what their gun was for. In a 2021 email, Ivan told me, "I don't like the notion of a large disparity in the capacity for violence between the state and it's [sic] subjects. Governments (or any centralized ruling power) is how you end up seeing the authority and capacity to carry out atrocities controlled by far too few hands."

Over time, JStark played with various designs as he worked on his goal of making a gun that would be accessible to the widest possible range of people. "It took a couple of different shapes. At one point it was a shotgun. It was a rifle at one point; it sort of changed around as far as what he was chasing as he was . . . hunting down a path of least resistance." That path would eventually lead to the mountains of Myanmar.

But first JStark and Ivan had to design the weapon. Both had concerns about the legal implications of their work, but they also understood the world-changing potential of ending the ability of the state to determine who does and does not have the right to use violence. In states that ban firearms for civilians or require a permit, making one would be a serious crime. In some places even possessing the means to make one could be considered evidence of criminal activity. Given that the explicit goal of their project was to challenge not just the state's right to control access to guns but its ability to do so, they would have been very naïve not to expect serious pushback.

After they met online, JStark and Ivan chatted for about six months before they began working together. As a basic design, they settled on a pistol caliber semi-automatic carbine that relied heavily on an existing design for a 3D-printed gun named the AP9, designed by an engineer using the pseudonym "Darwin." Darwin's design was reliable, but it used commercial Glock barrels, which are not accessible for most people outside the US.

From across the world, they exchanged ideas on how to take Darwin's model, improve it, and make it from parts anyone could access anywhere. Their largest hurdle was the barrel, which bears the pressure of the explosion and must be strong enough to allow that pressure to escape only by pushing the bullet forward. While they soon found out that they could use off-the-shelf piping, they had to find an accessible way to machine a chamber for the round to sit in, and a way to cut grooves into the barrel that would impart spin on the bullet to stabilize it and make it accurate enough for shots of 100 meters instead of three or four.

Eventually, Ivan came up with an idea. He'd seen a user named JeffRod in a 3D-printed firearms community named FOSSCAD (Free Open Source Software and Computer Aided Design) use electrochemical machining—a process by which a positively charged cathode is used to remove material from a negatively charged anode—to replace expensive and complicated rifling and chamber cutting machinery used in the industrial process of firearms manufacture. "I managed to get . . . a half hour of JeffRod's time," Ivan said, "and he data-dumped on me. [He told me] this is what he thought worked, this is what he thought didn't work with his trials, and this is what he would change. And I probably took about half of his good ideas and then half of his things that should change, and merged those together, and then came up with a solution that ended up working pretty darn well." The solution, it turned out, was a system of machining the barrel by using little more than a bucket, some wire, electricity, and a few other products accessible to almost anyone, anywhere.

With the highest hurdle overcome, JStark and Ivan set about refining the rest of the design and making sure the hardware store parts they relied upon were available globally. Ivan, scrolling on his phone to find the appropriate video, told me that on August 10, 2019, he test-fired the first prototype FGC9 at his house with some friends. It worked and didn't explode (as many online naysayers claimed 3D-printed weapons would). The greatest hurdle in making firearms accessible to people with a need to defend themselves was behind them. However, the weapon failed to extract the cases left behind after the bullet was fired.

Next, they focused on tweaking the design, both for the weapon and the magazines it fed from. "The magazines probably took a good six months," Ivan said. They kept working until they got to a point where "we thought the magazines were more reliable than the gun itself." After completing dozens of iterative reworks of various parts until they were happy, JStark and Ivan began working on a set of instructions. These had to be easy to understand and follow for someone with little to no firearms experience but still lay out how to construct the gun in enough detail that a novice could do so without risking a dangerous malfunction due to manufacturing errors. Having finished with their instructions, Ivan and JStark released them to a small group of beta testers. "We had. . . a group of maybe ten people who went through that documentation and gave us a comment on that process," Ivan told me. They tested not only for variation in printers and parts but also for variation in English fluency, rewording their instructions to make them easier to understand for nonnative speakers. They also had to make sure to include not only links to products but also search terms to use to find them; once a product was associated with homemade firearms it was often removed from stores like Ali-Express. The process of refining the instructions took a further six months but was just as valuable as the physical design in ensuring the weapon was as replicable as intended.

I asked an online weapons analyst and small arms expert who goes by Calibre Obscura exactly how effective the design that came out of this process was. "The thing that you find," Obscura told me "is that as soon as that as it is possible to, either build a weapons factory or steal a weapons factory or take the guns themselves, [3D-printed weapons are abandoned]." Despite these weapons not being as effective as factory-made rifles, an opinion Ivan agreed with, in many ways, Obscura went on to explain, they're still hugely important, not just for their battlefield abilities but also for their broader significance. Obscura went on to say that a gun could be considered culture, a tool, a fashion accessory, an expression of ideology, a method of personal protection, a project, and a hobby. "And they're, you know, almost all of these things. There isn't really anything else like that." However, until relatively recently, access to firearms that were useful beyond a few meters was gatekept, in many parts of the world, by wealth or power. While weapons like the PA Luty submachine gun did exist, they were complicated and time-consuming to make and rarely saw use beyond intimidating unarmed adversaries.[1] Now, the FGC9 can be downloaded and made by anyone with a broadband connection, a printer that costs around $200, and some hardware store materials. "It doesn't matter if you like them or you don't like them, you actually can't stop them," Obscura added.

With the design finalized, the FGC9 was finally posted online on Deterrence Dispensed and a file-sharing platform called Odysee. At the same time as the release, JStark and Ivan started a PR campaign of sorts. "We had been . . . combating the idea that 3D-printed guns explode," Ivan said. "Step one is changing public perception." Soon, public perception would be changed in a way that neither JStark nor Ivan had predicted.

It was on Reddit that Myanmar's young rebels first found out about the FGC9, the same place I found out about their using it. In December 2021, a Reddit user with the newly created profile "DaddyUMCD" began posting questions, and later photos, in the FOSSCAD subreddit. I noticed pretty quickly that his photos did not appear to have been taken in the US and that they seemed to be set in a jungle climate very similar to that of Myanmar. After seeing photos of the FGC9s pop up both on Reddit and in police reports from Myanmar that misidentified them as "Turkish shotguns," I was pretty convinced DaddyUMCD was not a member of the gun printing community

---

1. P. A. Luty was a British firearms enthusiast who designed a submachine gun that could be made with easily obtainable materials, and he detailed its construction in *Expedient Homemade Firearms* as an act of protest against the strict limits on gun ownership imposed by law. It lacked a rifled barrel and was thus effective only at a short range.

playing a prank or the dictatorial junta's secret police trying to con Western media into turning on the rebels out of a fear that such access to firearms could lead to more gun violence at home. So I set about crafting a direct message to DaddyUMCD: "Hey buddy, I am a journalist in the USA and I have been following your fight against the junta and the use of printed guns. I'd love to chat and write about it, and will obviously do my best to maintain your security and not ask questions about your location etc. If you want to talk, I set up an email . . . just for that. Either way, you're a brave person. Stay safe over there."

I've probably sent a dozen or so cold emails like this in my career as a journalist. I send them, and then I spend days nervously trying not to check my phone. Every Reddit push notification gave me a burst of adrenaline, only to find out that there was a popular post in r/camping or that people were arguing about grind size in r/espresso. But a few days later, I got a reply from DaddyUMCD. It read: "Let me consult with my team first. We are slowly trying to get more international attention on our causes. I will definitely get back to you."

I gave them some time before sending a polite check-in message. It's not unusual to encounter initial enthusiasm and then have a source ghost you. But in this case, I got a swift response.

"Hey, sorry for late reply. As you might already know the battle in our area got heated and, we are currently on the run now. Good news is my team is interested in answering your question tho. But we need to reach to safe area first."

Even in a fairly varied career, this was my first time Reddit DMing a fighter mid-retreat. But now that we were talking, I got my hopes up for an eventual journey to meet the people who, whether they knew it or not, had struck one of the most decisive blows to the state's monopoly on violence since the invention of modern breech-loading firearms in the nineteenth century.

Our conversations continued. One member of their group was arrested and detained by authorities crossing the border to a neighboring state, as they often had to in order to download their files and purchase new printers and more filament for them to use. I said I might request comment on the situation and write about it, letting the government know that the world was watching, but eventually they secured the person's release before I was able to find a single media outlet interested in my coverage.

Our messages back and forth were sporadic when DaddyUMCD was in the jungle, until the following exchange in March 2022:

Me: "Hey buddy, my colleague and I are going to be in [name omitted] next month, is there any chance we could meet you? We can talk on Signal or Telegram if you prefer."

DaddyUMCD: "Oh woah. That would be really cool to meet you in person. I wish I were there.

"One of my close colleagues who is also the important person in this project and revolution will be there next month. He recently got out of jail too. There will also be other colleagues who did a lot of missions on the ground in Yangon. If the timing is right, you might get to meet them together.

"I will notify them ahead if they are willing to do the interview.

"I believe that you can hide their identities well. However, I would like to urge you to get assurance for anonymity again because they are some of the most wanted by junta."

With the assurance offered, my plane tickets booked, and a hotel in a small border town reserved, I nervously began packing for the admittedly strange journalistic endeavor of flying across the world with my friend and colleague Robert Evans to meet an anonymous stranger whom I'd met on Reddit and knew nothing about other than that they smuggled firearms.

Once in town, I spent a few days nervously checking my phone in between interviews and long dinners and nights of pool and laughter fueled by cheap beer and the fast friendship my colleague and I formed with Andy, our photographer, fixer, and translator. On a morning after one of those nights spent sitting in child size plastic chairs drinking cold beer from insulated sippy cups—an attempted workaround for a COVID ban on the public sale of alcohol—I woke up to see a new encrypted message on my phone.

The message, I would learn later, came from Myauk. It has long since been autodeleted, a safety feature on the app we were using. In our short text conversation, Myauk offered a photo of himself, covered head to toe in black and wearing a balaclava, holding an FGC9 composed of several colors of plastic and looking for all the world like a harmless water pistol. To the educated, if somewhat hungover, guesses of myself and the colleague whose room I had just loudly barged into with the news, we knew we had found our guy.

After a few messages, we resolved to meet on one of the last days of our trip. Robert and I would walk to a café that had become one of our favorites for its delicious salad. Once there, a vehicle would arrive, and we would get in the back. That was our plan, and, in the words of our security consultant, it was "everything you're not supposed to do." But both of us trusted that we weren't being set up, and so we nervously walked to the tea shop on the appointed afternoon. I was pretty certain we were not being conned, but I couldn't shake intrusive thoughts about the possibility of this being our last dinner date if the junta had decided to pose as rebels and capture two Western journalists to make them look bad.

We hadn't been at the cafe more than a minute, not even long enough to pick up a cup of tea, when the truck arrived and we dutifully grabbed the handles on the doors, gazed at our nervous reflections on the tinted windows, and jumped in.

To our great surprise, we were met by Myauk, his fiance, and their "godfather," who was driving. We sat in the back seat, with Myauk—the guy who we knew exclusively as an international gun runner—in the middle, like kids being picked up from school. Unlike a kid on a school run, I had hundred-dollar bills hidden in my boots and a small satellite phone should something go awry, but with Myauk I felt immediately at ease. We chatted as they drove us to a modern restaurant that was throbbing with activity despite being down a dirt road twenty minutes outside town in an area we hadn't even seen before. Over the next few hours, we shared a delicious dinner and talked at length about how, in the single year since the revolution, young Burmese rebels had built and equipped a sizable army using YouTube, Reddit, and online shopping.

When the coup first occurred, Myauk was "Netflix and chilling"—his words—with his girlfriend. He had a 3D printer and was studying engineering, but he didn't print much more than key rings and desk toys. He was afraid of guns and the soldiers who carried them, he told me as we sat down for an interview the day after we met for dinner. Before recording our interview, we took a trip to a local range, built out of slab concrete, that had only two of its rental weapons actually functioning. Robert and I proved our bona fides as conflict reporters by joining them in using a comically bad Turkish shotgun to send a few shotgun cartridges downrange into a paper target. The gun was built out to appear like an AR15, but the adjustable stock rapidly collapsed to the shortest position under the recoil of the first round, sending my face directly into the receiver end plate, and it was a rare magazine that didn't jam repeatedly. The FGC9 began to make a pretty clear case for itself after the fourth or fifth time we removed the upper from the Turkish shotgun to extract a stuck casing.

"I'd never imagined having guns," Myauk said. "We were the same as North Korea [in the sense of having strict gun control]." Before the war, he thought gun ownership wouldn't work for Myanmar before the coup. "But after the coup, we must have our own guns." Even when the junta was defeated, civilians would have to own guns ("because we can't say there won't be another coup").[2] He said the moment he changed his opinion was when he took to the streets to peacefully protest against the coup only to see the military shooting protesters. "We couldn't stand it anymore," he said, "I thought we . . . need to have guns."

But before he printed guns, Myauk made explosives, which at first people didn't believe he could fabricate. They needed to "make a community," he said, rather than having individual groups work alone on the same process. The people interested in joining him all met up. "Other people, especially the old people, said we shouldn't do it, that peaceful protest was the way to go," Myauk said. "But the young people, especially Generation Z, decided to make explosives because of the emotions at that time." He eventually made more than two hundred bombs with his group. "Some explosives are for buildings, some are for bases, some are traps where they try and cut the wire and they die." His most successful operation was to build erythritol tetranitrate (ETN) bombs, which, he says, created such a big explosion at a checkpoint that five ambulances had to come to evacuate the soldiers. We asked how he learned to make ETN, which is a powerful explosive, and he said a fellow revolutionary taught him. He didn't know the person's name or their background. "We just met, and now we are brothers, like a second family," Myauk said.

This was our first interview, and it seemed odd to be talking about killing and dying while sitting in a vegetable garden surrounded by chirping songbirds, while occasionally scrambling to move our audio equipment out of the path of an automated sprinkler. Myauk's animated English, combined with the way he sometimes mispronounced words he must have learned by reading online rather than hearing, was charming, and if we'd been discussing any other topic this would have been an entirely pleasant afternoon of conversation, but the multicolored plastic guns we were discussing had been designed for serious business.

Myauk had no way of testing the guns in his apartment in Yangon, so he would send them to a warehouse to be assembled. Somehow the military

---

2. Myauk and others noted that the US model, while it might have prevented them from needing to print guns, was not without flaws and they were all well aware of the horrific impact of school shootings.

found the warehouse, and later they also arrested one of his team. It was during their interrogation of this team member, which may well have involved torture, that the military discovered what the little plastic guns were. The guns they captured from that warehouse were the ones I had seen the junta's police misidentify as Turkish shotguns.

Undeterred, Myauk and his team decided to scale up production, and they set up a print farm of twenty-five 3D printers. But the scale and electricity draw of this operation would leave it very vulnerable to being discovered in Yangon. Myauk is half Burmese and half Karenni, and Myauk said that before the revolution he thought Karenni ethnic revolutionary organizations were terrorists. Now he's sorry about that judgment, he says. He spent two months traveling between groups, and he grew his hair out as a form of disguise. "The military has so much gender inequality," he said, "and they hate gays." So Myauk pretended to be gay, and he says this alleviated any suspicions they had about him being a fighter. During this time, someone he was supposed to meet was captured in Yangon. The meeting was online, and nothing seemed awry until his friend subtly let them know he was in the infamous Insein jail and that his call was being monitored. "Oh shit," Myauk thought. His friends, knowing Myauk had the most experience with printing and the FGC9, told him to flee.

Like so many revolutionaries before them, Myauk and his friends set off for the mountains. His fiancé was able to connect him with the armorers of ethnic revolutionary organizations, many of whom have decades of experience hand-making weapons based on British World War II Sten guns or Chinese Type 81 assault rifles. Myauk showed the armorers his plan for a plastic sub-machine gun he could make using a roll of filament and a gadget they'd never heard of. "Nobody believed us at first," he said. The armorers told him that a plastic gun was impossible and that guns needed to be made of steel. Myauk and his team sent samples, which at first didn't work. The armorers made adjustments and very soon saw the potential for the weapons. Within a few months, there were print farms all around the country.

Since those first samples, Myauk and his team have experimented with some improvements to the gun. One area in which both they and Ivan have identified the need for improvement is the fire control group. Where the first FGC9 relied on an airsoft fire control group, or an AR15 group that was not restricted in much of Europe, these disappeared from the unrestricted market once word got out about their use in FGC9s. The FGC9 mkII, the model

Myauk and his friends made, relied on a printed fire control group. Designing a better version of this has been hard, largely due to material constraints. "I've picked up and quit probably four or five times out of frustration now because fire control groups are really hard," Ivan told me in late 2023, but he has since released a much-improved version. In Myanmar, where armorers in ethnic revolutionary organizations have a lot more experience with metallurgy than printing, they taught Myauk and his friends how to cast a fire control group from molten metals, which is more reliable and allows for a more precise trigger pull. They also added metal connectors, to give the weapon more stability. These developments in turn have been added to the open-source firearms community's list of methods and techniques, and they might one day help someone else pick up a more effective gun to secure their freedom and dignity.

Gunsmiths in Myanmar also experimented with longer barrels, hoping to give the projectile a bit more velocity and range, but they didn't gain much other than a more unwieldy gun. According to one post by DaddyUMCD, they also kept abreast of new developments by gun designers in the US, including Ivan and JStark. "For anything new and interesting, Reddit is our go-to source," DaddyUMCD said. Three production units with lathes were raided in Myanmar in late 2021, setting back some of their improvements, but, even as the war raged on, DadduUMCD and his team continued to look at new and better ways to arm themselves and openly discussed these ideas on Reddit.

One of the questions most often asked by DaddyUMCD and others was whether it was possible to convert the FGC9 to run on 5.56 NATO ammunition of the kind used by the bulk of the junta's troops. Where M16-type rifles cost up to $7,000, each FGC9 was being made for $100 by 2021. However, 9 mm ammunition was not as commonly found in captured military bases and was mostly obtained either from the police or by purchase in neighboring Thailand. To further complicate the supply situation, the ammunition captured from the junta wouldn't work reliably in their M16s; at first they theorized that it required an especially hard strike on the primer which their rifles didn't make. Later, they concluded that it was just low-quality ammunition manufacturing using poor-quality primers that meant captured ammunition was likely to misfire and result in a "click" rather than a "bang" as the primer failed to ignite the explosive powder that should propel the bullet out of the barrel in a well-made cartridge. At $2 per round, imported ammunition wasn't cheap, and sitting on a stockpile of rounds they couldn't use with fighters who didn't have weapons to join the fight became a major problem for the rebels.

I asked Ivan if it was possible to make an FGC9 in a rifle caliber. "Stark and I probably spent 100 hours talking about this," he said, "and the answer is no." It would be much easier to make a weapon capable of firing 9 mm ammunition, and then use that to capture a rifle, they concluded.

Certainly, obtaining rifles from dead adversaries or captured caches is an option in Myanmar, but the quality of government-made weapons is often so bad and maintenance so infrequent that fighters prefer almost any other weapons system. Over the years, ethnic revolutionary organizations have purchased M16s left by the United States in Vietnam, but many are now out of working order and in need of repairs. This problem, it turned out, was another one that they could solve using the internet.

This time the weapon used was based on a design by someone named Hoffman Tactical and then modified by Neutron_Nick, and it prominently featured a logo from the far-right militia the Three Percenters. Although it closely resembles an AR15-type rifle to the unskilled eye, the operating system was closer to the AK-style one used in the junta's rifles. It offered the pro-democracy rebels a way to take parts from old M16s and reequip them to work with captured ammunition by hitting the primers harder. In 2023, a joint team from the Karenni National People's Liberation Front (KNPLF) and the NUG, released a video of the weapon.[3] It was made using Hoffman's lower and a metal upper that they craft-produced or sourced from damaged weapons, and in field trials it fired whole magazines without issue. Each weapon costs $2,000, much lower than the $6,000 or more for a functioning M16, and the new weapon allows rebels to use ammunition that was previously a liability for them.

These developments were not happening in isolation. Myauk said teams meet to collaborate. "We share our knowledge. . . Now we have 3D printers, we can do anything," he said. Some teams might have more knowledge of conventional weapons, or a useful analog like model rockets or recreational drones, and they contact Myauk to simulate various designs with his powerful software and growing expertise in 3D printing. Now drone teams print

3. The KNPLF is a communist group that left the side of the junta in June 2023 and joined the rebels after some of their troops were murdered by junta troops who were engaged in war crimes that the KNPLF tried to prevent.

droppers to allow them to drop grenades directly on the targets, and fins to stabilize the bombs. The weapons innovation team's model, Myauk says, is one of "equality leadership," and anyone on a team can contribute an idea.

These new designs are shared on encrypted apps and can be printed at any of dozens of locations across the country. Filament, the plastic material used to create the prints, is purchased from online bulk retailers and carefully double wrapped to prevent it from becoming damp and useless as it is smuggled across an active war zone and into the remote print farms where dozens of Creality Ender 3 v2 printers hum away, creating perhaps the first arsenal to seriously challenge the monopoly of the state on arms production.

To get a sense of how unique this stateless system of weapons production was, I asked Obscura. The printed guns themselves, he told me, are a natural outgrowth of a long-term movement for making or modifying guns that has existed in the US for decades: "Going back to . . . the '70s, '80s, and '90s . . . there's loads of like printed guides out there. One of the famous . . . ones is, you know, converting your AR to be full auto or converting your Ruger to be full auto." These PDFs or printed guides weren't illegal in the US, even though following them might be, but they had very little impact in the rest of the world, where the problem was not converting the rifle but obtaining it in the first place. Other guides detailed very rudimentary firearms, like slam-fire shotguns, which can be made from commonly available pipes and nails but offer very little utility as a fighting weapon if one's adversary is armed. "The idea of putting together a gun at home is not something particular to the internet age or to 3D printers," Obscura said. But one of the areas where Obscura says that 3D printing did represent a sea change was in accessibility and the framing of the project: "The FGC9 is very clearly driven by a more internationalist outlook; it was made explicitly to avoid gun control, hence the name."

Of course, not all the weapons the people of Myanmar need can be downloaded just yet. "We are winning on the ground," Myauk said, "but we are always afraid of the air, the helicopters and planes. If we had MANPADS, we would win for sure." MANPADS refers to man-portable air-defense systems, the sort of guided missiles that the US sent to mujahideen in Afghanistan and UNITA in Chad and then struggled to reclaim after those conflicts. Used by a skilled operator, these missiles can destroy a fighter bomber of the kind used by the junta in Myanmar, and in doing so remove the ability of the regime to target schools, music festivals, and military formations with impunity as it has done since the coup. The problem with MANPADs is that there are very few of them on the global market and fewer still that can be purchased by a non-state actor without a state backer or access to huge amounts of money.

According to Calibre Obscura, "It's not that uncommon for missiles to pop up on the market, but do they have all the hardware [needed] to work? A battery on one of these things, should have a service life of, let's say, ten years, like a guarantee from the factory. If it's like a decent, fairly modern missile, chances are you could look at it at in ten years and either recondition or sort of re-certify if you'd like for another five or 10. Once you start getting over twenty-five to thirty years, these are thermal batteries, which are different to normal batteries, and they start dying." Because of this, many of the systems on the market may or may not work. Many of these missiles are also for sale in areas a long way from Myanmar, and the costs of smuggling one would likely be extreme. For cash-starved rebels in Myanmar, obtaining even one or two missiles would represent a huge resource strain.

In August 2021, the Karen National Union allegedly attempted to make just such a purchase. According to the US Department of Justice, using the encrypted messaging app Telegram, they met with a Japanese Yakuza arms dealer called Takeshi Ebisawa. Ebisawa, speaking through a translator who used the pseudonym "Bobby," offered the ethnic revolutionary organiza- tion access to several hundred US-made Stinger surface-to-air missiles. The missiles were part of a cache he had seen months before in Copenhagen. While there he'd met several associates and even posed for a photo with an anti-tank rocket launcher to show his clients he had the goods. Unfortunately, the men selling Ebisawa the "weapons" were undercover Danish Police joined by an undercover Drug Enforcement Agency (DEA) agent, and Ebisawa's right-hand man, identified in court documents at UC-1, had tipped off the Danish Police and the DEA about the whole deal. But, for a time, the DEA allowed Ebisawa to believe he really did have access to these weapons.

In a Telegram thread, Ebisawa sent photos of the Stingers to Bobby, who forwarded them to high-ranking KNU officers and Thai army officers who would help facilitate the deal. The Stingers, he said, had been left behind in Afghanistan following the bungled US withdrawal and smuggled out via Iran. Ebisawa asked if he could be paid with "sugar," which the US DEA alleges was understood to mean heroin. It is alleged that it was possible for the KNU to provide heroin, and a plan was hatched that would see Ebisawa's pilot land a plane in the jungles of Myanmar, drop off MANPADS, and fill up with drugs.

Ebisawa's associate, who had been passing information to the DEA for several years, suggested, quite ridiculously, that the amount of methamphetamine and heroin that he could obtain from this deal, which also included another ERO called the Shan State Army, "would be on the metric tons level."[6]

The mole then traveled to meet high-ranking KNU officers, and they promised to try to obtain samples of the drugs for the mole to test on the US market. After this, they would place a 20 percent deposit for the missiles. The total cost of the deal would be around $40 million. Sadly for Ebisawa, the mole managed to persuade Ebisawa to launder drug proceeds and finally gave the DEA a way to arrest him, which they did as he sat down to a meal at Morton's Steakhouse in Manhattan in the spring of 2022. Sadly, for the rebels of Myanmar, the missiles were never real to begin with, and their government continues to bomb them unchallenged.

Once again, where the market and the neoliberal world order failed them, young people in Myanmar turned to the internet for help. As Obscura explained, manufacturing an anti-aircraft system is rather more complicated than making a gun. Most semi-automatic firearms essentially create a small explosion and then use the force of that explosion, or the gasses generated by it, to push a bullet forward and cycle a mechanical action that loads another. These mechanisms require tight tolerances, but even someone with little to no engineering background can understand how they work. MANPADS, on the other hand, appear like some kind of black magic to all but experts. Obscura explained this: "Essentially, you do need some complicated electronics in order to get that it does that IR infrared homing. So, you need to have the infrared homing hardware, you need to have a missile that is packaged up and is reliable and can sit there, and you need to have a reliable power source. All of these things require complicated and sensitive electronics, as well as advanced technical skill."

Those complicated electronics are what stand between the people of Myanmar and a future where all people are equal and safe from genocidal violence. Rebels in Myanmar have experimented with solutions that rely on model rocket engines, an artificial intelligence autopilot, and a programmable microcomputer called an Arduino. They've mined the depths of academic journals and weapons blogs trying to work out how to reverse-engineer the missile's tracking system.

While their as-yet unsuccessful research into MANPADs keeps them away from the front lines, it isn't without risk. Myauk mentioned that several members of the production teams have lost their lives in building and testing weapons. One team member in Yangon died when the breach failed on a grenade launcher he was testing, causing the whole thing to explode rather than containing the explosion and forcing the projectile out of the barrel.

Obscura says that, while developments in MANPADs are possible, "something which can actually fire, locks on, and actually does track a target and hits it is extremely difficult. So, I personally don't think we are close to seeing that anytime soon." The closest anyone has come, he says, are the Houthis in Yemen adapting air-to-air missiles for ground launch.

Despite their frustrated attempts to print a surface-to-air missile, the young rebels I spoke to were effusive with respect and admiration for the strangers online who had helped them fight tyranny. JStark became the face of the FGC9 following his participation in the documentary *Plastic Defence*, made by independent journalist Jake Hanrahan and released in late 2020. JStark, whose face remains covered by a balaclava for the entire film and who speaks through a filter that masks his identity by making his voice sound like a robot, tragically died not long after the film was released. In 2021, German armed police raided JStark's apartment. They found nothing illegal there, or any firearms. However, just two days later, JStark, aged twenty-six, was found dead in his car.

News of his death became public not long before my trip to meet Myauk. I had noticed at our dinner the night before that Myauk's phone had a photo of JStark as the background, and when we sat down to our interview, I asked how he felt about the pseudonymous weapons designer who had unwittingly facilitated a Gen Z revolution on the other side of the world. "Thank you so much," Myauk effused. "Because of this guy, we knew we could print guns," Myauk told me. "Respect, rest in power."

German authorities claim that JStark's death, in a parked car in front of his parents' apartment in Hanover, was the result of a preexisting heart condition. Following JStark's death, Hanrahan revealed some of the outtakes from the documentary, including one of JStark muttering, "*Biji Serok Apo,*" a slogan of the Democratic Confederalists of Kurdistan that can be translated as "Long Live Leader Apo." It's a slogan I've heard myself, from the people I met in Rojava where Öcalan's face is a constant presence despite the decades he has spent in solitary confinement in Turkey. Although JStark wasn't well known in Kurdistan, and despite some claims that he was "in the process" of joining the YPG, he seems to have been unable to ever set foot in Rojava. Yet his contribution to the revolution in Myanmar serves as a reminder that even when the states of the world abandoned the people of Kurdistan and Rojava to their fates, the people of the world did not.

In March 2024, on Nowruz, the day Kurds celebrate the new year, Kurdish guerrillas in Iraq released a video of a Turkish Bayraktar drone, the kind I had seen destroy so many lives the previous year, lying in pieces in the mountains of Kurdistan. They followed up with videos of many more drones exploding and falling from the sky. The guerrillas claimed to have shot down fifteen, and they've shot down more since. The way they did so remains unclear, and the weapons did not appear in Rojava until the Assad regime collapsed in late 2024, when the guerrillas accidentally shot down a US Predator drone, but their technological advances offer a vision of a world in which such innovation is not the sole domain of the state.

Even with their impressive tally of drone kills, the Kurdish freedom movement hasn't been able to prevent Turkish warplanes from bombing Rojava, perhaps because the freedom movement's technologies are not capable of engaging them or perhaps because they know that doing so will force the US to choose between its allies in Turkey and its partner forces in Rojava. The special forces soldiers who first wore the YPG patches are now long gone from Rojava, and, while the US maintains a small footprint in the country, they only use their air defense assets to defend their own bases. In Hasakah, I saw the impact of drone bombings on civilians, after the US base a few kilometers away had just shot down a Turkish drone that came too close to the facility.

When the US's friendship with the people of Rojava has been tested, it's been found wanting. In my short time in Rojava, I was able to experience a fraction of the pain and fear the people have suffered from aerial bombardments to which they cannot respond. I can understand their desire to defend themselves and their revolution from the constant fear that the night sky might take their life at any moment. At the time of writing, I don't know how the movement obtained what seem to be loitering anti-aircraft munitions, whether they made them themselves, purchased them, or obtained them from a state ally.[4]

---

4. A loitering munition is one that takes off and "loiters" in the sky until a target is detected and then propels itself into the target in order to detonate. By contrast, MANPADS are launched from the ground once a target is identified and intercept it on its route. Many have noted their similarity to Iranian munitions, but I have seen no

But every day that the people of Myanmar don't have access to MANPADs is one day closer to the moment they work out how to make their own, and in doing so remove one of the last vestiges of the state's monopoly on violence. They are not alone in their fight against that monopoly; although developing missile systems might be more legally complex in the US, the 3D-printed gun movement offers a vision of a world where innovation is not just for profit and ideas are not constrained by markets. We need not rely on this vision only in wartime, and indeed 3D-printed tourniquets are saving lives in Gaza as the Israeli state drops bombs on children as I write this. Technology has been a mixed bag in the age of the internet, but in this one small area of people tinkering with layers of plastic, it really has brought people together and made some freedoms impossible for a tyrannical government to deny. It just so happens that those freedoms, the freedoms to speak and to defend oneself, are the ones young Burmese rebels can use to secure all the other freedoms.

Of course, these weapons can be used to build a new state that does not allow its citizens such freedoms. Many revolutions have been armed, but those arms have been seized by the new state the moment it accedes to power. In early 2025, I spoke to a PDF sniper and asked him what would happen if the state tried to reestablish itself and take back their weapons after the revolution. "We won't let them," he replied.

---

evidence of Iranian origin beyond their similarity, and members of the movement insist they were engineered in the mountains.

7

Solidarity

> In trenches dug on the side of the Aragon hillsides, men lived frater-
> nally and dangerously without the need for hope because they were
> fully alive, aware of being what they had wanted to be.
>
> —Louis Mercier-Vega, alias Ridel, *Refuting the Legend*, 1956

The southern border of the United States, and the northern border of Mexico,
protrudes from the desert landscape in the ancestral and current homeland
of the Kumeyaay people. Plants and animals that for centuries have eked
out a fragile existence in the arid landscape that is by turns freezing cold and
baking hot seem repelled by the ten-meter wall that cuts like a scar through
the landscape and then stops periodically in the places where funding or
initiative ran out. It is in many ways both a beautiful and tragic place, and
it's one where I have spent a lot of time (too much time, perhaps my editors
would argue) while working on this manuscript.

Since I began, tens of thousands of people have crossed the border in
the mountains and been detained in open-air concentration camps where
they received no food, water, or shelter from the state. They came from
China, Venezuela, Mauritania, Kurdistan, Punjab, and dozens other places
to seek refuge from violence, poverty, and persecution. The state ignored
their pleas for help, and people from the region stepped up and took on
the task of taking care for them. Mutual aid groups from the surrounding
area, joined and supported by nonprofits, have fed, sheltered, cared for,
and welcomed every single one of those people. We've worked nonstop
for months, through cold nights and witheringly hot days, carrying water,
building shelters, chopping and delivering wood, and making tens of thousands of vegan meals.

Days at the border can be long and nights cold, but at the end of each of them I am overcome not so much by exhaustion as by a deep feeling of fraternal love and appreciation for my friends. This feeling is what keeps me and dozens of others coming back, and it is a feeling that is facilitated not just by our important work but also by our mutual respect for each other and the people traveling this way.

It's this sense of mutual respect that is, I think, at the core of anarchist solidarity. The sine qua non of anarchism, at least as far as its on-the-ground implementation goes, is the building of ways to care for one another that are not also ways to *control* one another. If we are not doing this, we have strayed too far from the principles behind our work as anarchists. And, I would argue, if we are caring for one another we need not concern ourselves so much with theory or discourse because we are already putting these into action. On the border, I have experienced a feeling of overwhelming respect and happiness at being part of a collective that is neither above nor below the people we assist but with them in their time of hardship, and I've also had this feeling among anarchist fighters I have interviewed around the world. It's what keeps them coming back to the front lines, just as it keeps me driving across the desert several times a week to hand out beans and repair broken shelters.

During our time helping people in the desert, we received help from mutual aid groups around the country, and this gave me the chance to make several friends who had traveled to Rojava to participate in the revolution. I began to see that the two endeavors were not as distinct as they might seem and that both rested on the principle of mutual aid, which is to say assisting others because one wants to build a world where people help each other, and doing so without any expectation of reciprocity.

Mutual aid is a core concept of anarchism. It's often expressed with the phrase "solidarity, not charity." The implications are that mutual aid is delivered from one person to another as equals, that both are dehumanized by the unnecessary human suffering that is so often caused by the state, and that both feel compelled to alleviate suffering for others. In participating in mutual aid, we recover our dignity. In many cases, in most cases even, mutual aid is delivered by feeding the hungry, sheltering the unsheltered, or providing harm reduction supplies to individuals living through substance use. Sometimes, in cases where libertarian leftist projects or vulnerable people are under attack, mutual aid can take the form of picking up a weapon and risking one's life to defend a stranger's freedom. This is perhaps the ultimate act of solidarity, and it has been common among anarchists for more than a century.

Voluntarism as a form of revolutionary solidarity has always interested me from my early days reading Orwell and studying the Spanish Civil War. Fighting for someone else's freedom is anathema to many who feel that fighting is only appropriate if one is dying for one's state rather than one's convictions. Often the solidarity that led fighters to risk and sometimes lose their lives in Spain or Kurdistan is framed as being in opposition to something, for example anti-fascist or anti-ISIS. However, many also traveled to fight *for* something. Across the world in 1936, people who had been living hand to mouth for years, trying to build a revolution at home while they struggled to pay the rent, saw a chance to participate in something that offered a better future for working people. Orwell, after all his years of imperial travel, reflected that his arrival in Barcelona marked something of a threshold in this regard. "It was the first time," he wrote, "that I had ever been in a town where the working class was in the saddle."[1] The same is true of Kurdistan, where a society without the state is being built, and it must be defended, not just because the threats to it are evil but also because the revolution is good.

When one thinks of international volunteers in Spain, one thinks first of the International Brigades. This melting pot of fighters, from anarchists to Stalinists, has gone down in history as an example of selfless sacrifice and the pursuit of a noble cause. No doubt many of those fighters were and remain totemic examples of solidarity and sacrifice. However, in many cases, they returned from Spain scarred not only by war but also by the authoritarian overreach and paranoid fratricide that had come to engulf Soviet-style Marxism in the mid-1930s. Notable among this group is, of course, Orwell, who fought for the POUM, rather than in the International Brigades, and saw firsthand the events of May 1937 and spent the rest of his life criticizing totalitarian statism and as a result lived in fear of agents of the NKVD coming to kill him for having been willing to risk his life alongside them.

Less celebrated are the international anarchists who fought in Spain. Unlike the International Brigades, whose fighters were largely recruited and transported by the Comintern, the anarchists mostly arrived on their own initiative. The CNT's international propaganda and solidarity building apparatus was, at the start of the war, nonexistent outside of some networks shared with French anarchists. Links existed only where foreign anarchists, largely Germans and Italians seeking refuge from fascism at home, had come to the

Republic to take advantage of its relatively liberal asylum policies and found fellow ideologues in the Spanish CNT-FAI. It was one of these refugees, a Silesian anarchist named Augustin Souchy, who became a sort of de facto ambassador for the cause of the anarchists.

Before the war, some links had been forged when anarchists visited Spain, where the CNT existed legally from 1931, to witness the size and fortitude of the movement there. Germans, in particular, enjoyed this so-called "revolutionary tourism" and likely the pleasant climate of Barcelona during the early years of the Republic. Those who moved to Spain found solidarity in the CNT if they were able to make the considerable leap between the two languages and cultures. "They saw the comrade in me, not the German, the alien. In a word—I was one of them," wrote Karl Brauner, who came to Barcelona in 1934.[2]

On the day the fighting began, these German comrades would strike a decisive blow on behalf of the working people of Barcelona. Having learned from the CNT that the long-expected coup had begun, the German anarchists stole a march on their fascist fellow countrymen in Barcelona. Before dawn, armed with weapons provided by their defense committees, they rushed to the German Club on the Calle Caspe-Lauria. Without the constraints of the law, and finding themselves briefly and bizarrely allied with the police, they wasted no time in stealth and openly raided the building. They found not only machine guns and rifles but also membership lists of the Nazi Party (NSDAP) in Spain. In one single action, they had significantly hampered the efforts of foreign fascists to support the coup and significantly improved their own arsenal. The machine guns they captured were later repurposed in the street battle in the city, doubtless saving many lives with their ability to suppress and eliminate army positions.

Within days of the revolution, the Germans were joined by more international volunteers. Many of these were French anarchists like Louis Mercier-Vega (who was known by a variety of pseudonyms). Mercier-Vega, along with friends from his affinity group *"les Moules-à-gaufres"* (the Waffle Irons), set off for Spain as soon as they could cash their paychecks. Mercier-Vega traveled with Charles Carpentier, ten years his senior, and participated in the founding of the international group within the Durruti Column. There were three centuria in the international group, named for Sébastien Faure (composed of Italian and French anarchists), Erich Mühsam (for the Germans, Prussians, Poles, and Russians), and Sacco and Vanzetti (presumably for

English-speakers), and among them were many experienced militants. The Faure centuria included an Algerian named Mohamed Saïl, and a Frenchman named Émile Cottin who had tried to assassinate Georges Clemenceau in 1919. Antonio García Barón, who would go on to fight at Dunkirk, survive Mauthausen, and lose a hand in a fight with a jaguar in the Bolivian jungle also joined them, even though he was Spanish.

The CNT did not only benefit from international solidarity but also engaged in it. In July 1936, it began discussing ways to foment a revolution in Morocco, undermining the Spanish and French colonies there. The CNT even arranged for Moroccan delegates to meet with Largo Caballero, prime minister of the Second Spanish Republic, and propose that they help foment an uprising in Franco's rearguard. The Moroccan delegates wanted Largo Caballero to ensure that they would not be opposed by the French and in turn proposed they would not claim full independence but instead substantial autonomy. Largo Caballero did not agree to these terms, offering to arm them against Franco but making no promises to speak with the French, and the Republic lost a chance to open a second front out of its loyalty to a colonial power that had shown no such loyalty in return.

While many of their stories are told elsewhere in this book, it should be mentioned while discussing their differences with the Republic that the international anarchists faced particularly difficult choices at the time of militarization, and some of them, including Mercier-Vega, never forgave the CNT for its collaboration with the government. The Republic pursued many of them relentlessly, and those who chose to stay would always have to look over their shoulders. This meant the international anarchists faced a difficult choice between abandoning their comrades and risking being shot by those who were formerly their comrades when the anarchist units were subsumed into the Republican Army with significant Soviet control.

It was those anarchists who inspired Sam to volunteer in Rojava. He went to Rojava, he says, out of a sense of historical obligation. He'd read about the Spanish Civil War as an anarchist and a punk, and he saw the revolution in Rojava as a chance to participate in something equally significant. Initially, Sam didn't want to fight. "I don't know anything about fighting.... I was like, oh, yeah, [I'm] just gonna, like, go to garden." He even packed a shovel.

Sam found plenty of work for his shovel, but that didn't mean he wouldn't be fighting. Just getting to Rojava was a struggle. After flying to Iraq and spending time with other volunteers in a safe house, Sam set off for Rojava with a group of other recruits. They hid in the back of trucks, then rafted across rivers and hiked across the desert through the mountains to the Syrian border. Even once they were inside Rojava, they were stopped by Peshmerga from the Iraqi Kurdistan Regional Government, who have no jurisdiction outside Iraq, and one tense standoff ended only when YPG guerillas racked their weapons and made ready to fight. "The Peshmerga weren't ready to die," Sam said.

Sam would face a choice similar to the one the Pershmerga faced, and ultimately he did decide to risk his life fighting. But first, like all foreign volunteers, he had to take a course at what is known as "the academy." There, he received basic combat instruction, Kurdish lessons, and a course on the history and ideology of the Kurdish freedom movement. The instruction wasn't so much a body of dogma, he said, as a discussion of what the movement believed. Of course, many volunteers hadn't come out of an ideological commitment to horizontal organizing so much as out of a desire to fight the Islamic State. But the discussions and lessons taught them how important it was to speak Kurdish, a language that had been repressed for decades, and why the Kurdish freedom movement sees women's liberation as an integral part of national liberation. This time also gave the volunteers a chance to feel each other out, and for people who had obvious ideological or personal incompatibilities with the group to either leave or in some cases be asked to leave when their actions put others in danger.

Initially, there were conflicts between the volunteers, who had vastly different worldviews, but over time these disagreements became less important. "One of the great parts about being in service with all these guys," Sam said, "is that you learn about. . . what's important, and what's not so important." Fighting over ideology, he realized, was meaningless. "What are you doing with your hands?" Sam always asked himself, and he tried to make sure it was something useful. "Even the most apolitical fighter in Rojava is more of a revolutionary than an anarchist sitting at home," he said. "[When] there's an opportunity to do something bigger, they're not there. They don't show up." To Sam, this was important, and while his fight might be characterized as against ISIS, for him it was a fight for the revolution.

While falling out over ideology took a back seat, what could not be set aside was tactical and weapons training. The volunteers who had conventional military experience or training were not impressed with the level of training the inexperienced volunteers were receiving in the academy. "The shit they're teaching you, you're gonna get me killed," they told Sam. "We have to teach you how to move together, how to extricate from a firefight, and how to clear buildings," they said. And so they did, setting up extra classes in the evenings and teaching each other what they knew. The Kurdish fighters, Sam said, learned as they fought and placed a lot of faith in their superior ways of organizing and their dedication that came from ideology. It worked well for them, and Sam also stressed that many local fighters didn't have the luxury of months of training, which is standard for soldiers in the US and UK, because the fight was on their doorstep, and they needed to defend their homes, families, and communities. However, Sam's new comrades in arms wanted to pass along what they'd learned at the expense of the state, and, in return, Sam set about organizing them to tend to the academy's gardens.

In their free time when Sam and his friends at the academy were not teaching each other combat skills, they significantly improved the gardens around the academy. While Sam had no combat experience and approached the fighting lessons as a student, he was very experienced with gardening, so naturally he took the lead in that area. This was possible, in part, due to a flexible system in which nobody was inherently superior to anyone else, so Sam could be "commander of the plants," as he put it, but a student of war. This reflects the general approach of the YPG and YPJ in which being a commander is a job, rather than a status, and, although it might convey respect and even obedience on the front lines, it does not, in theory, offer any significant status benefit outside the military sphere.

After he graduated from the academy, Sam thought he might be sent to help with a tree planting campaign. But the commanders at the academy had other suggestions for him. "You're an anarchist, right?" they asked him, and Sam agreed that he was. "So you're a revolutionary?" It was hard for Sam to say no after having traveled around the world to participate in a revolution. "Then you should see combat," they said. They asked Sam to go to the front and keep an eye on another volunteer who they felt was becoming nihilistic.[1]

Sam came to Rojava to serve, and he emphasized to me that he could have said no. But he felt that he'd showed all his abilities and his knowledge of permaculture, and they had decided his best use would be at the front, so that's where Sam went. It took several days to get to the front in Deir ez-Zor.

---

1. It's not unusual to find people who arrive at these kinds of conflicts seeking to find purpose or die trying. However, the level of concern for the well-being of this volunteer that is shown here is more remarkable, and commendable.

The soldiers who were with him were convinced that a commander would send transport for them, but it never came. Sam, a punk with next to no combat experience, figured they should just hitchhike. It turned out he was right. "You really do have to like hitch rides," he said. "That part was really nice in terms of, like, the punk aesthetic to the whole revolution. . . . You hitchhike everywhere. You share everything you've got in an absolutely communal way. When we're passing through the mountains, everyone's, like, hanging out, like in the woods by a fire. When you're in Rojava, you're just kind of squatting buildings. You just break into them and that's . . . your place for the night, and then [you] move on to the next one. It was, like, punks in a war!"

Some of the veterans in the group, who had spent their formative years in boot camp, not at punk shows, found the punk style of self-direction hard. They were used to being given orders rather than having to collectively take responsibility for their own conduct and safety. One volunteer, Sam said, struggled to deal with this after having spent time in the British Army, where he had not seen combat. Rather than settling down with a unit, he jumped from one to another trying to find a chance at combat. In the end, he didn't see any fighting. Whereas Sam and his team, who settled down with a unit based in a hospital, saw as much fighting as they wanted and were respected by commanders, which allowed them to be able to decide how much risk they wished to be exposed to.

The first time he saw combat, Sam was surprised at how well he handled it. His group, known in Kurdish as a *tabûr*, was engaging a group of ISIS fighters at about 400 meters, a longer range than that at which most shooters can provide accurate fire with an assault rifle and no magnified optic. Nonetheless, bullets were flying around them, and Sam found himself moving to cover and returning fire. "You just do the thing," he said. "You have to shoot at them because they want to come kill you. It's not like you're trying to go after them and go hunt them down. They are right there. They're trying to come get you." Years later, a friend told Sam a bullet had missed his head by less than a foot, but at the time he didn't notice, he was too absorbed in firing his weapon and trying to keep himself and his friends alive.

This attitude wasn't mirrored by conventional forces. The risk of death was much higher for the volunteers than for the conventional forces deployed to Syria by the US and its allies. These forces provided assistance in the form of logistics, engineering, and airstrikes, and their assistance should not be underestimated in terms of the impact it had on the ability of the SDF to defeat IS. However, when it came to the up-close killing and dying, the states and governments of the world were absent aside from a few special forces units, and the majority of the blood being spilled was that of Kurds, Arabs, Assyrians, and their international volunteer allies.

Sam says he didn't really think too much about the states of the world shirking their obligation to fight ISIS, an evil that they were somewhat complicit in creating. "[Fighting IS] was work that needed to be done," he said. "I wouldn't ask anything of any government, and I'm an anarchist, that, you know, I expected more anarchists to be there. I was disappointed about that, yeah, that there were not more anarchists and revolutionaries who volunteered. I didn't expect anything from the international community. I mean, even though we were fighting their war for them; everyone knew it."

The "international community" Sam refers here means the community of states. The community of people is a distinct thing; that community has helped the democratic project in North and East Syria a great deal, as Sam showed with his willingness to fight and risk his life on their behalf. Volunteers also run the Rojava Information Center, a sort of public affairs and media liaison office for the revolution. Turkish Marxists have fought on behalf of the revolution against the Islamic State, and international volunteers have worked and shared their skills in civil engineering, network management, and many other areas where the revolution has had to replace the capacity once held by the state.

These volunteers are, of course, not above reproach. In some cases, volunteers have been accused of not fully embracing women's liberation, which is integral to the revolution, or simply of creating spaces that are outside of the revolution in some sense because they are exclusively populated by outsiders, however supportive they may be. This can weaken solidarity by not allowing the revolution and its principles to impact every part of the lives of the people there to support it. Volunteers can offer more solidarity and gain a better understanding of what the revolution really means by learning Kurdish and sharing space and their lives with local revolutionaries, as many did. International volunteers, of course, are not any more important a part of the revolution than the people of Syria who have taken up arms or positions to create and defend a better world.

While volunteers from outside Myanmar's borders may be rare, the revolution in Myanmar is an international revolution and always has been. The many ethnic nationalities of the country are fighting, sometimes side by side in the same units, against tyrannical centrism. The revolution was born in the spirit of the Milk Tea Alliance, an online solidarity movement between people across Southeast Asia fighting state oppression. From its earliest days it was shaped by solidarity. Protesters in Yangon airdropped infographics from Hong Kong about how to avoid tear gas and organize against state violence. They adopted the three-fingered salute that was first used in this context by Thai protesters in 2014, who in turn borrowed it from the Hunger Games series of novels. From the beginning, protesters in Myanmar not only demanded international solidarity with their signs and slogans, they also exemplified it when they put aside their differences and took the mountains with comrades from various marginalized ethnicities to fight against the junta.

Indeed, one could argue that the Myanmar revolution is perhaps the most internationalist of those I have mentioned. Despite the proclamations of Western "analysts" and "experts" that the ethnic revolutionary organizations were simply taking advantage of the revolution to bolster their territory and would stop once they reached what they saw as their ethnic boundaries, this has not been the case. PDF troops traveled from their homelands to fight alongside EROs in their offensives, and EROs pushed beyond what most would see as their homelands to further weaken the junta. PDF units are often composed of multiple nationalities or ethnic groups, fighting together side by side for a future where their differences won't matter and building that future as they fight.

This does not mean, of course, that within ethnic revolutionary organization–controlled territories there has not been the imposition of certain authoritarian policies and forced recruitment or abusive treatment and summary killing of people of other ethnicities; all these things have occurred. However, due to the increasing power of Ethnic Revolutionary Organizations in Myanmar, lines of communication and solidarity now run across the country. In some instances, this has had remarkable and beautiful results, but in others it amounts to horse trading between EROs to ensure that the groups they represent are not harmed by other groups within the broader revolution.

Even when I was half a world away in Qamişlo, the international solidarity of Myanmar's Spring Revolution reached out to me. To explain how, I'll first have to explain the situation in Rojava at that time. While I was there, the Turkish Air Force undertook a sustained campaign of bombing with drones and F16s against civilian infrastructure. The F16s, supplied by the US, were bombing fighters who were in theory US allies, but mostly they were bombing civilian infrastructure that makes life survivable in Rojava, from hospitals to power plants. But states have allies, not friends, and so when the SDF was not fighting an enemy of the US they were of no use to the US, and so the US government was willing to let them die. Because the Turkish drones and jets were also bombing hospitals, factories, warehouses, and power stations, lots of civilians would die as well. None of this was helping me get to sleep, and I spent my first night in Rojava nervously half-sleeping and moving between the three single beds in my hotel room trying to determine which was the least broken before giving up and sleeping on the floor.

Every morning came with a new list of horrors in the form of videos and photos of destroyed buildings, a press release detailing the number of people killed, and an appeal from the local hospital for blood donations. But at least the daylight was something of a respite from the bombing at night, and I was able to spend my days conducting interviews, walking through the market, and talking to one of the market stallholders who had appointed himself my Kurdish tutor and was enthusiastic about taking my arm and leading me around the market pointing at things and shouting Kurdish nouns in my ear above the din of the market in between tea breaks.

Every night, though, brought concern, not only (or not primarily) for my own well-being; it seemed that being caught in a drone bomb would be a case of extremely bad luck for me. But I worried for the people I had spoken to each day, who were often the targets of these drone attacks. The commanders and administrators on the military and civilian sides of society in Rojava were exactly the sort of people targeted by Turkey's campaign, and I was always nervous to hear whether they'd made it home safely after our interviews.

One night, I was lying on one of the beds in my hotel room, unable to sleep, and instead passed the time playing a game on my phone that involved driving a combine harvester, a distraction from anxiety I badly needed. At some point, I fell asleep. When I was woken up, it was not by my alarm or a bomb but by the buzzing of my phone on my chest, caused by incoming messages. When I looked at it through bleary, half-awake eyes, I saw that my virtual combine harvester had become irretrievably stuck in a ditch, and that I had received half a dozen encrypted messages from a friend in Myanmar.

While I'd been experimenting with the exact amount of sleeping pills I needed to fall asleep under threat of drone strike but also to not be so sleepy that I couldn't respond quickly if a drone strike did happen, my friends in Myanmar had been busy. The messages on my phone took several minutes to load, thanks chiefly to the intermittent wi-fi and power, and the fact that I was not standing on the chair in the corner that delivered the best signal. When the images eventually downloaded, I saw something I had not expected. A video showed a group of eighty or so young Burmese people, aligned in three ranks and wearing their green-patterned camouflage—aside from one soldier who appeared out of place in desert fatigues in the jungle. Behind them were the flags of the Karenni Nationalities Defense Force. I recognized them from the countless videos I had seen of the unit, who are famous not only for their fierce fighting but also for their large dance parties. Beneath their flags, and in front of the jungle they fought to liberate, a young Karenni man read from a script.

At the bottom of the screen, subtitles in English translated his speech. "Dear comrades in Rojava," began the commander of KNDF's Battalion 5, Sayar Richard. "We are saddened to hear about the recent air raids that targeted non-military objectives, including civilians and civil infrastructure in Rojava. We can relate to the difficulties, sacrifices, and bravery of our brothers and sisters in Rojava since we have endured the cruelty of a military dictatorship for more than seventy years." In the video, Sayar Richard went on to express the solidarity of the Karenni fighters with the people and revolution of Rojava. "From one revolutionary movement to another that the international community has turned a blind eye to," he went on. "We would like to say, 'We see your struggles, we see your fight for liberation and justice.'" The declaration went on to highlight the shared struggles for true democracy, gender equality, and an end to dictatorship.

The message was made public a few days later, and within a few hours, the video was traveling around Rojava. Later in the day, the video was all over local television and on the front pages of Kurdish news websites. In the days after I left Rojava to travel elsewhere in Kurdistan, the hevals I met would message me to ask to learn more about Myanmar. They asked for books, articles, histories, documentaries, and even podcasts, and they devoured them all voraciously before coming back with more questions. What struck me most was their genuine spirit of solidarity. One afternoon, as a heval walked me back from and interview, he said that it was important to connect with revolutionaries in Myanmar not just to teach them what the Kurdish people had learned but "so that we can learn from them because we don't have all the answers."

Shortly after I returned home from Kurdistan, I was once again awakened by my encrypted messaging app causing my phone to vibrate clean off my bedside table. The messages this time were from friends in Rojava, the YPJ, and the AANES. In response to the KNDF video, the men and women of the YPG and YPJ had come together, despite the threat of drone strikes, to express their solidarity with the people of Myanmar. The second part of this remarkable exchange began: "We salute you with our belief that building a free society is possible through the forefront of women's freedom and the brotherhood of peoples, which will create a more beautiful world with them. Therefore, with all determination and resolve, we will wage this struggle in the name of all humanity, and from here we send you our greetings filled with love and respect."

As with so many things in Rojava, what followed was a lengthy discourse on the meaning of the revolution and the primacy of women. Their greetings went further than those of the KNDF in outlining a future in which people can build a democracy without the state and outside of the hegemonic power of global capitalism. The statement of revolutionary solidarity included these encouraging words: "With this strength, your demand for freedom, and your continuous struggle, you will be able to thwart the plans of capitalist countries."

Immediately I sent the video to a Burmese friend and confessed that this exchange had brought tears to my eyes. To see two movements, with such little support and such lofty dreams, taking on the state at its own game and winning had already inestimably improved my hopes for the future. But seeing them take the time to express their fraternity and solidarity changed my outlook on life and the world. For nearly a decade I had traveled to report on crises and disasters, but often I had emerged from them hopeless. To see two of the most marginalized groups and unlikely victors I have ever been fortunate enough to spend time with beginning to forge an alliance between each other and against the cruelty of the state would have seemed a dream two years before. Now it was happening on the screen of my phone before I'd had time to make coffee.

Soon after, the KNDF sent a written response acknowledging that they admired the example of the YPJ and that they were "still on the journey toward full gender equality." The day they sent this message was the day they launched a major offensive, Operation 1111. The KNDF's letter ended with a message as much for the world as for each other: "May our shared struggle inspire others and contribute to a world where freedom, justice, and self-determination prevail. Solidarity in the face of adversity is a force that transcends borders, and our message serves as a beacon of hope for those fighting against oppression everywhere."

The next morning the KNDF embarked on their offensive, which would see them fighting on the campus of Loikaw University, where some of them had been students before the coup. The fighting was fierce, but they eventually captured the campus and the city. Sayar Richard, however, did not survive the battle. He stepped out from under cover to make a radio transmission and was killed by a bomb. The news of his death spread around Myanmar and quickly to Rojava, where the local press carried a short obituary, and friends sent me messages asking me to pass along their messages to his comrades. They all began the same way, "şehîd namirin," the phrase that translates as "martyrs never die" is probably the only Kurdish phrase my friends in Myanmar have learned, and then as now it offers a great deal of comfort in times of loss.

The solidarity between Myanmar and Rojava has gone beyond the merely symbolic. Although not without risk, especially as both movements have virtually no way to defend themselves against airborne attacks and so must avoid gathering, that the speeches were made at all was an act of extreme bravery and solidarity. More acts in the same vein came quickly in the weeks after the speeches, and some had even occurred in the weeks before and helped to build the relationship to the point at which public statements could be made. The "thickness" of this solidarity, to borrow a term from anthropologist Clifford Geertz, is what distinguishes it from the empty statements of "deep concern" pronounced by international bodies or "condemnation" from the US State Department, phrases reserved for acts both bodies could stop but choose not to. Instead, the revolutionary groups in Myanmar and Rojava chose action over appearances.[3]

One important action for any left libertarian group is building community, which plays a more important role in maintaining a healthy fighting force than might first appear. The incredible degree of alienation that many of us feel living under neoliberalism has been pointed at by many as the reason for our epidemic of post-traumatic stress disorder (PTSD) and related conditions. A 2020 meta-analysis in the *Journal of Traumatic Stress* showed a strong correlation between PTSD and alienation, but, of course, in this instance, the causal arrow could point in either direction, or both. While the United States has been at war for two decades, and one would expect some entirely predictable psychological trauma to have occurred due to this, it appears that levels of PTSD among veterans here are much higher than we find in places like Rojava, where the population has endured a decade of war with some of the most brutal adversaries on the planet. There's no doubt that many have lasting psychological scars, and estimates of PTSD among refugees from the war in Syria range from 75 to 99 percent. Despite this, the YPG veterans I have spoken to seem less likely to suffer the most debilitating forms of PTSD than their US military equivalents. While in Rojava, I asked YPG and SDF spokesman Siyamend Ali how the YPG and YPJ dealt with the wide range of psychological complications that can arise from combat.

"First of all," Ali told me, "the YPG comes from society. [The public] pay us respect. They really cherish us. You can go and knock . . . and they will open their door for you and they will actually have great hospitality if you're YPG. All of these things taken into consideration, it helps us. It helps us to have a high level of morale, and to be more proud of ourselves." The distinction he is highlighting here is, perhaps, the key differentiator between a state military and a people's defense force. The former exists to defend the state, but the state cannot be there for its fighters in the way they need it to be when the war is over. A people's defense force exists to defend the people, who can help their fighters heal.

"We're not only a force who's only practical on the battlefield. We're also practical in our social life as well. We sit with so many families, we share our life with them, share our knowledge, we share our pain with them. And they do the same thing," Ali told me. The state is a relatively recent phenomenon in human history; the full-time professional army of the state is more recent still. The model of the YPG and YPJ seems more aligned with conflict before the state existed, in which communities defended themselves rather than relying on a professional group of fighters to defend them. Perhaps the historical experiment that is the state, and especially the capitalist one, has created this profound isolation, and this isolation and uncertainty may result in high rates of PTSD among soldiers.

Ali told me that even injured troops still have a place in the YPG: "When someone gets injured or handicapped due to battle, like having an arm cut off or a foot cut off, we don't tell them their role is over and that they're useless. We don't have such a thing. Instead, we give them another role. We try to rehabilitate them, or maybe educate them more, or we give them a role—for example, writing news." Many of them live in Mala Brindar, homes for wounded former fighters where they can find community and purpose beyond the conflict. These communities used to be in most of the cities and towns of Rojava, but recent Turkish airstrikes on them have led to some closing down since 2023.

These societal explanations may go a long way to explaining the lower incidence of chronic PTSD in Rojava overall, but I wanted to ask Ali about the more acute instances, the ones I have experienced. What would they do, I asked, if a friend came back from a mission anxious or unable to sleep without unwanted and intrusive memories?

"This is a very good question," Ali replied. He said, of course, due to the horrific nature of the war they fought, many fighters experienced long-lasting trauma responses. "We try to sit with them and discuss it with them," he said. If group discussion doesn't help, fighters can be moved off the front line or referred to psychologists who can help them manage their PTSD. The fighters, he was keen to point out, are not useless because they are hurt, mentally or physically; they still remain part of the struggle.

Ali made the same point a number of ways in our conversation, that he sees his fellow fighters as an end in themselves, not a means to an end. While the YPG is not averse to risk, and its commanders know their soldiers will die—indeed some of them choose death in a way that is not really paralleled in western military culture, they are not "pawns in a chess game," as Ali put it. This is the same way I try to relate to my sources, as ends in themselves, against the advice of some of my colleagues, because not doing so seems fundamentally at odds with the reason I write in the first place. While it may be stressful to receive a phone call from a former source asking for help months or years after a story, being able to share my experiences with sources-turned-friends has been inestimably better for my overall sense of well-being.

Ali differentiated the YPG's approach from the one he believes exists in Ukraine. "Now if we talk about Ukraine, the way they fight there is they treat their soldiers just like numbers." Many international fighters who volunteered in Rojava went on to Ukraine afterward to fight the Russian state. Opinions on this are mixed in Rojava, but it is often seen as perpetuating conflict and seeking conflict for the sake of fighting rather than defending a revolution, a stance that my anarchist friends on the front line in Ukraine would strongly disagree with. Ali did not say this exactly, but he did say he felt the two wars treated their foreign friends differently. As he pointed out, parts of cities in Rojava are named for foreign martyrs, and their portraits can be seen across Kurdistan. Through fighting alongside each other, the volunteers came to know the people of Rojava, and the people of Rojava learned more about the world, he said. "It was a shared experience."

This concern for one another extended beyond the borders of the

AANES. When young women fighting in Myanmar have reached out to me after struggling with the burden of trauma, I have sometimes struggled to help them personally. My life experiences and theirs, while they overlap, are still very different. In my search for help for them, I reached out to the YPJ press office for suggestions. Within a few days, the Burmese and YPJ women were talking, and a Burmese friend related to me that she emerged from the exchange not only having shared her experiences but also feeling a greater sense of optimism for the potential of the revolution to change gender roles as well as political arrangements.

However, the solidarity between the two groups has not been limited to encrypted calls. The KNDF video sent to Rojava made an impact not just among the leadership of the YPG and YPJ but also among the ranks of the international volunteers. In March 2024, five months after the KNDF sent a message to the people of Rojava, two volunteers from Rojava arrived in Myanmar (international volunteers tend to be welcomed but not sought after). They were not fighting with the KNDF, although they had tried to reach out to them. Having received no response, they traveled to the north of the country to join the Chin Brotherhood.

The Chin are some of the poorest and most marginalized people in Myanmar, and they were among the first to rise up with muskets and shotguns against the junta. Since the coup, they have seen more support from other ethnic groups and have been able to significantly improve their fighting ability with weapons purchased on the black market, manufactured, or 3D-printed. In 2021, Chin fighters briefly went viral for their use of muzzle-loading muskets, which they call "tumis," a technology that was outdated by the beginning of the nineteenth century but was the best they could lay their hands on at the time. Now, with the help of two hevals from Kurdistan, the Chin are training snipers to make long-range shots from concealed positions using modern Ruger Precision Rifles and magnified optics.

One of these fighters, who uses the nom de guerre "Azad," is now fighting with the Chin Brotherhood. Azad says he'd always been aware of the revolution in Myanmar thanks to the presence of humanitarian groups like the Free Burma Rangers in Rojava as well as Myanmar, but it wasn't until the coup that people in Rojava began following affairs to the east. When the KNDF sent their message at the end of 2023, Azad says, "The structure, like, the actual organizational structure of the revolution in Rojava really paid attention. . . . For a lot of us, it was kind of a wake-up call."

Despite being very different places, Azad told me in a phone interview, the revolutions have much in common, "the idea that even without a state system, or under a kind of a unified federation of administration, that many different groups and with different beliefs, different backgrounds, different ethnicities, can come together for a bottom-up type system." The revolution in Myanmar has diverse politics, none of which really are explicitly democratic confederalist, but the revolution does share the goal of reimagining relations between community and state. "At the end of the day," Azad said, "it is very much the same struggle. It's many different peoples fighting back against an oppressive central regime that wants to erase them."

This solidarity, remarkable as it is, has continued to grow even after Sayar Richard's passing. As the Turkish-backed SNA began its 2024 campaign against the AANES along with its usual looting and war crimes, the KNDF sent a picture of them holding a sign that read "From Karenni to Rojava, em di tekosina, we de serkeftinê hêvî dikin,hevalno. Berxwedan Jiyane!" (From Karenni to Rojava, we wish you success in all your struggles, friends. Resistance is life!)

I received a message from Kurdistan, updating me on the situation in Rojava and reaching out to Myanmar in solidarity. "The Kurdistan Freedom Movement has formulated the democratic struggle of the peoples in the form of a paradigm, based on the pillars of Democracy, Ecology, and Women's Freedom," they wrote in response. "So wherever in the world people organize themselves and struggle for their democratic self-determination and for dignity, for the protection of the natural environment and for the freedom of women, we will regard this as a support and help for our Freedom Movement and part of our common struggle."

They also had a message for the KNDF:

First of all, I would like to honor the memory of Sayar Richard who read the message of solidarity for Rojava. The Kurdish people would never forget him and the struggle he represents. His voice will reverberate in the historical memory of the Kurdish people for ever. We know that they have hard times under a junta regime. As the Kurdish people we are not unfamiliar with such regimes. We have suffered a lot for more than one hundred years under the state terror of such regimes. Those who have similar experiences tend to identify and associate with each other easier. Unfortunately, we share hard experiences of being denied, suppressed, and massacred. But we should know that the way out of this authoritarian dictatorships is for the oppressed peoples to be in solidarity with each other and join their forces. If the fascist and authoritarian regimes help each other to repress the peoples, the peoples have the right and the revolutionary duty to help and support each other in solidarity.

As I said, earlier, all the peoples are on the same front, the front of democracy. The one thing they need to do is to organize and struggle to get the other front, the front of power and monopoly, retreat. A bridge of solidarity was built between the Kurdish people and the Karenni people of Myanmar after messages of support were exchanged between Rojava and KNDF (The Karenni Nationalities Defense Force). I think both peoples have a lot more to exchange other than solidarity messages. The KNDF and Rojava can share their experiences of resistance, community work, communal economy, communal democracy, women's emancipation, and political struggle. I would like to highlight the fact that we support the struggle of the Karenni people for justice and freedom and wish they will be successful in building their society through struggle against state terror.

As I am writing this sentence in 2025, almost every day sees a new example of the two revolutions' mutual affection. A 2023 translation of Öcalan's work into Burmese has begun circulating. Women snipers in Chinland flash the peace sign salute used by the YPJ, and fighters in the Anti-Fascist Internationalist Front in Chinland pose with messages of support for the YPJ on the anniversary of their founding. Karenni fighters pose with a scarf in the colors of the Kurdish flag that I sent to Andy as a gift when I got back from Rojava.

This solidarity has gone beyond the exchange between Rojava and Myanmar. In the spring of 2025, KNDF fighters filmed a video in which they read a message for the people of Gaza. Wearing their fatigues, and keffiyehs, they addressed the camera with their message. "We long for a future when your children don't have to be brave," they said. In their beautifully written address, they expressed compassion and solidarity with civilians half a world away being killed in their schools and hospitals, something they had seen in their own communities.

Solidarity has been a cornerstone of anarchism, and this does not change in times of war. Indeed, there is even more urgency to call for support of all kinds in these life-and-death struggles with which states divide people and set them against one another. States collaborate with capital to control people; by refusing the state's logic and fighting for all humanity we find true solidarity. When the states of the world ignored the Islamic State in Syria or refused to commit their troops to fighting it, anarchists, and other volunteers from around the world rushed to Rojava to stand alongside the people there in defense of the revolution. In Myanmar, where the state pushes ethnonationalism for its own benefit, people of different ethnic backgrounds fight side by side against the junta. We must not forget that anarchism is for everyone, and if we believe in creating a world without the state, we ought to be ready to defend the places where that world is being built and join others in creating a world a world where we do not need state allies because we have each other.

8

Logistics

In November 2023, while I should have been writing this book, I spent a significant amount of time volunteering with a mutual aid project on the southern border of the US, in a tiny mountain town an hour east of San Diego. We were an extremely mixed group of anarchists, Quakers, and others who couldn't stand to do nothing while Joe Biden's Department of Homeland Security kept people detained outdoors without food, water, or shelter in near-freezing temperatures. Together, we fed thousands of people, kept them warm, held their children, and offered what little welcome we could. These people, from all corners of the world, had entered the US to ask for asylum, crossing through gaps in the border wall. Once there they were told to stay in the desert before being collected for processing. Their stay often lasted days, a time in which they could not leave the little desert shantytowns that sprang up alongside the various holes in the wall. Despite this, the Biden administration claimed they were not being detained and thus didn't need to be treated according to minimum detention standards. As they were not detained, and often relatively accessible if you didn't mind driving the jarring dirt roads, volunteers could access them to provide aid. One night, just as it was getting dark, we were finishing up the daily routine of cleaning our food service vessels and preparing for the next day's breakfast. As we were locking up, a local lady pulled up to the side of the tiny and unkempt youth center we were using as an aid hub. "Who's in charge?" she asked. After a second of pause, two of us responded, "Everyone."

This answer might strike readers as cute or contrived, but it's not untrue. For months, our group cooked meals, fed strangers, attended to medical and shelter needs, and was the only humanitarian presence in a hostile and deadly environment. We gave out tens of thousands of sandwiches and bowls of hot food, and twice as many bottles of water on top of thousands of blankets, tents, and warm jackets. By contrast, a local NGO that received a $3 million grant from the county of San Diego ran out of money in a matter of months, after having spent much of that money on things formerly done by the government. Once given the grant, this NGO alienated the broad solidarity network of nonprofits and volunteers that had established itself to fill a social need that the government had ignored, without government funds or leadership. "From the beginning, there was no willingness to work collectively," Guerline Jozef, executive director of Haitian Bridge Alliance, told a local reporter.[1]

My own part in this mutual aid project, although relatively trivial, condensed for me many similar experiences over more than a decade of experience in conflicts and humanitarian crises. It is possible to organize horizontally on a large scale without corruption, inefficiencies, or chaos. When everyone is in charge, everyone's ideas have equal value. This allows for innovation from people who are less entrenched in the methods we have all grown used to. In our case, this might mean substituting zip lock bags to serve food in during a particularly hard night when we ran out of bowls, or perhaps providing shelter from harm in novel ways. One example is the Kurdish Freedom Movement adapting a tunnel system that began with six guerrillas digging a small shelter and now includes a volleyball court and tailor's shop while also providing room for gatherings safe from drone strikes. Despite the manifest evidence that almost all successful revolutions—and many less dramatic movements—begin and grow using horizontally organized and spontaneously funded networks for logistics, we must retread the very well-worn path of explaining such networks and their viability to people entrenched in the notion of the state as indispensable in logistics.

To demonstrate the viability of anarchist organizing in the field of logistics, we can, of course, point to the many national disasters in which the government has failed to take care of citizens, rugged individualists have overestimated their ruggedness, and communities have come together to take care of one another. However, we are concerning ourselves with conflict logistics here, and we must specifically address the ability of anarchists at war to move beyond the temporary and the small scale. The guerrilla and the partisan can supply themselves off the land and the people, and this is the model from which all anarchist warfighting begins. But, the skeptics would say, what happens when we go beyond this? What happens when anarchists have armies and those armies need to be fed, provisioned, and armed?

The obvious point to begin our journey is in revolutionary Barcelona. In July 1936, just a few days after the coup had been defeated in the streets of

Barcelona, CNT workers returned to their workplaces without their bosses. By the time the last shots were fired in the streets, more than 3,000 workplaces had been collectivized across Catalonia. Workers' committees ran the factories and, using the CNT, they coordinated between different industries to ensure a steady supply of parts and raw materials. In this, the CNT policy of organizing by type of industry rather than differentiating workers into different unions based on skill or job type played to their advantage. The CNT's long tradition of democratic and decentralized governance and focus on workers taking direct action to solve their problems also helped. Unlike top-down movements, the anarcho-syndicalists were experienced with taking matters into their own hands. When the revolution came, the workers did not wait for orders; instead, they acted spontaneously, with all the haste required of a people who must build a war economy from the ground up in a matter of days.

Initially, the collectivization of workplaces was not replicated on an industry-wide scale as the CNT would have wished, as geographical and circumstantial differences made the situation different in each town and workplace. This caused competition between workplaces, a surplus in some areas and a deficit in others. Collectives moved to remedy this either by sharing between industries or by sharing surpluses within their industry; for example, the Barcelona tram system was able to generate enough revenue that it could use some of the excess funds to support less successful operations in the rest of Catalonia.

Workers' committees ran the factory floors and sent delegates to a management committee that oversaw issues on a factory level. These in turn sent delegates to a centralized administrative committee, which included a delegate from each type of work within an industry. These committees also included experts and would help direct production according to the goals of a general assembly of workers. At all times, the syndicate general assembly retained power and the ultimate decision-making authority. It was this assembly that decided on a fair wage, and assemblies often accepted that, to begin with, there might be small differences in income as the economy transitioned.

Workers whose jobs required a large amount of formal education, such as doctors, were collectivized along with those in blue-collar lines of work. Barcelona's Syndicate for Sanitary Services included 1,000 doctors and 7,000 skilled workers. Previously, doctors had worked only where the wealthy could pay them, now they were sent by their syndicate to where people needed them. They occupied buildings, created hospitals for the population and the military casualties, and made sure that nobody across Catalonia was without healthcare. At the Ritz, the unionized waiters continued to wear their bow ties but now served meals to workers and militias in the renamed "Hotel Gastronomic number 1."

Meanwhile, women who may have previously been unable to participate in the wage economy were trained by *secciones de trabajo* led by the anarcho-feminist Mujeres Libres as drivers, mechanics, and apprentices in other fields. Some of them found work driving or repairing trams. However, they were still considered responsible for childcare, and this held them back from full participation in areas where the syndicate did not have collective childcare operations. As a result, women did not gain as much representation in committees as one would hope. However, in some syndicates, men took on women as apprentices and shared their skills with their comrades and welcomed them into the collectives. Perhaps, with more time, this solidarity would have helped address the historical gender imbalance in wages and workplace empowerment.

Because the workers were in control, workplace safety and welfare issues were now taken seriously. Inefficient, costly, and dangerous small workshops were an issue of concern for the workers, and they moved to collectivize and combine such operations. For example, in Granollers, collective hairdressers' shops were set up to replace kitchen-table and backroom operations around the city. It was common for the textile industry to rely on piecework by women, which was often conducted at home, but the collectives abolished this and incorporated women into factories and collectives. Meanwhile, the needs of the working class were also centered; by firing tram executives, workers were able to reduce fares, and some syndicates built on the longstanding anarchist idea of collective leisure and self-improvement with their own recreation areas, swimming pools, and daycare centers.

Collectivization of consumption proved difficult in the cities. Workers ran factories but then often sold the goods and shared the profit rather than distributing the goods according to need. It was only in rural areas where consumption too was collectivized. In the villages, people moved closer "to each according to their ability, from each according to their need." Rural people worked together in the fields and were joined by anarchist fighters rotating out of the front lines, who helped with the harvest. What they gathered, they shared. It was on this smaller scale that anarcho-communism flourished across

Catalonia. The goals of the movement—to have an entire economy organized by syndicates, in which each took according to their need and worked according to their ability—were never met. However in the time that the people controlled Barcelona they made progress toward their revolution in economic and domestic affairs as they fought the war, and all the while the state worked to return to the status quo ante. In the cities, the state remained and gradually clawed back its place through decrees and missives obliging collective workplaces to sell their goods and not distribute them according to need. Small-scale tradespeople and shopkeepers never socialized in some cities, making distribution capitalist even when production was socialized.

Nonetheless, the Catalan economy in the autumn of 1936 remains a case study in workers' control. In Barcelona, small optics workshops collectivized and built a new factory to make binoculars and repair the rare riflescopes in the militia's inventory. Sadly, the chemical industry struggled to pivot to manufacturing or remanufacturing rifle rounds in the time required, and it was not helped in this regard by the decision of the state to withhold supplies from anarchist columns, or by an international blockade. These external conditions can, and did, have a massive impact on the ability of a horizontally organized industry to meet the material needs of its people, be they at war or at peace.

Where supplies were more available, the workers prospered. Autoworkers collectivized the Hispano-Suiza automobile factory and turned the production line from luxury vehicles into one for armored cars.[1] By July 24, just five days after the coup, the first rudimentary armored vehicles, built without bosses or profit incentives, were in the hands of comrades headed to the front.

The vehicles produced by the collectives were known as "Tiznaos," from the adjective "tiznado," meaning "sooty" (a more fitting translation would be something along the lines of "Old Smoky"). While these vehicles look almost comical to the modern eye, they had already been an effective part of the people's arsenal for several years by the time war broke out in 1936. Tiznaos were first used in the Asturias revolt of 1934 and were essentially rudimentarily up-armored versions of regular vehicles. The first example was produced by the Duro Felguera metallurgical factory in October 1934. Soon,

---

1. The Catalan government had tried to order armored cars from the same factory in 1934, but it was not possible to produce them, and the contract ended up being fulfilled by a factory in Madrid. This may have been a political issue, considering the October 1934 Catalan independence uprising.

in addition to steel plates welded on the outside of vehicles, innovations such as covered wheels and a rotating turret were shared between workshops and incorporated into newer models.

On July 24, 1936, the Tiznaos rolled into battle again in Asturias. Two Asturian Tiznaos that had been built by the workers of the Constructora Gijonesa Juliana days before were used in the assault on the barracks in Gijón. Under the leadership of anarchist militant Victor Álvarez the two vehicles advanced on the barracks. The first was pinned down by fire, and its hastily added armor offered little protection; however, this provided cover for the second vehicle, carrying Álvarez, to spray gasoline on the walls of the barracks, which Álvarez himself then lit on fire.

By the end of July 1936, hundreds of collectivized factories had turned to support the war effort. In Madrid, *Tierra y Libertad* wrote, "Workers of the metallurgical union are working without rest to transform the workshops and factories. As of now, without a prior plan in place, they have armored vehicles to convert them into assault cars. . . . The production is directed by the defense committee."[2]

Cipriano Mera received a pair of armored cars on the first of August. Later he would recall that early models lacked much ballistic protection: "We did a test at two hundred meters with armor-piercing bullets and a Spanish rifle, and we were greatly astonished to see that the first shot dared to pass through the four plates on both sides. We carried out a new test with an ordinary bullet, giving us the same result."[3]

However, it was in Barcelona, the stronghold of the anarchists, where most Tiznaos were made. Barcelona had a small motor industry, but there were also many factories devoted to making textile machinery and naval equipment. On July 21, the metallurgy union elected Eugenio Vallejo as their delegate general to organize a war economy and began centralizing their work in the Hispano Suiza factory, with half a dozen other factories making parts for assembly there. The committee consulted with soldiers who had experience with armored vehicles to improve their designs. On July 23, less than a week after the revolution began, the POUM's newspaper *Avant* reported that the armored cars had begun to arrive from occupied workshops

At the Constructora Field boiler factory, at 254 Calle Pedro IV, workers took boilerplate metal and made it into something approximating an armored shell for various large-goods vehicles. The curved boiler sections, which can be seen in the company's advertisements in prewar newspapers, were welded or riveted together on a wooden superstructure, lending the vehicle the appearance of a partially submerged hippopotamus. Although it may have looked rather comical, the curved design increased the likelihood that a bullet would ricochet rather than pierce the armor of the vehicle, which was not the type of hardened steel that is better suited to armor plating. The armor likely offered some protection from the pistol and carbine rounds that were common, if not the full-power rifle rounds. At least nine individually numbered vehicles were produced, each slightly different, and many included a pivoting turret with a machine gun.

The slightly bizarre appearance of these vehicles drew the eyes of photographers, and thus their history is quite well documented. Constructora Fields vehicle no. 9, for example, was daubed with the Catalan slogans "Abaix el Feixisme!" (Down with fascism!) and "Visca livertat [sic] del poble!" (Long live the liberty of the people!), as well as the Spanish slogans "Teruel sera la tumba" (Teruel will be the tomb [of fascism]) and "No Pasarán." It saw service at Caspe before being captured in 1938.

The Durruti Column had at least seven armored vehicles, including a large armored command vehicle called "the louse," a Torras workshop vehicle called "King Kong," two vehicles made by Maquinista Terrestre y Marítima in Barcelona, and two made by the Volcano workshop.[2] Later in the war they also received vehicles made by a collective of railway workers in Girona.

The workers of Barcelona were by no means alone in turning their ploughshares into swords. In the Basque country, workers' committees even delegated specific elements of the armored vehicles to different factories and then had the parts delivered for assembly in a central location. In Asturias, six sets of workshops grouped together and began a uniform production of weapons and armored vehicles using a common pattern, allowing for much-improved field repair.

Without the constraint of patents, profits, and personal ego, and by using the structures of the CNT, these innovations could spread around the Republic at the speed of a telegraph, much in the same way 3D-printed guns now spread on Reddit. Thus innovations like wheel skirts and paired ventilation grates that allowed engines to cool but did not provide a possible "straight through" shot at the radiator were quickly diffused through the Republic.

---

2.   King Kong was driven by Antonio Bonilla, who was also the elected delegate of the column's armored section and who was with Durruti at the time he was fatally shot.

Alongside innovative design, the vehicles were decorated with common slogans. While some Tiznaos bore the names of the unions that had built them, many of them bore the initials "UHP" and appealed to the common cause of conscripted soldiers and the revolutionaries they were facing.[3] One proclaimed, "No tirar hermanos, estas peleando contra vuestros hermanos." (Don't shoot brothers, you are shooting at your brothers.) These lumbering behemoths were an encapsulation of the revolution: sometimes ineffective, sometimes used naively, but made by workers for workers and bearing dreams of the early days of the revolution into battle.

Such innovation would not have been possible without the support of the working classes of Barcelona. There is, after all, little to be learned about welding or suspension in the works of anarchist theory, but a great reservoir of such knowledge existed in the minds of the men and women practicing anarcho-syndicalism in the barrios of the Catalan capital. It is the support of the working classes that allows libertarian militaries to exist and function. This was driven home to me in Rojava as I sat in a civilian home sharing a kebab with Siyamend Ali of the SDF.

As we discussed how the SDF had grown from an irregular militia to a dominant force in the region, I shared with him the one Mao quote that has somehow stubbornly lodged itself in my mind despite my best efforts: "Many people think it impossible for guerrillas to exist for long in the enemy's rear. Such a belief reveals a lack of comprehension of the relationship that should exist between the people and the troops. The former may be likened to water, the latter to the fish who inhabit it. How may it be said that these two cannot exist together? It is only undisciplined troops who make the people their enemies and who, like the fish out of its native element, cannot live."[4] Heval Siyamend agreed this was a good analogy. "The YPG comes from society, from the people here," he told me. This allows them to move through society, and the two of them to be mutually reinforcing. It's a very different approach to that of the US or other NATO militaries, which make a point of considering themselves apart from and often superior to the rest of society.

Part of the SDF's uniqueness comes from its tactics, especially those used by the Kurdish freedom movement. Some of these are very common and even universal for the region, but others are unique and often a result of

---

3. UHP appears to have begun its life as "Union Horse Power" but over time many different expansions of the acronym, all suggesting proletarian unity, have been used.

innovation by individual fighters, not high-ranking commanders. For example, Hiwa told the that the sprawling tunnel systems that protect the YPG and YPJ from drones were initially developed in Zap, an area of Southern Kurdistan. Unhindered by the need to pass things through several corps and departments, they were able to quickly spread and have allowed the movement to survive years of air war. Today they span Rojava and other parts of Kurdistan, keeping fighters and their weapons safe from air attack.

Where the US military relied on a huge supply chain to bring the rations known as MREs, pizza, and even lobster tails to its troops in Iraq, it is more common for units in the SDF to cook for one another and provision themselves locally. In late 2024, I watched a video of Kurdish mothers in Aleppo preparing meals as their children prepared their weapons to defend their neighborhood against Turkish-backed Islamist rebels. It is the same way the Catalan anarchists provisioned themselves, with the international group undertaking trips across enemy lines to steal eggs, according to Antoine Gimenez's testimony. For much of the Aragon campaign, Gimenez stayed with a family in the collectivized village of Pina de Ebro, eating at their table and sleeping in their home. "Whenever I think of all the people I met in Spain before and during the war," he wrote, "and all the folk I lived alongside, mixed with, and had dealings with, the sweetest memory, the one closest to my heart, is of the Aragonese peasant woman who, amid the mayhem, opened her home to me and welcomed me like a lost child. Tía Pascuala. La Madre."[5]

In Myanmar, things are much the same. Instead of relying on long supply chains, rebels often buy and eat locally. PDF units swear allegiance to the people of Myanmar before eating and often benefit from those people's generosity as they sit down to eat their rice and fish paste. During my trip to meet PDF fighters, we shared meals with a local family, eating vegetables from their garden, tea leaf salad, and all manner of pickled and preserved foods they'd made on the small plot of land they owned. Sharing the meal with them was a much more profound welcome than I've felt slurping down an MRE, and, of course, substantially better tasting. However, it is not just food that the rebels in Myanmar have had to provide for themselves but also weapons. In this sense, their supply chain is unique.

While it is by no means true that all members of the 3D-printed firearms community consider themselves anarchists, it could be argued that the community's output and organization are inherently so. Creators do not charge for their designs and often collaborate with one another to improve on different iterartions. These are then hosted on decentralized platforms and shared with anyone who wants to download them, nearly always for free. Instructions, as I have documented here, are written specifically to be accessible to people in as many parts of the world as possible. Rebels in Myanmar have become part of this community, not only leaning on it for support and problem solving but also experimenting with new designs of their own making and sharing them with the community as a whole. The FGC9 as used in Myanmar has unique modifications such as a cast fire control group and reinforcement of the upper receiver, which make sense given the materials available to the rebels. These modifications could now be made by anyone, anywhere in the world, who wants to download the means of self- and community defense. Just like the anarchists of Spain, they are not hindered by patents, profit, or even laws, and as a result 3D-printed firearms technology is developing at an incredible rate.

The rapidly growing and very politically diverse 3D-printed gun community is not built on profit but on a shared affection for firearms and a commitment to the right to defend oneself. Its alliance with the people of Myanmar is as unlikely as it is important, and in my years of following the conflict I have found that members of the online 3D-printed firearms community have been among the very few groups in the US continuing to take an interest in the liberation struggles of the people of Myanmar, consistently standing in solidarity with them and even donating to some of the fundraisers for medical aid in the liberated areas. The connections I have seen develop, based in some cases in a shared passion for engineering and in others in a shared passion for freedom, offer a vision of a solidarity-based supply chain that delivers much more than weapons. Today in Myanmar, rebels print little key rings with the words "Live free or fucking die," a quotation from JStark in *Plastic Defence*, the Popular Front documentary on his work designing the FGC9.

As well as guns, rebels in Myanmar have innovated in the field of drone warfare, giving them an incredible degree of access to air power for a non-state entity. Groups like Federal Wings, Young Force, and Golden Tiger PDF, create their drones from scratch using parts purchased online, 3D-printed, and custom made in workshops. Their drones drop grenades with 3D-printed stabilizing fins, or mortar bombs rigged up underneath the fuselage of the drone. They've developed a powerful air presence without a single penny of state aid, relying instead on community workshops, purchase on the open market, and solidarity-based support from drone enthusiasts and fighters in

Ukraine and other conflicts who have shared drone techniques and technologies with them.

Of course, the 3D-printing is not the only way the revolutionaries of Myanmar obtain supplies. Most necessities are purchased using donations from the community (including the overseas diaspora), as well as raffles and lotteries. Anti-junta organizers have also used pay-per-click ads to raise funds by directing thousands of clicks to advertisements using Telegram channels. These ingenious fundraising methods have allowed the rebels to leverage the tools of global capitalism against the system it created, one that ignores their plight. A virtual PDF fighter videogame has also raised funds. Of course, ethnic revolutionary organizations also engage in more traditional fundraising and taxation and some previously sold drugs. These methods are not unique but nonetheless effective, and while they may represent a moral compromise, they typically also compromise the core principles of the groups involved.

Often weapons used by rebels in Myanmar are looted from the state, either seized in battle, brought over by deserters who receive a bounty for doing so, or captured in armories. The spoils of war, often known by the Arabic word "ghanima," should not be overlooked as a logistical solution for anarchists. The militia columns in Spain largely took, and improved, their armament in this fashion. The raid on Atarazanas Barracks in which Ascaso was killed resulted in the capture of a great many rifles, and thirty thousand rifles were captured at the San Andrés Barracks according to Agustín Guillamon. The better part of a century later I have received notice of the SDF capture of advanced surface-to-air missiles from the crumbling Assad regime. In this sense, anarchists must act like any other guerrilla group, even when the scale of their formations grows larger than that of guerrilla warfare. Where they are not able to make certain weapons, either through a lack of materials, knowledge, or fabrication facilities, they are compelled to consider the possibility of seizing them, and they must undertake—if possible—operations focused on arming themselves at the expense of their enemies.

Many more advanced weapons, those which cannot be fabricated by worker-run spaces at this time or 3D-printed at home, are gatekept by those with capital and power. To obtain such weapons, extremely difficult compromises must be made. The same is true when it comes to raw materials or supplies that cannot be obtained from within the liberated area. As we have seen in previous pages, antistate movements have been forced into alliances that, on the face of it, contradict their values. The SDF fought side by side with the United

States against IS, but the US was nowhere to be seen when Turkish-backed Islamists began a genocidal campaign of ethnic cleansing in Afrin, or six years later when they did the same in Manbij. The EROs of Myanmar have, at times in the past, relied on support from China, but today China supports the coup regime. Such movements have also relied on—if the US Department of Justice is to be believed—transnational criminal organizations. In Spain, even the most ardent anarchists of the FAI and the Iron Column mostly accepted the militarization that was heavily pushed by Moscow, in order to access weapons that would allow them to keep fighting fascism.

From our perspective today, many of these compromises may seem naive or ill-advised, or genius acts of realpolitik playing one state actor against another for the benefit of neither. But the debates I have recounted in Spain are not that different from the ones I see today in group chats from Myanmar. We have the advantage of knowing the outcomes of the concessions made in Spain, which those who made them did not. It is easy for us to judge these alliances based on their results, not on the information available to the people who made them. We should avoid this impulse because it trades the comfort of judgment for the discomfort of uncertainty, but it is the latter that we might find ourselves in, and the experiences of others can serve as a guide. We should not idealize the past, and, although it can be hard, we have to admit that some people died because of mistakes and that their best legacy will lie in our not repeating those mistakes. Each alliance I've mentioned, and many more besides, was entered into by people who knew it was a compromise. Sometimes it turned out to be too much of a compromise, and other times rebels were able to use the state for the benefit of their material needs and not give up what was core to them.

Of course, we go to history looking for answers, and there is much we can learn from war that we can apply elsewhere. But there is no easy set of guidelines to what we should and should not give up in such scenarios, no checklist for concessions. Instead, I think anarchists are best served by falling back on their processes. Consensus, or modified consensus organizing, allows all those impacted by such an important decision to have a say in it. On a larger scale, a system of delegates will be necessary to facilitate this, but it is still practical to undertake a consultative process during the time taken to deliberate an alliance as such things are rarely done quickly.

When anarchists enter an alliance, they are rarely associating with like-minded people. In anarchist organizations, we associate as equals; we must trust each other entirely or our organizing methods will not function. This is not the case in alliances, and our solidarity may have limits. Therefore, anarchists should not expect states to show loyalty or solidarity when we find ourselves in times of difficulty, if doing so is not in the states' interest. This is something the people of Rojava have learned time and again, as US troops sat in their bases with their surface-to-air missiles unused while children died in Turkish bombing raids outside their gates. However, the US was not in Syria to support the project of building democracy without the state in the AANES but rather to fight IS. This may have looked like an alliance at times, but the US has its own objectives and is not in full solidarity with its partner forces. For instance, it was politically advantageous to provide airstrikes against IS targets and avoid the deaths of US ground troops. Thus when entering into such alliances, anarchists must consider what is in the interests of potential allies and how they can best align the actions of allies with their own goals and interests.

Of course, much of this is very obvious, and it does not make difficult decisions any easier. In the fall of 2024, I watched a nonstop stream of war crimes being committed by Turkish-backed jihadists in Syria. The US, which relied on the people of the SDF to die in the thousands in the battle against IS, has not lifted a finger to help on the ground. In Spain, the militarization of many columns led to the persecution of anarchists, and in Myanmar people still fight with weapons they obtained via Reddit because the states of the world did not care about their struggle for liberty. However, one could argue very convincingly that the SDF would not have defeated IS without the air support of the US. Even with advances in drone technology, the air remains largely the domain of the state. Furthermore, through their interactions with US military personnel, the SDF was able to explain their ideology and build solidarity with people, even if that is not reflected in states. This solidarity, like that of the 3D-printed gun community and the rebels in Myanmar, has a benefit that is hard to measure but has resulted in a radical change in the politics of several US military veterans I have spoken to. We ought to exercise caution when judging their choices, while always trying to learn from them.

Anarchists may, as we have seen, organize at a scale commensurate with the state. However, to do so they must first organize in a manner that pre-supposes the absence of the state. The CNT, in particular, was able to fill the vacuum of the state and the bourgeoisie because it had spent decades orga-nizing the working class to act democratically, directly, and spontaneously. In situations where there is not such a strong workers' movement, it is unlikely that one can be built in an instant and even less likely in times of war. But even states often lack material resources and must trade for them, and the same is true for collectivized workers: no amount of solidarity will create steel in the absence of raw materials and furnaces. The need to trade offers states a chance to block access for non-state projects. In situations where they lack an existing movement or raw materials, anarchists must seek other ways to equip themselves as they build a libertarian society. These may be developed through solidarity, as has been the case in Myanmar; through alliances, as has been the case in AANES; or through the spoils of war, as has been the case in every region I have written about here and in many other conflicts. Hopefully this chapter has done some of the work of dispelling the myth that anarchists are incapable of organizing supply lines at scale. After all, the state has no hands of its own. Everything that is made is made by human hands, and those hands need not obey the state. Anything the state can do, people can do, because they already do it.

9

Gender

I did not come to the front lines to die for the revolution with a
dishcloth in my hand.

—Manuela

Sitting in a restaurant in Qamişlo, sipping on the endless chai that punctuates
every gathering there, it's easy to forget that the people here have been at war
for more than a decade. The plastic rock face molded into the wall reminds me
that, even down here in the plains, the mountains have always been a friend to
the Kurdish people as they faced repression from various states across space
and time. On the television in the corner of the room, a recruiting video
for the Yekîneyên Parastina Gel and Yekîneyên Parastina Jin, the People's
Protection Units and Women's Protection Units, is playing. In English, both
groups are better known by their initials YPG and YPJ respectively. On the
television screen in Qamişlo, women wear camouflage ghillie suits covered in
fake foliage to allow them to effectively blend in with their environment and
take long-range shots without being spotted. In their suits, which are a common aesthetic across the Kurdish freedom movement, they chant the Kurdish
women's movement's slogan, "Jin, Jiyan, Azadî" (Woman, Life, Freedom), as
part of the recruiting video.

Since it was first coined as part of the Kurdish liberation movement that
began in the mountains of Turkey, the slogan Jin, Jiyan, Azadî has echoed
around the world. Most notably, it became the de facto demand of the Iranian
women's movement in 2022. The Iranian movement took to the streets after
a twenty-two-year-old Kurdish woman named Masha Amini was killed by
morality police for allegedly improperly wearing her hijab. The chant went
beyond Kurdish people and was embraced by a wide range of ethnic and

language groups inside Iran who were demanding their liberty, and soon it was heard in solidarity protests all around the world.

In recent years, the slogan has gained some traction in the neoliberal core countries thanks to its use in those liberatory uprisings across Iran in 2022. Some of this globalization has been meaningful and profound: in late 2024 I shared a "Jin, Jiyan, Azadî" with Iranian women fleeing persecution through the deadly Darién Gap to seek asylum in the US. Regrettably, not every recitation is so sincere, and the slogan has been co-opted by groups who seem to pay little heed to the politics that gave rise to the women's movement in Kurdistan. But to some degree, just the globalization of the slogan is still a victory for a movement that has solidarity at its core, and every time I see it outside of a Kurdish context I still get a little electric jolt of excitement that perhaps someone else has heard of and learned from the Rojava revolution.

It's not uncommon for slogans to move from the streets to the state. Take, for example, the French national motto of "liberté, égalité, fraternité," which is unironically used by a government that at the time of writing has banned protests in solidarity with Palestine and once ruled over slave colonies without noting a hint of contradiction. In North America, Jin, Jiyan, Azadî became little more than an aesthetic, a hashtag, a bumper sticker divorced from context. The slogan was briefly co-opted by the kind of girlboss feminism that suggests women can overcome obstacles individually with hard work and the right connections, not together with collective struggle and a fundamental change in society. By way of example of just how much the Kurdish freedom movement has been reduced to an aesthetic for some actors, Hillary Clinton—whose time as secretary of state coincided with the gassing of civilians in Syria, which crossed a "red line" for the Obama administration but which resulted in no large-scale response—has acquired the film rights to Gayle Tzemach Lemmon's *The Daughters of Kobani*, a book about the YPJ. Often this representation of the movement, and the slogan, pays little attention to the desires, goals, and statements of women in the movement. Sometimes it objectifies them.

In the north and east of Syria, Jin, Jiyan, Azadî has retained its status as the North Star of the self-administration's politics, even if that sometimes creates friction with a more neoliberal feminism that the likes of Clinton want to imagine the YPJ is part of. During my time in Rojava, I met with Rîhan Loqo, the spokeswoman of the Kongra Star, the women's organization that has played a vital role in creating and sustaining a democratic system in which women enjoy equal rights and status with men from the military to the marketplace and everywhere else one looks in Rojava.

Loqo explained to me, with Diwar and Khabat taking turns translating, the order of obstacles that oppressed women: "This came first from the regime, second from society, and finally from the family." The revolution, she said, had to first liberate women. "If I can build a free woman, I'm going to be able to build a free family," she said. "If I can build a free family, I will be able to build a free society. If I can build a free society, we'll be able to build a free nation." Thus, the revolution in Kurdistan did not just include women, it was about women. Without free women, it lacked its keystone.

The model employed in the Kurdish freedom movement is one of strict equality. It's not that the revolution created an opening for women that could close again later; it's that women's liberation is what the revolution was about. For years before 2012, the Kurdish freedom movement had worked to build power and equality in its own institutions, and once the state showed weakness it was able to bring the same model to society. Every position of authority, from the military to the municipal council, is co-chaired by a man and a woman, to prevent them from replicating patriarchal structures.

The armed units of the Kurdish freedom movement in Syria have distinct but parallel units composed entirely of men in the case of the YPG and women in the case of the YPJ. The YPJ was formed as a distinct unit in April 2013. Earlier that year, the YPG formed the all-women's Martyr Rûken Battalion. Between April 2 and 4, the women who were fighting in the YPG organized a conference with delegates from all around the liberated areas to discuss the future of their units. On April 4, Öcalan's birthday, they announced the formation of the YPJ. The newly formed separate units would be commanded by women, many of whom cited patriarchal oppression as the main reason they picked up arms.

By the time the YPJ was formalized, women had been carrying arms for the Kurdish freedom movement for some time. As Öcalan's thinking moved towards what would become the basis for jineoloji, the philosophy that Loqo was explaining to me, the Kurdish freedom movement began to separate women from male command structures in order not to replicate the patriarchal hierarchies they saw as the root of inequality in many militaries and societies. The first women's units took shape in 1993, before Öcalan was imprisoned, under YJA Star (Yekîneyên Jinên Azad ên Star, or Free Women's

Units), and established themselves as confident and capable fighters in the mountains of Kurdistan.

As with the YPG, leaders in the YPJ do not wear badges of rank or hold billets that confer more power or income. All command positions are shared by one man and one woman. The Military Council of the YPJ consists of thirty-one people. It holds scheduled meetings once every six months and irregular meetings whenever emergencies dictate a need for them. The Military Council is responsible for all the activities of the YPJ. Beneath this are local councils which meet quarterly. The troops themselves are organized into platoons (*taxim*) of eight to nine people, companies (*bölüks*) of two platoons, and battalions (tabûr) of two companies. At its peak during the battle against ISIS, the YPJ had more than 20,000 fighters.

These fighters were not, as women in some Western militaries are, barred from certain high-risk jobs. In the battles of Kobani, Raqqa, and the dozens of other cities and villages liberated from IS since 2013, they played a vital role. Thousands of women gave their lives in battle against the particularly vicious misogyny practiced by ISIS. Many of them are not remembered by anyone other than their families, their comrades, and the communities they died to protect. However, one of the first and most famous was Arîn Mirkan. Almost a decade after her death, Mirkan's face still smiles at you from posters all over Rojava in places where people gather, and every time they march, a reminder of the sacrifice made by so many young women.

Mirkan smiled down at me from across the room in the Kongra Star offices in Qamişlo as speakers blared outside for the funeral of the twenty-nine internal security officers who had been killed by a Turkish bomb two days before. Her own death is what earned her a place in the pantheon of the Kurdish women's movement. When the photo of Mirkan was taken, she was young, smiling, and happy to be wearing her dark green uniform. At that time, in late 2014, the Islamic State seemed unstoppable. Having overrun Iraqi security forces in Mosul, Tel Afar, and Sinjar, they had swept through huge swaths of Syria and toward the outskirts of a small Kurdish majority town on the border with Turkey, called Kobani. It was there that they met their stiffest resistance in the form of the YPG and the YPJ. The latter was composed chiefly of young women like Mirkan, eager to defend the slice of liberty they'd carved out among the horrors of the Syrian Civil War. When Mirkan arrived, a battle was raging for the strategic high ground of Mishtenur Hill just outside town.

Perched on the other side of the border, on a hill that became known as "Media Hill," journalists from around the world and some of the 200,000 refugees who had fled the fighting looked on. Media Hill, which took on the aspect of a natural set of bleachers on which crowds could gather, had once been a place where local couples could take a romantic picnic, but the view now was anything but endearing. Between the hill and the border, Turkish security forces deployed teargas to prevent Kurdish volunteers from Turkey crossing the border to fight and locals from staying too close to the fighting. In one instance they fired tear gas grenades through the rear windscreen of a BBC reporting crew's car.[1] Across the border, binoculars and cameras could pick out the distinctive black flag of the Islamic State and the explosions caused by US fighter bombers dropping bombs on IS positions based on the on-the-ground intelligence gathered by YPG and YPJ fighters.

But despite the airstrikes, which were relatively sparse and sporadic, the YPG and YPJ on the ground were struggling to take out the tanks that ISIS had stolen from Assad's army. On Mishtenur Hill, they were losing ground. The Kurdish freedom movement desperately asked for help, even imploring their old enemies in Turkey to assist them. Despite public assurances that it would stop IS at Kobani, the government of Turkey only took active steps to prevent weapons from passing through its border to the YPG and YPJ, and the Kurdish fighters were left alone to face the terrors of the Islamic State. Pledging to fight to the last, they tried to secure the high points of the city to prevent ISIS artillery and tanks from shelling the town, thereby forcing IS to fight street by street, house by house, and room by room. Meanwhile snipers in the city's numerous apartment buildings made the jihadists pay for every yard they took with their blood.

Mirkan, whose given name was Dilar Gencxemis, reportedly ran out of ammunition in the fierce, often hand-to-hand fighting on Mishentur Hill. Like many of the fighters in the town, she knew that surrendering to IS would not mean survival. However, with ammunition dwindling and IS using tanks that the YPG and YPJ had little means to stopping with their few anti-tank weapons, the fight did not look like one she could win. Instead, she chose to end her life on her own terms. Mirkan ran toward the enemy, getting close enough to a tank and the infantry supporting it that when she detonated explosives in a vest she was wearing, she killed ten enemy fighters.

Mirkan's sacrifice extended the battle for some time and struck a blow against the Islamic State, but it did not prevent the hill from falling.

Nonetheless, it earned her a place among the martyrs who are so cherished by the Kurdish freedom movement that it is impossible to spend any time in the region without seeing their portraits and hearing their stories. As the hill was lost, things became desperate in Kobani. Salih Moslem, a co-chair of the PYD, visited Turkey to plead for help and was told that he would receive it only if the PYD abandoned its claims to autonomy and disbanded its canton system. He refused. The fighters trapped in the town had spent days without sleep, had little food left, and their ammunition was dwindling. Some fighters chose to carry more hand grenades and less rifle ammunition due to the close-up and devastating combat that has been likened to the hellish Battle of Stalingrad in the Second World War. The city was reduced to fields of rubble, but the fighters held on for weeks. The US dropped them ammunition and supplies from the air and bombed ISIS targets in the city. The Kurdish fighters faced daily ISIS suicide bombs and the small arms of nearly 9,000 ISIS fighters. After a month of fighting, reinforcements from the Arab-majority Free Syrian Army, some Kurdish groups from Iran, and then the Peshmerga of Iraqi Kurdistan joined the Syrian Kurdish fighters, entering via the Turkish border and showing a vision of the possibility of a popular front.

Slowly the combined anti-ISIS forces gained ground. Fighting street by street to liberate Kobani from the Islamic State, they captured Mishtenur Hill five weeks after Mirkan had died there. They set up an ambush and killed ISIS commander Abu Khattab, and over several more weeks, they fought for Mishtenur Hill and the rest of Kobani. On January 19, 2015, YPG and YPJ fighters cleared out the last of the resistance on Mishtenur Hill and raised their flag above the city of Kobani. A week later, ISIS would admit that it had lost the city and the battle.

It's easy to see how Mirkan became a hero. Just as many other nations and groups around the world do, the Kurdish women's movement salutes a martyr who gave everything she had, including her life, to the battle against IS's Islamist misogyny and repression. Her sacrifice did not turn the tides of the battle, but over time hundreds of other fighters' sacrifices did.

Alongside a picture of Mirkan on the wall of the small meeting room are pictures of Sakine Cansız, a founder of the PKK who was murdered in Paris in 2012, and Rosa Luxemburg. Beneath these pictures and offering me my third cup of chai of the interview sat Rîhan Loqo. As she explained to me, many narratives of the women's movement in Rojava begin in 2012. In doing so, they miss the vital groundwork that women organizers had put in for decades before. "Women have not joined the revolution," Heval Rîhan told me. "They created their own revolution." She went on to explain why this was so important: "Internationally wherever there was a war or there was a revolution, women were playing an essential role. It's the same as France, the same as Vietnam, also in Cuba, internationally, but after the war was finished, they . . . said, 'You can go home now.'" Rojava, she says, is different because "the [women's] revolution came first"; it wasn't possible to restrict the women to domestic roles after the war and the revolution because without them there was no revolution.

In Myanmar, the war certainly came first, but it's very difficult to see the free women of Myanmar going back. Before the coup, and despite the prominence of Aung San Suu Kyi, the country was still deeply misogynistic. Andy shared a story with me that illustrated exactly how the Spring Revolution became a gender revolution in Myanmar. In the early days, protesters in the streets of Yangon were behind a barricade that was about to be stormed by the police. In traditional culture, he said, it would be emasculating for men to pass beneath a woman's undergarments that were hanging out to dry. Feminist activists realized that the machismo of the police could be exploited, and the women in the group threw htamein (sarongs) up on the washing lines and cables that hang above Yangon's crowded streets. The police, they thought, wouldn't pass underneath them, and so their barricade held until the cops eventually pulled down the clotheslines. In a single afternoon, hundreds of young Burmese realized how sexism holds everyone back.

Myauk experienced a similar revelation. He first met his girlfriend (now fiancée) in a meeting in which activists were brainstorming to plan protests and clandestine actions. "She was very respected," he said. "In Myanmar culture, there is some gender stuff," he said and then paused to find the right words: "Boys are always good." But that was the culture he left behind when he joined the revolution. "This was before," he said. As the revolution continued, he realized that his girlfriend was really smart and that her intelligence didn't need to be qualified with her gender; she was just as valuable a fighter as he was. Soon she was his backup for on-the-ground operations, the person he wanted by his side if he had to fight for his life. He said he didn't worry about her in the revolution because "she is very clever. . . she is more clever than me." This pivot on gender roles is something I heard from almost every young man and woman I spoke to who had been part of the revolution in Myanmar. Despite their country being famous for Aung San Suu Kyi, the woman much lauded for leading them on the path to democracy, everyday life was deeply misogynist in Myanmar in 2021. By the next year, things were changing among the young men and women fighting in the Spring Revolution.

Women in Myanmar have been part of the revolution from the start. Though women's lot in a future Myanmar, one without the junta, remains to be seen. Not all those fighting the junta share the front-line feminism that saw the revolutionaries in the streets of Yangon hang their htamein on clotheslines or young men and women of the KGZA fight side by side in the early months of the war. A key tenet of the feminism that drives the Kurdish freedom movement is the belief that revolution cannot be made for people, that they must make it for themselves. Rather than men arming themselves and carrying out a revolution on their own, women must liberate themselves if the liberation is to be of any value. Women's liberation must be central to the revolution, not tangential. Certainly, the liberation of the women of Western Kurdistan has been of very great value, and the YPJ played an integral role in the defeat of the Islamic State, one of the most misogynist movements of the twenty-first century. Without their contribution, the toll on men might have been unbearable, and having twice the number of young, enthusiastic, and brave fighters should not be overlooked when we assess the victory of the SDF in their battle against IS and their parallel victory in building a new society.

If we compare Kurdish women's liberation to that which was proclaimed on behalf of the women of Afghanistan, we can tease out the differences between self-liberation and liberation from above. Just two months after 9/11, following a speech by First Lady Laura Bush, the State Department released an eleven-page report on the Afghan Taliban's "War Against Women." The report, issued by the department's Bureau of Democracy, Human Rights, and Labor, claimed the systematic repression of women in Afghanistan was "particularly appalling."[2] The plight of women and girls in Afghanistan, which was indeed both dire and disgusting, gave cover to two decades of war in their country, and to many discussions on the lot of Afghan women that notably didn't include any Afghan women. After twenty years of war and thousands of lost lives, the US abandoned the women of Afghanistan to the same "particularly appalling" treatment that it had cited as a reason for its invasion. The Kurdish, Assyrian, and Arab women I met in my time in Rojava, who had played active roles in the struggle against ISIS, cannot be abandoned by their liberators because they liberated themselves. They, and their Kalashnikov rifles, provide their own security and their own guarantee that there will be no going back to the misogynist terror of the Islamic State.

The women of Myanmar aren't going back either. Zaw's girlfriend had been with him at the front lines when we spoke, but in our final conversation he shared that she was recovering after being injured by a mortar. "It landed near her, and it hit her leg," he told me through a translator. "The bone broke, so she had to go to the hospital. But until that moment, she was with me all the time and we were fighting together." In the early days of the war, many young women like her found roles in mixed-gender units. As Zaw told us, this created some problems. While the young men might have accepted gender equality in theory, the lingering legacy of separate spheres sometimes raised its head in combat. Often men would try to show off their bravery in front of the women or take great risks to reduce the danger to the women in their group.

Over time, as the revolution matured, so did the gender politics of the dozens of rebel groups fighting in it. Groups like Myaung Women's Warriors and KNDF's Battalion 5 established separate women's units, which allowed women and men to fight for their liberation together but avoided some of the issues Zaw had seen when they fought in the same teams and units. In Chinland, women fight as snipers, just like the women of the YPJ. Other areas, especially those where young rebels joined more established ethnic revolutionary organizations, saw relatively little change in gender roles.

These single-gender units mirror the organization of the YPG and YPJ, and indeed this is no coincidence. Moreover, the links between Myanmar and Rojava go a lot deeper than sharing the same method of organizing columns by gender. In early 2023, a young woman fighter in Myanmar whom I had interviewed for a previous story reached out to me over an encrypted messaging app. She'd been having a difficult time dealing with the trauma and dislocation of war. This was made more difficult by the fact that her family had sided with the junta, leaving her without a support system. After two years of fighting and seeing her friends die, the horrors of war had caught up with her, and she was reaching out for help. I'm not a therapist, but I have been to see one, and sometimes it's helped. Often what has helped me is speaking to friends with similar experiences.

Yet as a conflict reporter in my mid-thirties, my experiences have been very different from those of a young woman guerrilla. I was fortunate to know a few people who might be able to relate to the woman's experience; I reached out to contacts around the world and got a response from Rojava. The women of the YPJ were happy to talk, so I passed along their number. A few hours later I got a message from my friend in Myanmar, saying how much better she felt and how the people she spoke with had reminded her of the importance of women's role in the revolution and inspired her to keep fighting for a free and equal future (the exact message was auto-deleted from my phone before I thought to archive it). Since then, they've continued to talk, and often when I can't get in touch with her, I have to reach out to someone in Rojava to check if she's okay.

The solidarity between the KNDF and the YPJ has been, in large part, driven by the women within KNDF, especially Battalion 5. But that solidarity has also spread. In Chinland in 2025, across the country from the KNDF, young women of the Chinland Defense Force sent greetings to the YPJ on the anniversary of their founding. The women of the YPJ serve as an example of the women's revolution being integral to the anti-fascist struggle against the Islamic state as well as the Syrian state that they and others in the Spring Revolution can aspire to.

Women's international solidarity has a long history. The better part of a century before the conflict began in Myanmar, women were already on the front lines in Spain, including women from all around the world. The *milicianas* of Spain have been much celebrated. Names like those of Rosario Sánchez Mora, the seventeen-year-old sapper better known as La Dinamitera, are well known in Spain today. But by the winter of 1936 the Republic had ordered women removed from front line roles in the units it controlled, and Sánchez Mora was forced to deliver mail after she returned to the front line having recovered from the loss of her right hand in an accident.

Less well known are the women of the anarchist militias. Women had long been participants in the anarchist movement and had fought alongside their male comrades in the streets and their workplaces, though they faced an uphill struggle against a deeply patriarchal society. In Catalonia, the "popular sport" movement had sought to empower women across the left through explicitly anti-fascist sporting clubs. Many of these women athletes went on to form their own columns (or join mixed-gender columns) and headed to the front lines in 1936. Arguably the most famous miliciana, who was in fact not a fighter at all but a translator, is Marina Ginestà. Her smiling photo, taken by Juan Guzmán atop the Hotel Colon, has become an iconic depiction of the early days of the war. Ginestà has a Mauser rifle slung over her shoulder in the photo, but the seventeen-year-old translator never carried a rifle into battle.

Less famous is a photo of her running a hurdles race, which I found during my dissertation research, but sport played a powerful role in empowering women like Ginestà who later found their way to the front lines.

The experiences of milicianas in Spain fall into two distinct categories: those of the front-line fighters, and those in the rearguard. The former fought and died, just like their male comrades in mixed-gender units. The latter tended to fight only when their hometowns were attacked and were organized in women-only units.

Concha Pérez Collado, an adherent of the FAI who had been arrested before the war for concealing a weapon during a strike, fought on the front with the FAI's Aguiluchos de Les Corts. She was one of seven women in her unit. In a 1999 interview, she detailed the unit's role: "Exactly what the men did, well, that's what we women did . . . we always took on some extra work, like cleaning or cooking or something. But then we stood guard equally with the men. When there was the attack at Belchite, we went into the attack equally with the men. We did what we humanly could, some of us [women] were stronger than others, same as the men."[3] As Pérez Collado mentions, women often took on the double burden of fighting and caregiving. The social revolution was constructed every day the anarchists were at the front, and reconceptualizing gender roles took time. But in the months that the conflict continued, these women fought on the front line of gender equality. They were helped by the presence of international women, many of whom had not been raised in societies where patriarchy was quite as woven into the social fabric as it was in Spain at the time.

This double burden was also a barrier to women's integration into rear echelon roles. While Mujeres Libres set up apprenticeships and anarcho-feminist workshops, they were never able to gain complete wage or participation parity. This does not mean they did not encounter success and solidarity. As Pura Pérez Arcos, one of the first women to work as a tram driver remembered, "They took people on as apprentices, mechanics, and drivers, and really taught us what to do. If you could only have seen the faces of the passengers [when women started their work as drivers], I think the companeros [sic] in Transport, who were so kind and cooperative toward us, really got a kick out of that."[4]

While many women entered the economy informally, and thus were not fully integrated into the structure of syndicates, Pérez Collado joined the fight at the front lines. She served with the Ortiz Column, and on the Aragon front she met many other women fighting in various anarchist columns. One Basque anarchist woman noted that on this front the anti-fascist forces were overwhelmingly anarchist in their character, so that her identity there changed from woman to fighter. In 1938, Sofia Blasco interviewed a miliciana named Carmen who had joined an anarchist unit to lend her skills as a seamstress, but on seeing the importance of the fight she had taken up arms instead. By participating as an equal, she began to conceive of herself as one, physically as well as intellectually. "Fancy me," she told Blasco, "a weak woman, and now I can manage a gun with the ease that I used to wield a needle."[5]

Among the Durruti Column, there were many women, including international volunteers from the UK and Germany. They fought alongside their male comrades and suffered heavy casualties. In the case of Suzanne Hans and her partner Louis Recoulis, they died side by side in the fight for Farlete. Georgette Kokoczinski, known by the nom de guerre "Mimosa," which she had initially taken as part of an anarchist theater troupe that traveled around France, served as a nurse in the unit's medical team but also undertook daring missions behind enemy lines with the Durruti Column's international group. She had joined the troupe after fleeing a middle-class home at sixteen and finding a chosen family among the anarchists and thespians of Montmartre. When she decided to join the fight, she recorded her feelings in her journal, writing, "The die is cast and I too am on my way to the front, as I expressly requested. I reckon I will not be coming back, but that doesn't matter, my life has always been sour and there is no such thing as happiness."[6]

Perhaps she found happiness among the international group of the column. In one of their raids in Perdiguera, she was captured and executed. Her journal ends mid-sentence: "I have found myself a mattress, alone in a room, hoping for some peace and quiet, but it is not long before I am disappointed and soon there comes a scratching at the door; I have barricaded myself inside with everything I could find. Everything repugnant that man has about him is in. . . ."[7] In a tribute to her, an FAI affinity group in the Barcelona neighborhood of Gracia took the name "Mimosa."

Women like Mimosa were not protected by their gender if captured. Indeed, the Francoist military made explicit its intent to sexually assault Republican women, be they civilian or military, broadcasting these threats over the radio to intimidate the women. Famously, even the Nazi advisors embedded with Franco expressed shock at his willingness to sign the death orders of several women combatants with little more than a flick of the wrist before continuing his breakfast. The records of the militias include several instances of women who, surrounded and running low on ammunition, chose suicide over capture, just as the women of the YPJ would in the fight against ISIS eighty years later.

The Iron Column also counted milicianas among its ranks. Their names appear relatively infrequently in histories of the column, and to be certain the column was by no means entirely enlightened in its gender ideology. One record of their presence is the debate on militarization within the column, in which one fighter, named Falomir, suggests that they concede to the government's demands that they remove women from frontline roles. Women were a distraction, he said, and only looking for a husband at the front. The assembly unanimously rejected this his proposal; any woman who could bring her own rifle was welcome, they said.[8] Indeed, the Iron Column's marching song included a verse that Paz records as

> Downtrodden women,
> sisters and mothers!
> Bold female comrades
> who have written their motto
> of love and labor
> in blood
> on our banners;
> downtrodden women![9]

Even after militarization, the 26th Division continued to accept women into its ranks. Antoine Gimenez recounts that at least four women fought alongside him in the months after his unit was militarized, including one whom he calls "Rosario," who went forward with a group of fighters to seize an enemy cannon, which turned out to be an ambush. Fighting fiercely, but against more soldiers than she could subdue in hand-to-hand combat, she screamed for her comrades back in the trench to shoot her, which they did.

The anarchists' theoretical commitment to gender equality was not always carried out, and certainly women had to combine the burdens of cleaning, cooking, and caring along with their combat role. Even in Rojava, it seems that women still take on the burden of most domestic work. Famously, one woman in the communist 5th Regiment in Spain angrily proclaimed, "I did not come to the front to die for the revolution with a dishcloth in my hand."[10]

In the anarchist case, we see women like Kokoczinski, who played a dual role as a nurse and a fighter. Perhaps, to use more modern language, Kokoczinski is better seen as a combat medic, who carried and fired a weapon while recovering her wounded comrades from the front line and who accompanied them on missions to provide both medical and fire support.

The history of gender bias at the front was long, and after an initial flurry of support, by the winter of 1936 women fighters were, in some instances, assumed to be sex workers by the press, by the opposition, and even by comrades who did not know them. This moralizing discourse had the dual effect of undervaluing their contribution to the cause and inhibiting their sexual liberation. Even some anarchist women's groups did not place an emphasis on sexual education or liberation, and the majority of their discussion on sex focused on the causes of and "solutions" to sex work.

However, in the first months of the war, the attitude on the front lines seems to have been more liberated in this regard. Certainly, Gimenez, who was married at the time of his entry into the Durruti Column and remained so throughout the conflict, recounts several romantic liaisons with fellow fighters, their partners, and other anarchists. These amorous episodes, at least as he recounts them, did little to hinder the effectiveness of Gimenez or his female comrades in arms. He was not alone in openly documenting his romantic relationships with his fellow anarchists. Basque anarchist fighter Casilda Hernáez Vargas pushed back against the idea that fighters should not have sexual relations. "The days of women being confined to household chores and the bed for the pleasure of her husband are gone," she claimed. "That women are going to the front lines to sleep with men is a false claim. That said, if the two came into contact with each other, there was no avoiding certain affections and affinities.... Physical, moral, and spiritual connections between men and women could take place on the front. Anything else would be a real aberration."[11]

This stance is one that diverges from that of the YPG and YPJ, who remain distinct and generally do not socialize with fighters from the other group when by themselves (for example, a YPJ fighter might ask another woman to accompany her to have tea with YPG comrades). They must also remain celibate during their time in service. Anecdotes suggest that, for some, this has sometimes meant a very difficult decision between the movement and someone they love, and it has forced some to leave to pursue romantic or family goals. It is, of course, understandable that as the Kurdish freedom movement works to move past centuries of patriarchy, it needs to create spaces where men are not present so that women can talk freely and deconstruct the institutions of patriarchy. Striking the balance between this and the human tendency towards love is perhaps a question that remains to be answered satisfactorily but one that we can answer more completely once we have built truly equal gender spaces.

Of course, love does not occur between men and women only. Again, this is an area where many of the groups cited here have progress to make. In Spain, queer people appear rarely in the historical record, aside from the persecution of gay volunteers like William Aalst by the Comintern and its affiliated organizations. One hopes that the anarchists would have been better, and there was some embrace of lesbians by the anarcho-feminist movement, but homophobic slurs also seem sadly common in primary sources.

The argument that the Rojava revolution's feminism is somehow inherently transphobic or homophobic is occasionally raised, and so it bears addressing here. Both during the Raqqa offensive and afterward, commanders in the SDF have shown solidarity with queer people. In Rojava, I asked Rîhan Loqo about the role for trans and nonbinary people in the women's movement. "They [the women's movement] don't care about the body," Khabat translated. "They are with Kongra Star with their mentality and their soul, if you, like, agree to do what Kongra Star is doing, like, as a mentality and also with this ideology, so we'll accept you. If you are not with us, we will not accept you."

The ideology of the Kurdish freedom movement differs from that of anarchism in terms of sexuality, and this is not something it seeks to hide. While women and men may fight on the front lines, cadres of the movement are expected to remain largely celibate. In a more doctrinal anarchism, and in the Spanish example, this was not the case. In Myanmar, I have seen examples of fighters getting married while their friends look on in fatigues, with their rifles slung over their shoulders. Both approaches certainly will have their detractors. One can acknowledge that relationships between fighters may cause issues on the front line, but with sufficient trust and commitment, these issues can perhaps be overcome. After all, the whole basis of left libertarian thought is that people don't need coercion to do what is right. Certainly, of the many issues impacting the effectiveness of the Spanish anarchist columns, their libertarian approach to relationships was not a decisive one.

Celibacy among fighters is not by any means the same thing as "don't ask, don't tell," a US policy that essentially forced LGBTQIA members into the closet and their leaders into silence. In Rojava, the Queer Insurrection and Liberation Army was formed as part of the International Freedom Battalion and pictured with leaders while flying their pride flag, but queer people's everyday lives and experiences in the AANES are likely difficult. Decades of oppression under various visions of the state will take time to heal, and although it is not forbidden for anyone to be LGBTQIA in AANES, this does not mean they will not encounter discrimination. Being celibate to begin with makes it even harder for gay fighters to be out, and the experiences of foreign volunteers in the Queer Insurrection and Liberation Army (TQILA) might not reflect those of local queer people.

Similarly, the LGBTQIA community in Myanmar has been embraced by the revolution, and even some ethnic revolutionary organizations whose religions have tended to be rather conservative on such topics have accepted that their queer siblings in arms are no less valuable than any others as people or fighters. When trans rights activist Saw Han Nway Oo died, she was mourned by her comrades. However, again, there are still likely day-to-day difficulties for LGBTQIA fighters in the PDFs. One hopes that the progress we have seen continues, as there can be no end to the revolution until everyone is free. Now that now that queer people are armed, organized, and embraced within their units, any repression on the part of the state will be more difficult.

Following through on ideological stances on gender and sexuality has been a major failure of movements in the left libertarian sphere. In Spain, where milicianas were celebrated, women on the front line still faced a double burden of domestic and military labor. They were, in many cases, equal and important parts of the anarchist columns, but in far too many other cases they were treated differently from their male comrades and expected to fulfill roles supposedly suited to their gender. In Myanmar too, the rhetorical commitment to women's equality has not translated to battlefield reality in far too many cases, although this is a changing dynamic and one that some groups have acknowledged needs to change more. The YPJ, of course, stands out as one of the most notable women's formations in history and has shown beyond doubt that women are more than capable of fighting on the front lines and winning. Because women have fought as much as men in Rojava, and because the revolution was made by them, not for them, women now enjoy a much more prominent role in civil society in Rojava than in other polities in the same region. Although in some cases this has not translated to domestic equality, the co-chair system ensures that women are prominent in all echelons of society and types of organizing in the AANES. The women of Rojava offer an example for women everywhere to follow, as many of the women in Myanmar have chosen to. This does not mean that Rojava is perfect, nowhere is, and the inclusion of and pride in LGBTQIA people is an area where all the revolutions I have studied could improve.

Despite the gains made by women in all three conflicts, we should not suggest that complete gender equality was established in any of them, certainly not in Myanmar and Spain. Anarchists have historically struggled to undo their gender biases and those around sexuality; this becomes only more evident in times of conflict and violence. While gender is often seen in binary terms in historical documents, it bears repeating that nonbinary individuals have been part of every liberatory movement, even those that lacked the vocabulary to name them as such. The liberation of trans, queer, and nonbinary people is something that has been promised and not delivered by far too many groups for far too long. Even in this book, the majority of my sources are cisgender heterosexual men. Undoing the assumption that fighting is male-gendered and that the struggle for liberation can only be undertaken by men should be an ongoing struggle for anyone on the libertarian left, myself included.

10

Death and Other Endings

It is not necessary to conquer the world. It is sufficient to make a
new one. Us. Today.

—Subcomandante Marcos

In all my time writing and researching this book, the closest I came to being
shot was on a hike near my home in Southern California. I was out looking
for areas where migrants might be detained, and I was walking off-trail to find
them. While walking along a ridgeline, I noticed a strange buzzing noise, like a
giant bumblebee. "Odd," I thought to myself, "it sounds like bullets flying by."
Moments later one hit the dirt a few yards away, kicking up dust. Moments
after that, I also hit the dirt, crawling down the far side of the ridge, muttering,
"head down, ass down" to myself and wondering if I was about to die saying
something that sounded like misremembered lyrics to a 2 Live Crew song.
After a few moments of reflection and an assessment of the situation, I made
my way down the far side of the hill and away from what I assume was an
inexpert target shooter.

My brushes with death have been relatively trivial: a goring in a bull run
when I was younger, an encounter with an idiot with a gun, another with a
distracted driver, a couple of overestimations of my skill at mountain biking
on cliff-side trails. But I am sadly all too familiar with the finality of death. I
have a little folder on my computer with voice messages from sources who
became friends and, ultimately, what my Kurdish friends would call martyrs.
Sometimes, when I want to feel closer to them, I listen to their voices or
scroll their social media pages and I feel like they're still here. I listened to
these messages while I was writing this book, to get quotes right, and then
I lost them in a software update, and now they're gone forever. They were

little digital ephemera of the kind we will all leave behind, but they make me wonder about what else we leave behind and what those of us still here owe to people who aren't.

I found considerable solace when reflecting on loss in the writings of Louis Mercier-Vega, a French anarchist who fought in Spain. His piece "Refuting the Legend" gave elegant expression to such an emotionally fraught issue that I felt compelled to translate it into English for a zine that my friends put out. "In the fox holes dug into the hillsides of Aragon," he wrote, "men lived fraternally and dangerously and without the need for hope because they were living fully conscious of being what they had always wanted to be. We have tried to enter into a dialogue with them, with the dead, to [preserve] whatever of their truth can be useful for the survivors and the living."[1]

Mercier-Vega listed a few of his fallen friends, their names, and their strengths, before concluding: "All that remains are trace chemicals, the residues of bodies burned with petrol, and the memory of brotherhood. We were shown proof that a collective life with neither god nor master, alongside people as they actually are in the context of a world such as people have made it, is possible."[2]

What we owe our fallen friends, he argued, is not the obfuscation of their mistakes or the construction of hagiographies that paint them as saints but rather the truth. Ultimately, the revolution in which he fought and in which his friends died didn't succeed. Their lasting contribution, then, must be to teach us from their failure. Otherwise, their sacrifice will be little more than a heroic myth, a story we tell each other to make the defeat seem like one without dishonor, an elevation to a pantheon in which they sit alongside Durruti, Mahkno, and the other fighting anarchists who lost their lives in the struggle against the state.

Mercier-Vega's argument is sound, and I hope in this final chapter to extract what I can from the experiences and lives of the people in my stories. But first I want to talk about how we deal with death and how we ought to remember the friends who are no longer with us to celebrate our victories.

I don't wish to fall into the tautology of saying regional cultures of martyrdom are heavily influenced by the dominant religions in the region, because one could easily argue the same point backwards, that religious attitudes are downstream of cultural norms. However, there are certainly tendencies towards the elevation of martyrs in left libertarian movements that parallel those we see in faith-based movements. Anarchists in Spain were quick to embrace the myth of the heroic martyr in the civil war, with fallen fighters lauded for their seemingly impossible acts and incredible bravery. If stripped of ideology, the articles of some contemporary anarchist newspapers would not read that differently from those of the state communists or even the Francoists. Some of the martyrs, like Antonio Coll, the sailor turned "tank hunter" who was said to have destroyed four enemy vehicles in Madrid before losing his life, may never have existed at all. José Cabeza San Deogracias argues that Coll may have been created in an attempt to replicate elements of the propaganda film *We Are from Kronstadt* but with a CNT flair.[3] Coll represents not so much reverence for a fellow worker who laid down their life for the cause as the need for hypermasculine, morale-raising anarchist superheroes, which is what martyrs can often become. Certainly, Coll represents a sort of high-water mark of the anti-fascist militant as hypermasculine hero. Numerous anarchist dailies lauded his achievements in rendering enemy armor obsolete through the force of his will and courage.

No doubt this myth was inspiring, but it also obscured the fact that destroying modern German and Italian armor was a serious problem for the militias. In urban combat, the pistoleros of the CNT and FAI arguably had more experience than many of their foes. But in combined arms warfare where tanks, planes, and belt-fed weapons were bought into play, the militias had to think on their feet. Their military advisers, when trusted and trustworthy, helped them, but by March 1937 it was not only the Republic and its Soviet backers demanding a change. Seeing so many friends die made many militants in the anarchist columns wonder what they could learn from military tactics, and what they could accept without compromising their ideology.

The Kurdish freedom movement has likewise had to balance ideology with modern tactics and methods. However, its approach to martyrdom remains distinct from that of its allies in the coalition against the Islamic State. A friend once told me that the acceptance of death that seems so commonplace among SDF fighters is due to the common perception that one only gets one death and must spend it wisely. This differs from the idea that one has only one life and must preserve it at all costs. Certainly, spending one's death wisely in the Kurdish freedom struggle grants an element of immortality to fighters, as conveyed in the phrase "*şehîd namirin.*" More than just a phrase, these words are a clarion call, and the constant presence of martyrs in Rojava is very striking. Every home and most places of businesses I visited displayed portraits, backed in yellow for men and green for women, of people who had been lost. Their faces still smile down on their families, who also tend to the plants on their graves. Martyrs are said to have "ascended" to martyrdom in the movement's lexicon, and in a real sense they are seen as venerated figures who demonstrated their ultimate commitment to the cause. Units in the SDF are named after their fallen predecessors, carrying their names and legacies into battle. Martyrs are often said to light the way for others to follow. In this sense, they show that one can die and live on, and that death needn't be feared.

While the hypermasculine hero is less present in the Rojava movement, arguably the most notable martyr is Arîn Mirkan, who detonated herself to destroy an ISIS vehicle on Mishtenur Hill outside Kobani. To this day, her face smiles down at visitors to numerous official buildings in Rojava. Unlike the hypermasculine Western military heroes who make up the ranks of recipients of the Victoria Cross or Medal of Honor, Mirkan was a woman and a mother of two. The archetype of the military hero in much of the world is a young man who gave up his future, perhaps for his country or his friends. Gendered perceptions of childcare might cause a woman who does the same, especially a mother, to be seen very differently. In Rojava, Mirkan's decision to die was seen as exemplary.

Death, of course, leaves loved ones behind, and, in the case of so many people in Rojava, it leaves parents burying their children. When I met with grieving families in Rojava, I heard about the importance of the martyr's families' association in coping with their grief. One mother who had lost a fourteen-year-old son told me, "When someone is martyred, we go and visit their houses. We offer our sympathies, and we try to support them in every way possible. Because we can feel that they are also heartbroken, the same as us, so it's our duty to do this." She went on to say that participating in the group offered her some relief from her grief. "When we share our sorrow and cry together, it kind of helps us to feel a bit relieved from the pain," she said.

This sense of a shared burden among the community for which fighters laid down their lives is possible only in a movement that is as out in the open as the Kurdish freedom movement. More clandestine freedom struggles will likely be unable to replicate the support structures and veneration for fallen fighters that exist in Rojava. Of course, many people had to die for the movement to get to this point, something that its adherents will remind you of at the first opportunity. The armed Kurdish freedom struggle has been ongoing for half a century, and the freedom the people of Rojava enjoy today is due in part to the people who lost their lives to establish it.

I'm not certain that martyr culture in Rojava could be replicated elsewhere, even if it were possible for anarchists to grieve in public without concern for more state violence. The special affection and tolerance that the people of Rojava have for such a gargantuan human toll seems to me to come from a generational understanding that such losses are part of the struggle for freedom, the struggle against several states vying to oppress them. For those of us for whom dying is something of a choice, even if capitalism in its neoliberal form is killing many of us slowly, it may be hard to accept such a heavy toll. Even among the people of Rojava, who have borne so much loss, I couldn't help but notice the entirely understandable and universal desire to offer their younger children the chance to emigrate and have an opportunity for a better life.

"My son, he wasn't a fighter," Aheng's mom told me as we sat on cushions that doubled as pillows on the living room floor where not so long ago her son had played. "He wasn't a warrior, he wasn't carrying a gun. And it was unfair for him to get killed. He didn't have anything to do with it." These deaths of children whose only crime is existing in an area liberated from the control of the state are particularly hard to bear. Myanmar's ethnic revolutionary organizations have also faced the senseless and indiscriminate use of state violence for more than half a century. Like the people of Rojava, they have seen their civilian infrastructure in Myanmar, including hospitals and even schools and places of worship, bombed by a government that considers existence outside of its control to be a crime worthy of capital punishment.

The first time I saw a KGZA fighter's funeral in Myanmar, the video of his friends firing their rifles into the air and placing his remains on a funeral pyre was accompanied by a country music song, in English, with lyrics about US troops dying in Iraq. It seemed a combination of traditional Buddhist rites and the aesthetic of a twenty-first-century US version of "Dulce et decorum est pro patria mori."[1] This bizarre juxtaposition of rites seems to have been concocted in the moment by young people raised on the internet and suddenly finding themselves confronting the realities of war.

---

1. This famous line by the Latin poet Horace—and used in Wilfred Owen's poem by the same name about the folly of the First World War—can be translated as "It is sweet and fitting to die for one's country."

The dead in Myanmar do not seem to live forever as they do in Rojava, at least not in the same way. Zaw, a fighter I spoke to regularly and who lost his life shortly before I traveled to Myanmar, is sometimes memorialized on his unit's Facebook page on the anniversary of his death, but his name hasn't been taken by the unit, a common practice in Rojava, where everything from tabûrs to clinics might be named after a martyr. Likewise, Sayar Richard, while greatly missed, is not as present in the iconography of the KNDF as the martyrs of Rojava are. Nonetheless, PDF commander Saw Dar Ko, in a televised interview, teared up when asked what he would do after the revolution. He said he would visit the families of the fighters who did not live to see their victory, and thank them. The grief expressed in the martyr culture of Rojava might not be as visible in Myanmar—there are no posters of the dead in the jungle—but fighters in Myanmar still carry their fallen comrades in their hearts and memories, and in the versions of themselves they have become, every day.

The nature of the civil war in Myanmar is particularly brutal as families are often split between the junta and the resistance. This leaves parents sometimes supporting the very forces that would kill their children. Perhaps in part this is because of the strength of the junta's propaganda machine, which involves print, film, and online media spewing an incredible variety of fabricated nonsense. Some younger PDF fighters have also suggested that Buddhist perspectives on reincarnation play a part, but in reality this division within families is not as uncommon as it might at first seem. In Spain too families were often split by ideology or circumstance and found themselves on opposite sides of a brutal conflict. The death of a sibling or child was at once a victory and a crushing blow there, just as it must be for the parents in Myanmar who see their sons drafted into junta service and perhaps indoctrinated into its worldview despite the parents' own support for the revolution.

Of course, there is another way out of even forced conscription, and I have interviewed several deserters from the junta's military. Many of them say they would have left sooner if it had not been for the fact that their commanding officers held their wives and children hostage to prevent just such a possibility. The way to treat these deserters is a topic of much debate among the resistance. Currently they are paid a bounty to surrender and live as IDPs or leave the country, and a larger sum if they can bring their own weapons. But after the war, there is a need to reintegrate them into the society that many can see on the horizon. Currently, many of these deserters live in makeshift refugee camps in terrible conditions in neighboring states, but this is not a sustainable solution. Nor do the fighters I talk with wish to arrive at a situation like the one in Rojava, where fighters guard make-shift prisons that serve as a breeding ground for radicalism and resentment. Instead, they are looking to the model of restorative justice that has been upheld as the ideal for the progressive left for some time. The KNU, which has trained, equipped, and deployed a column of ex-junta deserters against the junta offers an example of this ideology in practice. In Rojava, this model is used for community policing of general antisocial behavior and gendered violence. The community often turns to its elder women to help resolve disputes or find a restorative solution to antisocial behavior. For example, a divorce might be mediated first by a hyperlocal committee, and if a resolu-tion cannot be arrived at, the couple might then ask a Mala Jin to mediate. In a case of domestic violence by a husband against his wife, the woman could either ask for divorce, as is her right in Rojava, or perhaps the dispute could be mediated at a Mala Jin and then women Asayish would check in with the married woman on a regular basis to ensure violence had not continued. The underlying principle is that communities are better suited to resolving disputes than courts.

Several groups in Myanmar are watching with interest to see how the same model could be applied in post-conflict communities there. After hear-ing stories of their parents, grandparents, and friends being locked up in Insein and the junta's other horrific prisons, they're searching for a solution that does not rely on cruelty, resentment, and fear. This is an example for all of us to follow, in war zones and at home. The carceral state and its apparatuses, despite the claims of politicians, have done little to reduce antisocial behavior, and punishing people does not help them change. If people who once tried to kill each other can entertain the idea of one day living alongside each other in Myanmar, the rest of us ought to be able to do the same in a less violent setting.

For many, though, there is no "after the war." Death is a part of war, per-haps the worst part of it. Every death is a tragedy, but, as Mercier-Vega argued, each one can also be a chance to learn. I hope that in this book I have offered examples that can be instructive in the future and an analysis that can help us as we look at movements of the past. None of us is a creation only of our own work; we are all formed through our interactions with each other. I took a great deal of comfort from the friends of Tekoşer Piling who told me that the criticism he gave them, coming as it did from a place of love, made them better revolutionaries and that this was how they carried him with them after his death.

I lost a dear friend when writing this book. He'd fought in Myanmar, the former Yugoslavia, and in many other places before being killed at the front line in Ukraine. He died using the call sign "Orwell," because George Orwell was someone whose own decision to fight fascism and totalitarian communism a century before was something we both greatly admired. The process of grieving has not been easy; it never is. By doing the work I do, in the places I do it, I have exposed myself to more death than many will see. I have also been extraordinarily fortunate to have known so many people who believed in a better world so strongly that they were willing to die for it. The sacrifices of friends who died for struggles they had not been born into but which they chose have taught me how profound solidarity can be. Their conviction has reinforced my own, and even in their absence they continue to inspire me to be brave and hopeful, even in the face of so much suffering.

Their sacrifices, and those of many people I never knew, remind me that we must not compromise in our goals. This is especially true in Myanmar, where it is imperative that the revolution does not end until it has created a system where genocide is not possible. This can be achieved by refusing to allow any entity a monopoly on violence; empowering people, not institutions; and removing the structures of the state that allowed a genocide to happen amid Myanmar's so-called "democratic" opening. If this does not happen, and instead the current junta is replaced with a new group of men in suits in Nay Pyi Taw, all those deaths will have been in vain, and another generation will have to rise up and buy its freedom with blood.

Of the teachings that have come to us through so much death and violence over so many years, I think the notion of a "minimum necessary discipline" is one that has been developed through hard lessons learned and friends lost. It's a lesson that, I think, has promise for a future where commanders on the battlefield may issue orders and quickly make decisions that cannot be made through the consensus process, but once the fight is over they do not retain authority or status.

Having a commander who relies not on authority but instead on the self-discipline of their troops and their commitment to a mutually agreeable set of norms allows for a quick response when one is needed. This is something that even the anarchists of the FAI realized was necessary. What is crucial is that the discipline come from within, from commitment to the cause, not from fear of punishment or arbitrary justifications arising out of rank and status. In this way, discipline does not sacrifice the autonomy that makes the fight worth fighting.

If a top-down and permanent authority structure is not needed on the battlefield, it follows that the economy need not accept such a structure either, even in times of war. I have shown, I hope, that anarchists can and have and do supply themselves with weapons and other necessary supplies without the structure of the state. While this may not be universally possible, it should not be dismissed, as it often is. The ease of both commandeering state materiel and importing it past state restrictions will be a determining factor in the ability of anarchist groups to build their own supply chains, and it can often be the difference between success and failure. When they do not secure their own supply lines, as we saw in revolutionary Spain, anarchists risk being cut off from arms and ammunition and left to die. Staying armed and securing supply lines are vital to the survival of any revolution, and anarchist ones are no different. Thus, for practical and ideological reasons, anarchists should not concede this terrain, and doing so seems to undermine the claim that it is possible for humans to not only survive but also thrive without the state and authority. An economy based on solidarity and mutual aid is possible, and we have seen this not only in peacetime but also in the context of war and natural disasters worldwide.

The most prominent example of an anarchist war economy is that of revolutionary Catalonia, where committees ran workplaces and vertically integrated syndicates ensured coordination between them. This method, however, only works because of the ability of pre-organized structures to replace those of the state and ensure that production and resources are allotted in such a way that there are not significant bottlenecks or failures, and in such a fashion as to ensure that workers remain in control. We should avoid at all costs the situation where workers take control of their workplaces only to hand that control over to committees who in theory represent the workers but do not contain any workers. With its vertical union structure and delegate system, the CNT usually avoided this situation. As numerous instances of worker control have shown us and continue to show us, obtaining consensus in these environments is not the tortuous process of endless meetings that many imagine it to be. Because decisions are small and largely practical rather than ideological, consensus can be arrived at quickly. Procedures such as the "modified consensus" method, which seems similar to the one described to me by Zaw in the early days of the revolution in Myanmar, allow those who do not wholeheartedly agree to go along with a decision without endorsing it, or veto it if they feel it isn't responsible.

The mountains, as Scott argues in *The Art of Not Being Governed*, will always remain fertile terrain for anarchism. But this does not mean that one cannot exist ungoverned in cities, plains, and on the front line. Indeed, the reporting for this book has taken me across the plains of northern Syria, into the mountains of Iraq and the rivers of Southeast Asia, and through many major cities. While the mountains are undoubtedly a terrain hostile to the state and favorable to the guerrilla, I hope I have shown that the anarchist military can exist outside of the familiar guerrilla-in-the-mountains model. That growth may not always be easy, and this book is by no means a guide. But I hope it can at least offer some information on which to build a frame of analysis.

I do not wish to present portraits of the movements I have covered here as frozen in time, or to exclude Ukrainian, East African, Chinese, or Korean anarchists, to name some of the anarchists who have taken up arms. Indeed, as I am writing this sentence I am in the process of booking travel to visit more of them and return to visit old friends. I am sure I will learn more from them than I have had to offer to readers here. However, I would like to close with a suggestion that readers genuinely interested in building a world without state violence in service to capitalism participate in projects that make the state irrelevant, destroy patriarchy, and end ethnic strife. These projects need not, and in almost all cases should not, have anything to do with warfare or armed conflict. It is in the doing of such things—making the state irrelevant, destroying patriarchy, and ending ethnic strife—that we learn how to do them better. What I have tried to do here is chronicle the way these things have been done in a few conflicts, so that these ways are not forgotten or ignored. But none of this matters if hungry people are not being fed, unsheltered people are not being cared for, and workers are being abused, and even at a time where the states of the world are engaging in an increasing number of proxy wars, the vast bulk of what needs to be done is entirely peaceful. We ought not to assign any particular value to armed combat over other forms of struggle; it is just another way of doing what needs to be done. I have learned more about anarchism from making sandwiches for strangers and dropping jugs of water in the desert than I have from the substantial pile of books I have read on the topic. At the time when the Islamic State was murdering Yezidis, they needed to be defended, and so people went to defend them. At the time you are reading this, the state and capitalism are depriving your neighbors of housing, food, hope, and a chance at a beautiful life. These are wrongs that need to be addressed, and you can address the horrors of capitalism without—one hopes—experiencing the horrors of war.

Glossary

Spain

CCMAC ...... Central Committee of Antifascist Militias of Catalonia

CEDA .... Spanish Confederation of the Autonomous Right

CNT .... National Confederation of Labor

ERC .... Republican Left of Catalonia

FAI .... Iberian Anarchist Federation

POUM .... Party of Marxist Workers Unity

UGT .... General Workers Union

UHP .... United [or Unite!] Proletarian Brothers; Union Horse Power

Rojava

DAESH .... Islamic State of Iraq and the Levant

FSA .... Free Syrian Army

HTS .... Ha'yat Tahrir al-Sham

IS .... Islamic State

ISIS .... Islamic State of Iraq and al-Sham (the Levant)

KCK .... Kurdistan Communities Union

KRG .... Kurdistan Regional Government

PKK.......... Kurdistan Workers Party

PYD .... Democratic Union Party

SAA .... Syrian Arab Army

SNA .... Syrian National Army

SDF.......... Syrian Democratic Forces

TQILA .... Queer Insurrection and Liberation Army

YBŞ.......... Sinjar Resistance Units

YPG .... People's Protection Units

YPJ .... Women's Protection Units

Myanmar

DEA .... Drug Enforcement Agency

ERO .... Ethnic revolutionary organization

ETN.......... Erythritol tetranitrate, an explosive that can be plasticized

FGC9 .... Fuck Gun Control 9 mm

FOSSCAD.... Free Open Source Software and Computer Aided Design

KGZA........ Karenni Generation Z Army

KNDF........ Karenni Nationalities Defense Force

KNLA........ Karen National Liberation Army

KNU .... Karen National Union

MANPADS... Man-portable air-defense system

NLD .... National League for Democracy

NUG.......... National Unity Government

PDF........... People's Defense Force

SAC .... State Administration Council

TNLA........ Ta'ang National Liberation Army

Suggested Further Reading

Please note, this is not an exhaustive bibliography. It's a very short reading list that hopefully will encourage readers to begin educating themselves and their reading circles about the movements discussed here.

Spain

Beevor, Antony. *The Battle for Spain: The Spanish Civil War, 1936–1939*. New York: Penguin, 2006.

Carroll, Peter N. *The Odyssey of the Abraham Lincoln Brigade: Americans in the Spanish Civil War*. Stanford, CA: Stanford University Press, 1994.

Casanova, J. *De la calle al frente: El anarcosindicalismo en España (1931– 1939)*. Crítica, 1997.

Ealham, C. *Class, Culture, and Conflict in Barcelona, 1898–1937*. Routledge, 2005. (Published in paperback as *Anarchism and the City: Revolution and Counter-Revolution in Barcelona, 1898–1937*. Oakland, CA: AK Press, 2010.)

Gimenez, Antoine. *The Sons of Night: Antoine Gimenez's Memories of the War in Spain*. Chico, CA: AK Press, 2019.

Manzanera, Elias. *The Iron Column: Testimony of an Anarchist*. Anarchist Library Series 15. London: Kate Sharpley Library, 2006.

Martínez Catalán, Roberto. *Rumbo a Zaragoza: crónica de la Columna Durruti*. Colección Exergo, no 2. [Zaragoza]: Rasmia Ediciones, 2019. (Published in English as *Zaragoza Bound: A Chronicle of the Durruti Column*. Chico, CA: AK Press, 2025.)

Orwell, George. *Homage to Catalonia*. New York: Mariner Books, 1952.

Paz, Abel. *Durruti in the Spanish Revolution*. Oakland, CA: AK Press, 2007.

————. *Story of the Iron Column: Militant Anarchism in the Spanish Civil War*. Translated by Paul Sharkey. Oakland, CA: AK Press, 2011.

Peirats, José. *The CNT in the Spanish Revolution*. Edited by Chris Ealham, translated by Paul Sharkey and Chris Ealham. 3 vols. Hastings, UK: Meltzer Press, 2001.

Myanmar

Combs, Daniel. *Until the World Shatters: Truth, Lies, and the Looting of Myanmar*. Brooklyn: Melville House, 2021.

Ralph, Saw and Naw Sheera. *Fifty Years in the Karen Revolution in Burma: The Soldier and the Teacher*. Edited by Stephanie Olinga-Shannon. Ithaca: Southeast Asia Program Publications, 2020.

Scott, James C. *The Art of Not Being Governed: An Anarchist History of Upland Southeast Asia*. Yale Agrarian Studies Series. New Haven: Yale University Press, 2009.

Thant Myint-U. *The Hidden History of Burma: Race, Capitalism, and the Crisis of Democracy in the 21st Century*. New York: W. W. Norton, 2020.

Rojava

Biehl, Janet. *Their Blood Got Mixed: Revolutionary Rojava and the War on ISIS*. Kairos. Oakland, CA: PM Press, 2022.

Bookchin, Debbie "How My Father's Ideas Helped the Kurds Create a New Democracy." *New York Review of Books*, June 15, 2018. https://www.nybooks.com/online/2018/06/15/how-my-fathers-ideas-helped-the-kurds-create-a-new-democracy.

Cudi, Azad. *Long Shot: The Inside Story of the Kurdish Snipers Who Broke ISIS*. New York: Grove Press, 2020.

Internationalist Commune of Rojava. *Social Ecology and the Rojava Revolution*. London: Dog Section Press, 2022.

Knapp, Michael, Anja Flach, and Ercan Ayboga, eds. *Revolution in Rojava: Democratic Autonomy and Women's Liberation in Syrian Kurdistan*. London: Pluto Press, 2016.

Nash, Ed. *Desert Sniper: How One Ordinary Brit Went to War against ISIS.* London: Little, Brown, 2018.

Öcalan, Abdullah. *Liberating Life: Woman's Revolution.* Cologne: Mesopotamian, 2013.

General and Theoretical Works

Graeber, David. "The New Anarchists." *New Left Review,* no. 13 (February 1, 2002): 61–73.

Graeber, David, and David Wengrow. *The Dawn of Everything: A New History of Humanity.* New York: Farrar, Straus and Giroux, 2021.

Scott, James C. *The Art of Not Being Governed: An Anarchist History of Upland Southeast Asia.* New Haven, CT: Yale University Press, 2009.

———. *Seeing Like a State: How Certain Schemes to Improve the Human Condition Have Failed.* New Haven, CT: Yale University Press, 2020.

———. *Two Cheers for Anarchism: Six Easy Pieces on Autonomy, Dignity, and Meaningful Work and Play.* Princeton, NJ: Princeton University Press, 2014.

———. *Weapons of the Weak: Everyday Forms of Peasant Resistance.* New Haven, CT: Yale University Press, 1987.

Subcomandante Marcos. *Our Word Is Our Weapon.* New York: Seven Stories Press, 2004.

Notes

Introduction

1. See, for example, Antony Beevor, *The Battle for Spain: The Spanish Civil War, 1936–1939* (New York: Penguin, 2006).
2. For histories of the Column, see Antoine Gimenez, *The Sons of Night: Antoine Gimenez's Memories of the War in Spain* (Chico, CA: AK Press, 2019); Roberto Martínez Catalán, *Rumbo a Zaragoza: crónica de la Columna Durruti*. Primera edición. Colección Exergo, no 2 ([Zaragoza]: Rasmia Ediciones, 2019).
3. "Remembering Omar Aziz, Syrian Revolutionary," Anarchist Federation, March 4, 2025, https://www.anarchistfederation.net/remembering-omar-aziz-syrian -revolutionary.
4. David Graeber, "The New Anarchists," *New Left Review*, no. 13 (February 1, 2002): 68.
5. James C. Scott, *Two Cheers for Anarchism: Six Easy Pieces on Autonomy, Dignity, and Meaningful Work and Play* (Princeton, NJ: Princeton University Press, 2014).
6. Andrej Grubačić and David Graeber, "Anarchism, or the Revolutionary Movement of the Twenty-First Century," *Z Mag*, 2004, 1.

2. Spain

1. Pablo Casals and Albert Eugene Kahn, *Joys and Sorrows: Reflections* (London: Macdonald, 1970), 130.
2. Chris Ealham, *Class, Culture, and Conflict in Barcelona, 1898–1937* (London: Routledge, 2005).
3. Abel Paz, *Durruti in the Spanish Revolution*, trans. Chuck Morse (Oakland, CA: AK Press, 2007), 467.
4. Paz, *Durruti in the Spanish Revolution*, 474.
5. For further reading on these groups, see Martínez Catalán, *Rumbo a Zaragoza*, 62.
6. Roberto Martínez Catalán, "La organización armada anarquista, debates y propuestas durante la II República española," *Ser Histórico*, January 29, 2025, https://serhistorico .net/2025/01/29/la-organizacion-armada-anarquista-debates-y-propuestas-durante -la-ii-republica-espanola.
7. Martínez Catalán, *Rumbo a Zaragoza*, 35.
8. Martínez Catalán, *Rumbo a Zaragoza*, 55.

9.   Chris Ealham, "An Imagined Geography: Ideology, Urban Space, and Protest in the Creation of Barcelona's 'Chinatown', c. 1835–1936," *International Review of Social History* 50, no. 3 (2005): 373–97.

10.   Paz, *Durruti in the Spanish Revolution*, 433. This is also recounted in Antony Beevor, *The Battle for Spain: The Spanish Civil War, 1936–1939* (New York: Penguin, 2006).

11.   Paz, *Durruti in the Spanish Revolution*, 487.

12.   COOP, *Press Service. English Edition*, No. 5, June 1, 1936.

13.   COOP, *Press Service. English Edition*, No. 5.

14.   George Orwell, "The Sporting Spirit," in *The Collected Essays, Journalism and Letters of George Orwell*, vol. 4 (1968), 42

15.   Paz, *Durruti in the Spanish Revolution*, 446–49.

16.   Frederico Escofet, *De una derrota a una victoria: 6 de octubre de 1934–19 de julio de 1936* (Barcelona: Argos Vergara, 1984), 352.

17.   José Peirats, *The CNT in the Spanish Revolution*, vol. 1, ed. Chris Ealham, trans. Paul Sharkey and Chris Ealham (Hastings, UK: Meltzer Press, 2001), 132.

18.   "El Micrófono de Queipo de Llano" Guerra Civil Española: Un museo virtual, https://vscw.ca/es/node/119.

19.   John Kersh, "Influence of Naval Power on the Course of The Spanish Civil War, 1936–1939," United States Army War College, March 15, 2001, https://apps.dtic.mil/sti/tr/pdf/ADA389113.pdf.

20.   Paz, *Durruti in the Spanish Revolution*, 464.

21.   Paz, *Durruti in the Spanish Revolution*, 473.

22.   Paz, *Durruti in the Spanish Revolution*, 496.

23.   "Ireland and the Spanish Civil War—Police Report on SPNI Meeting on Spain, April 1937," http://irelandscw.com/ibvol-ScottSPNI.htm.

24.   Paz, *in the Spanish Revolution*, 476.

25.   Paz, *in the Spanish Revolution*, 483.

26.   "'Los Hijos de la Noche': Los Anarquistas que Salvaron A 4.000 Personas de ser Ejecutadas por Franco – Kaos en la Red," *CNT Vitoria-Gasteiz*, July 22, 2020, https://vitoria.cnt.es/blog/2020/07/22/los-hijos-de-la-noche-los-anarquistas-que-salvaron-a-4-000-personas-de-ser-ejecutadas-por-franco-kaos-en-la-red.

27.   Elias Manzanera, *The Iron Column: Testimony of an Anarchist*, Anarchist Library Series 15 (London: Kate Sharpley Library, 2006), 13.

28.   Miguel Íñiguez, *Enciclopedia Histórica del Anarquismo Español* (Vitoria-Gasteiz: Asociación Isaac Puente, 2008), 197.

29.   Paz, *Durruti in the Spanish Revolution*, 538.

30.   Paz, *Durruti in the Spanish Revolution*, 494.

31.   Paz, *Durruti in the Spanish Revolution*, 506.

32.   Paz, *Durruti in the Spanish Revolution*, 506.

33.   Paz, *Durruti in the Spanish Revolution*, 549.

34.   Antoine Gimenez, *Sons of Night*, 148.

35.   Gimenez, *Sons of Night*, 148.

36.   Gimenez, *Sons of Night*, 316.

37.   Paz, *Durruti in the Spanish Revolution*, 474.

38. Paz, *Durruti in the Spanish Revolution*, 554.

39. Abel Paz, *Story of the Iron Column: Militant Anarchism in the Spanish Civil War*, trans. by Paul Sharkey (Oakland, CA: AK Press, 2011), 159–66.

40. Martínez Catalán, *Rumbo a Zaragoza*, 207.

41. Martínez Catalán, *Rumbo a Zaragoza*, 210.

42. George Orwell, *Homage to Catalonia* (New York: Mariner Books, 1952), chapter 5.

43. Orwell, *Homage to Catalonia*, chapter 10.

44. Orwell, *Homage to Catalonia*, chapter 10.

45. Orwell, *Homage to Catalonia*, chapter 5.

46. For more on La Nueve, see Raymond Dronne, *Carnets de route d'un croisé de la France libre* (Paris: Éditions France-Empire), 1984.

3. Myanmar

1. Amnesty International, "Myanmar: Facebook's Systems Promoted Violence against Rohingya; Meta Owes Reparations – New Report," September 29, 2022, https://www .amnesty.org/en/latest/news/2022/09/myanmar-facebooks-systems-promoted -violence-against-rohingya-meta-owes-reparations-new-report.

2. "Family of Protester Shot by Myanmar Police Agree to Remove Life Support," *The Irrawaddy*, February 13, 2021, https://www.irrawaddy.com/news/burma/family -protester-shot-myanmar-police-agree-remove-life-support.html.

3. Lwin Mar Htun, "Songwriter Who Provided 'Theme Song' to 8888 Uprising Finally Honored," *The Irrawaddy*, August 9, 2018, https://www.irrawaddy.com/news/burma/ songwriter-provided-theme-song-8888-uprising-finally-honored.html.

4. "Statement by Thomas H. Andrews UN Special Rapporteur on the Situation of Human Rights in Myanmar United Nations Human Rights Council," Relief Web, March 11, 2021, https://reliefweb.int/report/myanmar/statement-thomas-h-andrews-un-special -rapporteur-situation-human-rights-myanmar.

5. James C. Scott, *Two Cheers for Anarchism: Six Easy Pieces on Autonomy, Dignity, and Meaningful Work and Play* (Princeton, NJ: Princeton University Press, 2014).

6. George Orwell, "Don't Let Colonel Blimp Ruin the Home Guard," *Evening Standard*, January 8, 1941.

7. Kyaw Kha, "Operation 1111 'Close to Securing All of Kayah State for Myanmar Resistance,'" *The Irrawaddy*, November 28, 2023, https://www.irrawaddy.com/in-person/interview /operation-1111-close-to-securing-all-of-kayah-state-for-myanmar-resistance.html.

8. "Joint Statement by 195 Revolutionary Forces and Civil Society Organisations on the Situation in Northern Rakhine | Justice For Myanmar," https://www .justiceformyanmar.org/press-releases/joint-statement-by-195-revolutionary-forces -and-civil-society-organisations-on-the-situation-in-northern-rakhine.

4. Rojava

1. Abdullah Öcalan, *Liberating Life* (Cologne: International Initiative, 2013), 57.

2.   "Syria: Unprecedented Investigation Reveals US-Led Coalition Killed More Than 1,600 Civilians in Raqqa 'Death Trap,'" Amnesty International Press Release, April 25, 2019, https://www.amnesty.org/en/latest/press-release/2019/04/syria-unprecedented -investigation-reveals-us-led-coalition-killed-more-than-1600-civilians-in-raqqa -death-trap.

3.   Clare Maxwell, "Anarchy in the YPG: Foreign Volunteers Vow Turkish 'Revolution,'" *Middle East Eye*, May 11, 2017, https://www.middleeasteye.net/news/anarchy-ypg -foreign-volunteers-vow-turkish-revolution.

4.   Quentin Sommerville and Riam Dalati, "The City Fit for No-One," BBC, https:// www.bbc.co.uk/news/resources/idt-sh/the_city_fit_for_no_one_raqqa_syria_ islamic_state_group.

5.   Dave Philipps and Eric Schmitt, "How the U.S. Hid an Airstrike That Killed Dozens of Civilians in Syria," *New York Times*, November 13, 2021, https://www.nytimes .com/2021/11/13/us/us-airstrikes-civilian-deaths.html.

5. Discipline Among the Anarchists

1.   Quoted in Abel Paz, *Durruti in the Spanish Revolution*, trans. Chuck Morse (Oakland, CA: AK Press, 2007), 509.

2.   Gimenez, *Sons of Night*, 141.

3.   Gimenez, *Sons of Night*, 187.

4.   Paz, *Story of the Iron Column*, 164.

5.   Cipriano Mera, *Guerra, Exilio y Cárcel de un anarchosyndicalista* (Madrid: CNT, 2006).

6.   Gimenez, *Sons of Night*, 108.

7.   José Peirats Valls, *La CNT en la revolución española*, vol. 2 (Cali: Ed. Madre Tierra, 1988).

8.   "Un Día Lúgubre y Nublado," *Nosotros*, March 1937.

9.   "Un Día Lúgubre y Nublado."

10.   Emma Goldman, "Durruti Is Dead, Yet Living," Hoover Institution on War, Revolution and Peace, Stanford University, 1936, https://theanarchistlibrary.org/library/emma -goldman-durruti-is-dead-yet-living.

11.   Paz, *Durruti in the Spanish Revolution*, 538–39.

12.   Goldman, "Durruti Is Dead, Yet Living."

13.   Martínez Catalán, *Rumbo a Zaragoza*, 162.

14.   Martínez Catalán, *Rumbo a Zaragoza*, 163.

15.   Martínez Catalán, *Rumbo a Zaragoza*, 164.

16.   Martínez Catalán, *Rumbo a Zaragoza*, 164.

17.   Gimenez, *Sons of Night*, 75.

18.   Gimenez, *Sons of Night*, 106.

19.   Tekoşîna Anarşist, "Tekmil: A Tool for Collective Reflection," the Anarchist Library, April 28, 2022, https://theanarchistlibrary.org/library/tekosina-anarsist -tekmil-a-tool-for-collective-reflection.

6. Arming the Anarchists

1. "US Troops' Use of YPG Insignia in Syria 'Unauthorised,'" *Al Jazeera*, May 28, 2016, https://www.aljazeera.com/news/2016/5/28/us-troops-use-of-ypg-insignia-in-syria -unauthorised.
2. Hannah Beech, "Phyo Zeya Thaw, Burmese Pro-Democracy Rapper, 41, Is Executed," *New York Times*, July 27, 2022, https://www.nytimes.com/2022/07/27/world/asia/ 27phyo-zeya-thaw-dead.html.
3. Beech, "Phyo Zeya Thaw."
4. Richard Paddock, "Myanmar's Protesters Face Down the Military with Slingshots and Rocks," *New York Times*, April 17, 2021, https://www.nytimes.com/2021/04/17/ world/asia/myanmar-protests-coup-slingshots.html.
5. Andrew Wilson, "3D Gun Printer Advocate Cody Wilson, Accused of Having Sex with Underage Girl, Pleads Guilty," *KVUE*, August 9, 2019, https://www.kvue.com/ article/news/cody-wilson-pleads-guilty-to-new-charges/269-cb4bfa9d-1479-46ea -93bd-0ba1705f51ac; Rebecca Flores and Terrellyn Moffett, "3D-printed Gun Pioneer Cody Wilson Sentenced to Probation After Plea Deal in Sex with Teen Case," *KVUE*, September 12, 2019, https://www.kvue.com/article/news/local/3d-printed-gun-pioneer -cody-wilson-sentenced-to-probation-after-plea-deal-in-sex-with-teen-case/269 -4313d612-537c-4c2f-9f85-063194d8aa7c.
6. "U.S. v. Ebisawa and Singhasiri Superseding Indictment," Southern District of New York, https://www.justice.gov/usao-sdny/media/1339151/dl.

7. Solidarity

1. Orwell, *Homage to Catalonia*, chapter 1.
2. Dieter Nelles, "The Foreign Legion of the Revolution: German Anarcho-Syndicalist and Volunteers in Anarchist Militias during the Spanish Civil War," LibCom.org, http://libcom.org/library/the-foreign-legion-revolution.
3. Clifford Geertz, *The Interpretation of Cultures: Selected Essays* (New York: Basic Books, 1973).

8. Logistics

1. Gustavo Solis, "Migrant Advocates Say County-Funded Center Is Mismanaged and Lacks Transparency," *KPBS*, November 21, 2023, https://www.kpbs.org/news/border -immigration/2023/11/21/migrant-advocates-say-county-funded-center-is-mismanaged -and-lacks-transparency.
2. Eduardo de Guzmán, "Madrid Rojo y Negro," *Tierra y Libertad*, 1938.
3. Mera, *Guerra, Exilio y Cárcel de un anarchosyndicalista*.
4. Mao Zedong, *On Guerilla Warfare* (New York: Praeger, 1937).
5. Gimenez, *Sons of Night*, 49.

9. Gender

1. "BBC Crew Come under Attack Near Kobane," *BBC News* video, October 5, 2014, https://www.bbc.com/news/av/world-middle-east-29499683.
2. Bureau of Democracy, Human Rights and Labor, "Report on the Taliban's War against Women," US Department of State, November 17, 2001, https://2001-2009.state.gov/g/drl/rls/6185.htm.
3. Rocío Negrete Peña, "'Mira, ¿ves mis manos?' Militancia y trabajo de las mujeres exiliadas," *Impossibilia. Revista Internacional de Estudios Literarios*, no. 20 (2020): 54–77.
4. "The People Armed: The Role of Women in the Spanish Revolution," *Fighting Talk* 15, November 1996.
5. Sofia Blasco, *Peuple d'Espagne* (Paris: Editions De La Nouvelle Revue Critique, 1938).
6. Gimenez, *Sons of Night*, 606.
7. Gimenez, *Sons of Night*, 606.
8. Paz, *Story of the Iron Column*, 176.
9. Paz, *Story of the Iron Column*, 57.
10. Mika Etchebéhère, *Mi Guerra De España* (Buenos Aires: Eudeba, 2014).
11. Mary Nash, *Defying Male Civilization: Women in the Spanish Civil War* (Denver: Arden Press, 1999).

10. Death and Other Endings

1. Louis Mercier-Vega, "Refuting the Legend: On the Words and Life of Louis Mercier-Vega," Strangers in a Tangled Wilderness, trans. James Stout, September 2024, https://www.tangledwilderness.org/features/refuting-the-legend.
2. Mercier-Vega, "Refuting the Legend."
3. Henry Brown, "The Anarchist in Uniform: The Militarisation of Anarchist Culture during the Spanish Civil War (1936–1939)," *Contemporary European History* 33, no. 1 (2024): 305–22.

Index

"Passim" (literally "scattered") indicates intermittent discussion of a topic over a cluster of pages.

Abu Layla, 134
Afghanistan, 192, 193, 240
Al-Hawl refugee camp, 145, 146
Ali, Siyamend, 126, 128–30, 151–52, 160, 213, 226
Álvarez, Victor, 224
Anarchist Federation of Iberia. *See* FAI (Federación Anarquista Ibérica)
Anarchist International Revolutionary People's Guerrilla Forces (IRPGF), 139
"anarchist squint," 11, 19, 97
Anarchist Struggle. *See* Tekoşîna Anarşîst
Andrews, Tom, 91
anti-aircraft systems, shoulder-fired. *See* MANPADS (man-portable air-defense systems)
Arakan Army (AA), 82, 103, 104, 106–7
Arakan Rohingya Salvation Army (ARSA), 81
armored vehicles: Spanish Civil War, 10, 44, 47, 223–25
The Art of Not Being Governed (Scott), 18, 21, 260
Ascaso, Domingo, 65–66, 71
Ascaso, Francisco, 26, 29, 35, 39–40,

65, 67–68; flag design, 30; namesake pistol, 175, 177
Ashin Wirathu, 80–81
Assad, Bashar al-, 118, 122, 125, 147
Assad, Hafez al-, 125
Assault Guard (Spain), 29–36 passim, 69–70, 71
Aung San, 76, 77
Aung San Suu Kyi, 76–78 passim, 79, 81, 83, 173

Bali, Mustafa, 144–45
Bamar people, 21–23, 77, 78, 82, 103, 104, 108, 174
Bamar People's Liberation Army (BPLA), 104
Barbieri, Francesco, 71
Barcelona Popular Olympics, 1936 (planned). *See* Popular Olympics, Barcelona, 1936 (planned)
Bayo y Giroud, Alberto, 52n10
Berneri, Camillo, 71
Bonilla, Antonio, 225n2
Bookchin, Murray, 123
Border Guard Forces (BGH) (Myanmar), 102–3, 106
Bosch, Otto, 45
Brauner, Karl, 202
Britain. *See* United Kingdom
Bueno Perez, José, 49
Burley, Charley, 38
Burman people. *See* Bamar people

capital punishment and executions, 167; ISIS, 127, 167, Myanmar, 174, 255; Rojava, 147; Spanish Civil War, 36, 41, 50, 56, 60n15, 62, 68, 164–67 passim, 244–45; Turkey, 143

carbines: FGC9, 179–95 passim, 228; Spanish Civil War, 29, 33

Carlists, 33, 50, 58

Casals, Pau (Pablo), 25–26

Catholic Church: Spain, 27, 36

Çavuşoğlu, Mevlüt, 172

CCMAC (Comité Central de Milícies Antifeixistes de Catalunya), 42–44, 52, 55, 69

CEDA (Confederación Española de Derecha Autónomas), 27

China, 78, 86, 102, 103, 109–10, 230

Chin Brotherhood, 215

Chinland, 217, 241, 242

Civil Guard (Spain), 29, 33, 34, 48, 60

Clinton, Hillary, 79, 234

CNT (Confederación Nacional del Trabajo), 27–36 passim, 40, 44, 62–65 passim, 162, 201–3, 221–23 passim, 231; Coll, 253; vertical structure, 259

Coll, Antonio, 253

collectivization: Spanish Civil War, 53, 54, 69–72 passim, 221–24 passim, 232

Communist International (Comintern), 35, 45, 63, 201

Companys, Lluís, 32, 36, 40, 42, 62, 65, 69

consensus, 7, 96, 259–60

Cuerpo de Seguridad y Asalto. *See* Assault Guard (Spain)

La Dinamitera. *See* Sánchez Mora, Rosario (La Dinamitera)

DIY weapons. *See* homemade weapons

Durruti, Buenaventura, 29, 46–49 passim, 55–57 passim, 61–68, 161–63; death, 66–68, 225n2; Goldman on, 58n13, 161, 163; Nosotros, 26, 31, 39–40; Zaragoza, 43–44

Durutti Column, 47–66 passim, 154–63 passim, 202, 225; women, 244

Ei Thinzar Maung, 101

enlistees and officers. *See* military rank

ERC (Esquerra Republicana de Catalunya), 27, 42, 162

Erdoğan, Recep Tayyip, 142, 143

erythritol tetranitrate (ETN) bombs, 188

Escofet, Federico, 40

executions. *See* capital punishment and executions

Facebook: Cheryl Sandberg, 120; Myanmar, 6, 80–81, 84, 95–97 passim, 101, 102, 174, 256; Rojava, 131; Stout, 14

FAI (Federación Anarquista Ibérica), 31, 32, 34, 40, 71, 155, 165, 230; Aguiluchos de Les Corts, 243; CNT-FAI house, 44; Montseny, 62

Falange, 50, 58, 164–65

feminism, 234; Myanmar, 240; Rojava, 120, 126–27, 240, 247. *See also* jineoloji; Mujeres Libres

Fernández, Aurelio, 26, 39

firearms, 99, 130, 177–86 passim, 190–94 passim. *See also* machine guns; pistols; rifles; 3D-printed firearms

First International: Spanish section, 27
France: national motto, 234; Spanish Civil War, 55, 56, 175
Franco, Francisco, 30, 42, 49, 244–45
Free Syrian Army (FSA), 118, 136, 177, 238
Friends of Durruti, 68, 70, 72, 73

García Barón, Antonio, 203
García Oliver, Joan, 26, 31, 35, 39, 40, 48, 71
Gassol, Ventura, 25–26
gays. See LGBTQIA people
Gaza, 197, 217
genocide: Afrin and Manbij, 230; Kurds, 20; Myanmar (Rohingya people), 22, 81–82, 106–7, 110, 258; Turkey, 143, 230; UN, 90n7; Yezidis, 127–28, 131
Germans in Spanish Civil War, 35, 39, 45
Germany: Berlin Olympics, 1936, 37; Second World War, 58; Spanish Civil War, 55, 56, 58, 175, 244, 253; Thälmann, 45n7
Gil Ruiz, Rodrigo, 32
Gimenez, Antoine, 52, 58–59, 154, 156, 164–65, 245, 246
Ginestà, Marina, 242–43
Giral, José, 32, 42
Goded, Manuel, 35–36
Goldman, Emma, 4, 145, 167; on Durruti, 58n13, 161, 163
Graeber, David, 8–11 passim, 148
Grubačić, Andrej, 11
Guardia Civil. See Civil Guard (Spain)
Guardia de Asalto. See Assault Guard (Spain)
guns. See firearms

Habur, Avesta, 141

Hawl refugee camp. See Al-Hawl refugee camp
Hay'at Tahrir al-Sham (HTS), 146–47
Hernáez Vargas, Casilda, 246
Hisen, Aheng, 114–15
Hiwa, Zagros, 19–20, 119–24 passim, 130–31, 143, 227
Homage to Catalonia (Orwell), 70
homemade weapons, 95, 101, 177–78, 189; bombs, 188; drones, 104. See also 3D-printed firearms
Hong Kong, 86–87

Iberian Federation of Libertarian Youth. See Libertarian Youth (Spain)
International Brigades (Spanish Civil War), 35, 52, 58–64 passim, 68, 154–56 passim, 164, 201, 202
International Freedom Battalion, 138–39, 248
international solidarity, 109, 148; Rojava, 131–32, 138–39, 167, 248; Rojava-Myanmar, 105, 109, 149, 166, 210–17 passim. See also International Brigades (Spanish Civil war)
Iran, 233–34
Iraq, 13, 15, 131; KRG, 127, 131, 132. See also Peshmerga
Iron Column (Spanish Civil War), 50, 51, 60, 155–59 passim, 163, 230
Islamic State (IS; ISIS), 14–18 passim, 117–18, 127–48 passim, 171–72, 176, 206–7, 231, 236–39 passim; ARSA and, 81; misogyny, 236
Islamophobia, 80
Israel, 110, 121, 147, 197
Italy, 10; Spanish Civil War, 55, 56, 175, 253

jineoloji, 120, 121, 132, 235
Jover, Gregorio, 26, 29
Jozef, Guerline, 220
Juventudes Libertarias. *See* Libertar-
ian Youth (Spain)

Kachin Independence Army, 104
Karen Buddhist Army, 102
Karen National Army, 106
Karen National Liberation Army
    (KNLA), 105–6, 167
Karen National Union (KNU), 78,
    102, 103, 105, 193, 257
Karen people, 23, 105–6, 107, 167.
    See also Karen National Union
    (KNU); Karenni people
Karenni Generation Z Army
    (KGZA), 95–101, 166, 240, 255;
    funerals, 255
Karenni Nationalities Defense Force
    (KNDF), 24, 95–105 passim,
    166, 210–17 passim; women's
    units, 241; YPJ solidarity, 242. *See
    also* Karenni Generation Z Army
    (KGZA)
Karenni National People's Liberation
    Front (KNPLF), 191
Karenni people, 94, 166
Karen Women's Organization, 107
KCK (Koma Civakên Kurdistanê),
    19–20, 119, 220
KGZA. *See* Karenni Generation Z
    Army (KGZA)
Khalaf, Hevrin, 143
KNLA. *See* Karen National Libera-
    tion Army (KNLA)
KNU. *See* Karen National Union
    (KNU)
Kobani, Syria, 133–36, 236–38
Kokoczinski, Georgette (Mimosa),
    244, 245, 246
Kongra Star, 234–35, 236, 247

Kurdistan Communities Union. *See*
    KCK (Koma Civakên Kurdis-
    tanê)
Kurdistan Regional Government
    (KRG), 127, 131, 132
Kurdistan Workers Party. *See* PKK
    (Partiya Karkerên Kurdistanê)
Kurds and Kurdistan. *See* Iran; Iraq;
    Rojava; Syria; Turkey

Largo Caballero, Francisco, 52–53,
    62, 63, 72, 203
Legrier, François-Régis, 144n5
LGBTQIA people, 108, 139, 189,
    247–48, 249
Libertarian Youth (Spain), 71
López, Juan, 62
Loqo, Rihan, 120–21, 126, 172,
    234–35, 238–39, 247

machine guns: anti-aircraft, 105, 130,
    165, 176; homemade, 189; Luty,
    184; Myanmar, 85, 87, 93, 105,
    189; Rojava, 130, 176; Spanish
    Civil War, 29, 35–39 passim, 51,
    58, 67, 165, 202, 225
Mae Sot, Thailand, 22, 23, 101
Makhnovists, 156
Malraux, André, 57
Mandalay PDF. *See* People's Defense
    Force (PDF) (Myanmar): Man-
    dalay
MANPADS (man-portable air-de-
    fense systems), 192–95, 197
Manzana, José, 35, 47
Manzanera, Elias, 51–52, 163
Maoism: Myanmar, 78, 86; Rojava,
    167
Mao Zedong, 226
Martínez, Antonio, 26
Martínez Catalan, Roberto, 164
martyrs, 252; Myanmar, 89, 174,

212; Rojava, 114–16, 141, 212, 236–38, 253–55; Spanish Civil War, 156, 252–53
Marxist Workers Unity Party. *See* POUM (Partido Obrero de Unificación Marxista)
Marzani, Carl, 60
Maung Saung Khaa, 104n11
Mera, Cipriano, 32, 66, 155, 224
Mercader, Caridad, 36
Mercier-Vega, Louis, 202, 203, 252
Mexico-US border region, 199–200, 219–20, 251
military rank, 153, 157–61 passim, 167, 236, 259
Milk Tea Alliance, 86, 208
Mimosa. *See* Kokoczinski, Georgette (Mimosa)
Min Aung Hlaing, 79, 81, 83
Minn Latt Yekhaun, 98
Mira, José, 57
Miravitlles, Jaume, 42–43
Mirkan, Arîn, 141, 236–38, 254
Mohn Tine, Sayar, 21–22
Molotov cocktails: Myanmar, 90–93 passim, 178
Montseny, Federica, 62, 71
Morocco, 27, 28, 42, 203
Moslem, Saleh, 238
Mujeres Libres, 37, 222, 243
mutual aid, 199–201, 219–20
Myanmar, 6–8 passim, 21–24, 75–111, 165–67, 172–73, 207–12 passim, 227–32 passim, 256–60 passim; deserters from junta's military, 256–57; drone warfare, 191–92, 220, 228–29; 8888 uprising, 76–77, 78, 84, 89; gender and, 239–42; LGBTQIA people, 108, 189, 248; Rojava solidarity, 105, 109, 149, 166, 210–17 passim; 3D-printed weapons, 179–97 passim, 228–29; tunnel defense, 220
Myanmar National Democratic Alliance Army (MNDAA), 78, 82, 103, 167
Mya Thwe Thwe Khaing, 87

Naing Myanmar: "Kabar Makyay Bu," 90
National League for Democracy (NLD) (Myanmar), 23, 77–78, 79, 81, 83, 97
National Unity Government (NUG) (Myanmar), 23, 97, 98, 107; Ei Thinzar Maung, 101
Nine Nine, 22
nongovernmental organizations (NGOs), 219–20
Nosotros (anarchist group), 26, 29, 31, 35, 39–40
La Nueve (9th Company of the Régiment de Marche du Tchad), 73

Obama, Barack, 79, 135, 234
Öcalan, Abdullah, 15–16, 20, 116–23 passim, 132; capture and trial, 123; feminism and women's units, 120, 235; images of, 116, 195; translation into Burmese, 217
officers and enlistees. *See* military rank
Olimpiada Popular, Barcelona, 1936 (planned). *See* Popular Olympics, Barcelona, 1936 (planned)
Ortiz, Antonio, 26, 47
Orwell, George, 38, 70–71, 72, 99, 107, 201, 258
Orzetti, Lorenzo. *See* Piling, Tekoşer

Palestine and Palestinians, 109, 121; Gaza, 197, 217
Patrullas de Control, 69, 70

Paz, Abel, 54, 155
PDFs. *See* Mandalay People's Defense
  Forces (PDFs)
Peiró, Juan, 62
People's Defense Force (PDF)
  (Myanmar), 21, 23n2, 76, 97, 98,
  101, 197, 208, 227; Mandalay, 21,
  103, 104, 108, 110, 167
People's Olympics, Barcelona, 1936
  (planned). *See* Popular Olympics,
  Barcelona, 1936 (planned)
Pérez Arcos, Pura, 243–44
Pérez Collado, Concha, 243–44
Pérez i Farràs, Enric, 44
Pérez Salas, Joaquín, 51
Peshmerga, 15, 20, 127, 130, 134–35,
  204, 238
Phyo Zeya Thaw, 173–74
Piling, Tekoşer, 148–49, 168, 257
pistols: Astra 400, 174–75, 177
PKK (Partiya Karkerên Kurdis-
  tanê), 15, 118–22 passim, 128,
  131, 136, 172; Sakine Cansız,
  238; suicide bombing, 141n4;
  tekmil, 167
Popular Olympics, Barcelona, 1936
  (planned), 25–26, 37–39, 45
post-traumatic stress disorder
  (PTSD), 212–14
POUM (Partido Obrero de Unificación Marxista), 45–46, 58, 70,
  71, 154, 155, 201
Prieto, Horacio, 31, 62, 63
Prieto, Indalecio, 52–53, 69
prisons and prison camps: Rojava,
  145, 146
PTSD. *See* post-traumatic stress
  disorder (PTSD)
PYD (Democratic Union Party),
  118, 122, 123, 238

Qamişlo, 17

Queer Insurrection and Liberation
  Army (TQILA), 139, 248
Queipo de Llano, Gonzalo, 41

Reddit, 131, 177–79 passim, 184–85,
  190
refugee camps: Rojava, 145, 146
Requeté, 33, 50
rifles: homemade, 177, 178; M16s,
  97, 173, 190, 191; Myanmar, 110,
  165, 173, 174, 177, 191; Rojava,
  130, 143, 176–78 passim; Spanish Civil War, 51, 156–57, 174,
  229. *See also* carbines
Rohingya people, 80, 97; genocide,
  22, 81–82, 106–7
Roman Catholic Church. *See* Catholic Church
Rojava, 8, 13–20, 113–49, 159–61,
  167–70, 175–77, 195–96,
  203–10, 226–27; martyrs,
  114–16, 141, 212, 236–38,
  253–55; Myanmar solidarity, 105,
  109, 149, 166, 210–17 passim;
  Tekoşîna Anarşîst, 118, 127, 132,
  133, 149, 154, 160, 167–69 passim; TQILA, 139, 248; US and,
  118, 128n2, 130, 135–48 passim,
  159, 171–75 passim, 196, 208–10,
  229–38 passim; YBŞ, 128; YJA
  Star, 235–36. *See also* PKK (Partiya Karkerên Kurdistanê); YPG
  (People's Protection Units); YPJ
  (Women's Protection Units)
Ruana, Lucio, 60
Rufat Llop, Ramon, 5, 49–50
Russia: Myanmar, 173; Rojava, 141,
  147; Ukraine, 173, 214

SAA. *See* Syrian Arab Army (SAA)
Sánchez Mora, Rosario (La Dinamitera), 242

Sanz, Ricardo, 26, 39
Saw Dar Ko, 256
Sayar Richard, 105, 210, 212, 216, 256
Scott, Bill, 45
Scott, James C.: *Art of Not Being Governed*, 18, 21, 260; *Seeing Like a State*, 18–19; *Two Cheers for Anarchism*, 19, 97
SDF. *See* Syrian Democratic Forces (SDF)
Second Spanish Republic, 26–27, 30
Second World War, 57–58, 114; Liberator pistol, 122; Maquis, 10; La Nueve, 10, 73; Sten gun, 189
Seeing Like a State (Scott), 18–19
Serra, Moisés, 32
Sinjar Resistance Units. *See* YBŞ (Yekîneyên Berxwedana Şengalê)
Smith, Pio, 109
solidarity, international. *See* international solidarity
Souchy, Augustin, 202
Soviet Union, 31; Spain Civil War, 55, 57, 61, 64, 71, 72, 203, 230
Spanish Civil War, 1–2, 25–74, 153–65 passim, 201–3, 220–26, 252–53; armored vehicles, 10, 44, 47, 223–25; border checkpoints, 16; firearms, 51, 156–57, 174–75, 229; Goldman, 58n13, 145, 161, 163; Guernica, 175; International Brigades, 35, 52, 58–64 passim, 68, 154–56 passim, 164, 201, 202; women fighters, 242–48 passim
Spanish Confederation of the Autonomous Right. *See* CEDA (Confederación Española de Derecha Autónomas)
Spanish Second Republic. *See* Second Spanish Republic
Spring Revolution, Myanmar,

88–111 passim, 208–12 passim; women in, 239–42 passim
statue-toppling, 54, 125, 147
Stinger (MANPAD), 193
suicide attacks, 138, 140, 141, 144, 176
Sunni Islam, 127
surface-to-air missile systems, portable. *See* MANPADS (man-portable air-defense systems)
Syria, 9, 121; Bashar al-Assad, 118, 122, 125, 147; Deir ez-Zor, 114, 127, 140–44 passim, 205–6; Kobani, 133–36, 236–38; Raqqa, 135–42 passim, 247; revolution and civil war, 118, 236; Tabqa Dam, 138; Tishreen Dam, 137, 148. *See also* Rojava
Syrian Arab Army (SAA), 123, 125, 137, 141, 147
Syrian Democratic Forces (SDF), 117, 125, 136–51 passim, 168, 172, 209, 226–27, 231; Ali, 126, 128–30, 151–52, 213, 226; anti-materiel rifles, 176; martyrs, 141, 236–38, 253–54; Myanmar solidarity, 105. *See also* Tekoşîna Anarşîst
Syrian National Army (SNA), 140–43 passim, 147–48, 216

Ta'ang National Liberation Army (TNLA), 21–22, 82–83, 103, 127
tekmil, 167–68
Tekoşîna Anarşîst, 118, 127, 132, 133, 149, 154, 160, 167–69 passim
Thaelmann, Clara, 45–46
Third International. *See* Communist International
3D-printed firearms, 95, 178–92 passim, 197, 227–29

3D-printed tourniquets, 197
TNLA. *See* Ta'ang National Liberation Army (TNLA)
TQILA. *See* Queer Insurrection and Liberation Army (TQILA)
Trump, Donald, 142, 148
Turkey: 1980 coup, 119; Rojava revolution and, 8, 13–19 passim, 113–26 passim, 131–43 passim, 147–51 passim, 171–75 passim, 208–9, 237–31 passim
Two Cheers for Anarchism (Scott), 19
Twan Mrat Naing, 106

UGT (Unión General de Trabajadores), 32, 63
UHP, 30, 36–37
Ukraine, 173, 214, 258
United Kingdom, 160; British Army, 153, 206; British in Burma, 77; Rojava, 128n2, 130, 137
United Nations, 90–91, 109–10
United States: Afghanistan, 193, 240; DEA, 193–94; Department of Justice, 230; "don't ask, don't tell," 247; Mexico border region, 199–200, 219–20, 251; Myanmar, 79, 193–94; Rojava, 128n2, 130, 135–48 passim, 159, 171–75 passim, 196, 208–10, 229–38 passim; US Army, 153; US Army Special Forces, 118, 130, 159, 171

Van Paassen, Pierre, 46n9
Vivancos, Eduardo, 39

weapons. *See* firearms; homemade weapons
Wilson, Cody, 180–81
Win Myint, 83
women's movement: Iran, 233–34;

Rojava, 120–21, 126–27, 133, 172, 234–35, 236, 247
Women's Protection Units. *See* YPJ (Women's Protection Units)
World War II. *See* Second World War

YBŞ (Yekîneyên Berxwedana Şengalê), 128
Yezidis, 127–28, 131, 134, 144
YJA Star (Yekîneyên Jinên Azad ên Star) (Free Women's Units), 235–36
YPG (People's Protection Units), 117, 118, 126–43 passim, 168, 171–72, 226–27, 233–41 passim; absence of rank, 159; cemetery markers, 114; "commander" position, 205; fatigues, 151; gender relations, 246; Martyr Rûken Battalion, 235; Myanmar solidarity, 211; PTSD, 213; suicide, 141n4
YPJ (Women's Protection Units), 114, 117–18, 126–37 passim, 141–42, 151, 168, 233–41 passim; absence of rank, 159; "commander" position, 205; fatigues, 151; gender relations, 246; Myanmar solidarity, 211, 217, 242; PTSD, 213

Zaw Lin Htun, 6–7, 75–76, 82, 83, 87–97 passim, 256; death, 100–101; girlfriend, 101, 241; rifles, 110, 174
Zhou Min, 78n3